ROMAN KRZNARIC is an author, cultural thinker and founding faculty member of The School of Life, where he teaches courses about work. He has been named by the *Observer* as one of Britain's leading lifestyle thinkers, and advises organizations including Oxfam and the United Nations on using empathy and conversation to create social change. For more, see www.romankrznaric.com

PHILIPPA PERRY is a psychotherapist and writer who has written for the *Guardian*, the *Observer*, *Time Out* and *Healthy Living* magazine and has a column in *Psychologies* magazine. In 2010 she wrote the graphic novel *Couch Fiction*, in an attempt to demystify psychotherapy. She lives in London and Sussex with her husband, the artist Grayson Perry, and enjoys gardening, cooking, parties, walking, tweeting and watching telly.

JOHN-PAUL FLINTOFF is an author, writer and broadcaster. He trained as an investigative reporter, worked for several years at the *Financial Times*, then for the *Sunday Times*, and has written for many other newspapers and magazines around the world. His work has won several awards, and has led directly to changes to UK government policy. For more, see www.flintoff.org

THE SCHOOL OF LIFE is dedicated to exploring life's big questions: *How can we fulfil our potential? Can work be inspiring? Why does community matter? Can relationships last a lifetime?* We don't have all the answers, but we will direct you towards a variety of useful ideas – from philosophy to literature, psychology to the visual arts – that are guaranteed to stimulate, provoke, nourish and console.

www.theschooloflife.com

Volume 2
Edited by
Alain de Botton

THE
SCHOOL
OF LIFE

First published 2013 by Macmillan
an imprint of Pan Macmillan, a division
of Macmillan Publishers Limited

Pan Macmillan
20 New Wharf Road, London N1 9RR
Basingstoke and Oxford
Associated companies throughout the world
www.panmacmillan.com

ISBN 9781447227724

Copyright © The School of Life, 2012

The right of Roman Krznaric, Philippa Perry and John-Paul Flintoff to be identified as the authors of this work has been asserted by them in accordance with the Copyright, Designs and Patents Act 1988.

The picture and text acknowledgements on pages 156 and 442–43 constitute an extension of this copyright page.

Every effort has been made to contact the copyright holders of the material reproduced in this book. If any have been inadvertently overlooked, the publisher will be pleased to make restitution at the earliest opportunity.

All rights reserved. No part of this publication may be reproduced, stored in or introduced into a retrieval system, or transmitted, in any form, or by any means (electronic, mechanical, photocopying, recording or otherwise) without the prior written permission of the publisher. Any person who does any unauthorized act in relation to this publication may be liable to criminal prosecution and civil claims for damages.

9 8 7 6 5 4 3 2 1

A CIP catalogue record for this book is available from the British Library.

Cover designed by Marcia Mihotich
Text design and setting by seagulls.net
Printed and bound in Austraila by McPherson's Printing Group

This book is sold subject to the condition that it shall not, by way of trade or otherwise, be lent, re-sold, hired out, or otherwise circulated without the publisher's prior consent in any form of binding or cover other than that in which it is published and without a similar condition, including this condition, being imposed on the subsequent purchaser.

Visit www.panmacmillan.com to read more about all our books and to buy them. You will also find features, author interviews and news of any author events, and you can sign up for e-newsletters so that you're always first to hear about our new releases.

Contents

Introduction: The New Self-Help   vii
Alain de Botton

How to Find Fulfilling Work   1
Roman Krznaric

How to Stay Sane   157
Philippa Perry

How to Change the World   293
John-Paul Flintoff

Introduction:
The New Self-Help
Alain de Botton

There is no more ridiculed literary genre than the self-help book. These titles may sometimes sell well, but they are never taken seriously – usually for very good reasons. Admit that you regularly turn to such books to help you cope with existence and you are liable to attract the scorn and suspicion of all who aspire to look well educated and well bred.

It wasn't always like this. For two thousand years in the history of the West, the self-help book stood as a pinnacle of literary achievement. The Ancients were particularly adept practitioners. Epicurus wrote some three hundred self-help books on almost every topic, including *On Love*, *On Justice* and *On Human Life*. The Stoic philosopher Seneca wrote volumes advising his fellow Romans how to cope with anger (the still very readable *On Anger*), how to deal with the death of a child (*Consolation to Marcia*) and how to overcome political and financial disgrace (*Letter to Lucilius*). It is no injustice to describe Marcus Aurelius's *Meditations* as one of the finest works of self-help ever written, as relevant to someone facing a financial meltdown as the disintegration of an empire.

Christianity continued in this vein. The Benedictines and Jesuits poured out handbooks to help one navigate the perils of earthly life.

In his medieval bestseller, *The Imitation of Christ*, the theologian Thomas à Kempis recommended that one note down sentences from the text, learn them by heart and repeat them at moments of crisis. Great self-help writers were still dispensing advice down to the early nineteenth century. Consider that master of pithy and useful phrases, Arthur Schopenhauer, author of *On the Wisdom of Life*, who explained in 1823, 'A man must swallow a toad every morning to be sure of not meeting with anything more disgusting in the day ahead.' The assumption behind this long tradition was that the words of others can benefit us not only by giving us practical advice, but also – and more subtly – by recasting our private confusions and griefs into eloquent communal sentences. We feel at once less alone and less afraid.

A key catalyst for the decline of the serious, intelligent self-help book has been the development of the modern university system, a system that in the mid-nineteenth century became the main employer for philosophers and intellectuals and started to reward them not for being useful or consoling, but for being objective and rigorous. There began an obsession with accuracy and a corresponding neglect of utility. The idea of turning to a philosopher or historian in order to become *wise* (an entirely natural assumption for our ancestors) started to seem laughably idealistic and adolescent. Alongside this came a growing secularization of society, which emphasised that the modern human being could do the business of living and dying by relying on sheer common sense, a good accountant, a sympathetic doctor and hearty doses of faith in science. The citizens of the future weren't supposed to need lectures in how to stay calm or free of anxiety.

And so the self-help field was abandoned to the many curious types who thrive in it today: people who are reclothing the Christian message so as to promise us financial heaven if we believe in ourselves, have faith, work hard and don't despair. Or else those with a passing acquaintance with Buddhism, psychoanalysis or Daoism. What unites modern practitioners is their fierce optimism. They make the grave assumption that the best way to cheer someone up is to tell them that all will be well. They are utterly cut off from the spirit of their more noble predecessors, who knew that realism could also have its therapeutic benefits. Or, as Seneca put it so well, 'What need is there to weep over parts of life? The whole of it calls for tears.'

We need self-help books like never before, and that is why The School of Life, in conjunction with Pan Macmillan, has launched a groundbreaking experiment: a series of intelligent, rigorous, well-written self-help books, put together by some of the leading minds in the field. In this volume, comprising three books in one, we examine some of the great issues of life – and we do so in a way that is at once highly accessible and conceptually bold.

In an age of moral and practical confusions, the self-help book is crying out to be redesigned and rehabilitated. We are proud to announce its rebirth.

Alain de Botton is the author of How Proust can Change Your Life *and the founder of The School of Life: www.theschooloflife.com*

How to Find Fulfilling Work
Roman Krznaric

By the same author:

The Wonderbox: Curious Histories of How To Live

The First Beautiful Game: Stories of Obsession in Real Tennis

Contents

1. The Age of Fulfilment — 5
2. A Short History of Career Confusion — 19
3. Giving Meaning to Work — 43
4. Act First, Reflect Later — 73
5. The Longing for Freedom — 97
6. How to Grow a Vocation — 129

Homework — 143

Notes — 147

Acknowledgements — 154

The thought once occurred to me that if one wanted to crush and destroy a man entirely, to mete out to him the most terrible punishment, one at which the most fearsome murderer would tremble, shrinking from it in advance, all one would have to do would be to make him do work that was completely and utterly devoid of usefulness and meaning.
– Fyodor Dostoyevsky

1. The Age of Fulfilment

Three Career Tales

Rob Archer grew up on a housing estate in Liverpool where there was 50 per cent unemployment and the main industry was heroin. He fought his way out, studying hard and getting to university, and found a great job as a management consultant in London. He was earning plenty of money, he had interesting clients and his family was proud of him. 'I should have been very happy, but I was utterly miserable,' he recalls. 'I remember being put on assignments in which I had no background but was presented as an expert. I was supposed to know about knowledge management and IT, but it all left me cold, and I always felt like an outsider.' He did his best to ignore his feelings:

> I assumed I should be grateful to just have a job, let alone a 'good' one. So I focused harder on trying to fit in and when that didn't work, I lived for the weekend. I did this for ten years, burning the candle at both ends. Eventually it caught up with me. I became chronically stressed and anxious. Then one day I had to ask the CEO's personal assistant to call me an ambulance because I thought I was having a heart attack. It turned out to be a panic attack. That's when I knew I couldn't go on.

The problem was that all the alternatives – changing career, starting over again – seemed impossible. How could I trade in the security of my comfortable life for uncertainty? Wouldn't I be risking all the progress I had made? I also felt guilt that I should even be searching for such luxuries as 'meaning' and 'fulfilment'. Would my grandfather have complained at such fortune? Life appeared to offer an awful choice: money or meaning.

At the age of sixteen, Sameera Khan decided that she wanted to become a lawyer. She was driven partly by her interest in human rights and Amnesty International, and partly by the enticing glamour of her favourite TV series, *LA Law*. But she also wanted to do something that would please her parents, Pakistani and East African Indian immigrants, who had arrived in Britain in the 1960s, her dad working his way up from a factory job, and both of them becoming successful social-worker managers. 'For them, success is measured through tangible career rungs in a profession like law, medicine or accountancy,' says Sameera, who is now in her early thirties. 'Their expectations influenced my decision 150 per cent.' She followed her plan, getting a law degree, then spending her twenties qualifying as a solicitor. She found a position as an in-house corporate lawyer for a hedge fund. 'I had it all, I was a City Girl earning megabucks, and loved the way law used my brain.' But after five years in the job, it all suddenly changed:

I was on honeymoon, sitting on a beach in Sicily, when I had an epiphany. I realized something wasn't right. I'd just got married, which was a huge rite of passage in my life and I should have been ecstatic. I'd achieved my dream of becoming a lawyer, and I had my partner by my side. Yet I felt totally unfulfilled. Where were the 'my life is now perfect' sparks? And as I sat there I worked out that the problem must be my career. I could see its future so clearly laid out before me and it filled me with dread. I realized that I wasn't going to be happy sitting behind a desk for the next forty years – for the rest of my life – making rich people richer. I had worked really hard to get this qualification in a respected profession, but was now left thinking, 'Surely my career should offer me more than this. Is this it? Is this all I get from life?' When it dawned on me that my career to date felt somewhat meaningless, it was devastating.

I was really scared about contemplating anything but law. Law identified me; indeed, I thought it defined me. A lot of lawyers are like this – it's your label, it's who you are. To lose that identity was going to make me feel naked and completely empty. If you're not a lawyer, what are you? *Who* are you? When I got back from my honeymoon, I could see that I was getting myself into a downward spiral of job-related despair, but I didn't know how to fix it. I literally went to Google and typed in something like 'What to do if you hate your career'.

Iain King has never been conventional. When he left secondary school, he spent a year busking around Europe – playing the guitar standing on his head. One summer while at college in the early 1990s, he and a friend crossed into northern Iraq from Turkey, where they befriended a group of Kurdish freedom fighters, travelled around with them in a Jeep full of machine guns and hand-held missile launchers, and narrowly escaped being kidnapped. Later, Iain started up a national student newspaper, which folded after half a dozen issues, then volunteered as a researcher for a political party. Never having had much of a career plan, he ended up as an expert on peace-building for the United Nations and other international organizations. He helped introduce a new currency in Kosovo and has worked alongside soldiers on the battlefront in Afghanistan. He has also found time to write a philosophy book, and to spend a year as a househusband in Syria, the lone father at baby groups in the Damascus expatriate community.

When Iain's wife was pregnant with their second child, he decided it was time to give up his precarious freelance career and get a steady job back in London to support his family. He found a post in the civil service, and now advises the government on its overseas humanitarian policies. He describes it with great enthusiasm: the issues are fascinating, the people stimulating, and he is using his first-hand knowledge of conflict situations. Yet there is a lurking discomfort. Somehow being a civil servant doesn't quite fit with how he sees himself. Work and self are out of alignment:

> The job is interesting but it's rather conventional for the kind of person I am. I feel it isn't the permanent me. When I sit on the tube in the morning, I sometimes notice that I'm wearing a suit, and I'm forty, I'm middle-class, I'm white, I'm male, and I live in one of the more conventional suburbs of London. And I think, 'Where's the guy who used to stand on his head in the tube and play the guitar?'

On the face of it I look like a very conventional person, yet I still regard myself as deeply unconventional. Paradox is too strong a word, but there's a tension there. At this time in my life, I have to accept the tension. I'm more conventional than I might otherwise be because I've got young kids and I'm the single breadwinner. I'm not about to leave my job, but I sometimes wonder, 'Should I really stick with this forever?'

Great Expectations

The desire for fulfilling work – a job that provides a deep sense of purpose, and reflects our values, passions and personality – is a modern invention. Open Samuel Johnson's celebrated *Dictionary*, published in 1755, and you will discover that the word 'fulfilment' does not even appear.[1] For centuries, most inhabitants of the Western world were too busy struggling to meet their subsistence needs to worry about whether they had an exciting career that used their talents and nurtured their wellbeing. But today, the spread of material prosperity has freed our minds to expect much more from the adventure of life.

We have entered a new age of fulfilment, in which the great dream is to trade up from money to meaning. For Rob, Sameera and Iain, it is not enough to have a respectable career offering the old-fashioned benefits of a healthy salary and job security. Paying the mortgage still matters, but they need more to feed their existential hungers. And they are not the only ones. In the course of researching this book I spoke to scores of people, from over a dozen countries, about their career journeys. From stressed bankers to tired waitresses, from young graduates burdened by student loans to mothers attempting to return to the paid workforce, almost all of them aspired to have a job that was worth far more than the pay check.

Yet for most of them, the task of finding a fulfilling career was one of the biggest challenges of their lives. Some were stuck in uninspiring jobs they felt unable to escape, trapped by a lack of opportunity or a lack of self-confidence. Others had, after trial and error, eventually found work they loved. Many were still engaged in the search, while there were those who didn't know where to begin. Nearly all had faced moments when they realized that work wasn't working for them, whether the trigger for this was a panic attack, an epiphany, or a creeping recognition that they were on a treadmill that was taking them nowhere. The wisdom in their career-change stories emerges from them not being golden tales full of smooth transitions and happy endings, but rather complex, challenging and often arduous personal struggles.

Their experiences reflect the emergence of two new afflictions in the modern workplace, both unprecedented in history: a plague of job dissatisfaction, and a related epidemic of uncertainty about how to choose the right career. Never have so many people felt so unfulfilled in their career roles, and been so unsure what to do about it. Most surveys in the West reveal that at least half the workforce are unhappy in their jobs. One cross-European study showed that 60 per cent of workers would choose a different career if they could start again. In the United States, job satisfaction is at its lowest level – 45 per cent – since record-keeping began over two decades ago.[2] Added to this is the death of the 'job for life', now a quaint relic of the twentieth century. In its place is a world of short-term contracts, temping, and nomadic career wanderings, where the average job lasts only four years, forcing us to make more and more choices, often against our wishes.[3] Choosing a career is no longer just a decision we make – often frighteningly uninformed – as a spotty teenager or wide-eyed twenty-something. It has become a dilemma we will face repeatedly throughout our working lives.

The yearning for a fulfilling career may have begun to permeate our expectations, but is it really possible to find a job in which we can thrive and feel fully alive? Is it not a utopian ideal reserved for the privileged few who can afford fancy education, who have the financial means to risk opening a baby-yoga cafe, or who have the social connections required to win the coveted prize of a job they love?

There are two broad ways of thinking about these questions. The first is the 'grin and bear it' approach. This is the view that we should get our expectations under control and recognize that work, for the vast majority of humanity – including ourselves – is mostly drudgery and always will be. Forget the heady dream of fulfilment and remember Mark Twain's maxim, 'Work is a necessary evil to be avoided.' From the forced labour used to build the pyramids through to the soulless McJobs of the twenty-first-century service sector, the story of work has been one of hardship and tedium. This history is captured in the word itself. The Russian for work, *robota*, comes from the word for slave, *rab*. The Latin *labor* means drudgery or toil, while the French *travail* derives from the *tripalium*, an ancient Roman instrument of torture made of three sticks.[4] We might therefore adopt the early Christian view that work is a curse, a punishment for the sins of the Garden of Eden, when God condemned us to getting our daily bread by the sweat of our brows. If the Bible isn't to your spiritual taste, try Buddhism, which upholds the belief that all life is suffering. 'Anguish,' writes the Buddhist thinker Stephen Batchelor, 'emerges from craving for life to be other than it is.'[5] The message of the 'grin and bear it' school of thought is that we need to accept the inevitable and put up with whatever job we can get, as long as it meets our financial needs and leaves us enough time to pursue our 'real life' outside office hours. The best way to protect ourselves from all the optimistic pundits pedalling fulfilment is to develop a hardy philosophy of acceptance, even resignation, and not set our hearts on finding a meaningful career.

I am more hopeful than this, and subscribe to a different approach, which is that it is possible to find work that is life-enhancing, that broadens our horizons and makes us feel more human. Although the search for a fulfilling career has only become a widespread aspiration in the West since the end of the Second World War, it has its roots in the rise of individualism in Renaissance Europe. This was the era in which celebrating your uniqueness first became fashionable. The Renaissance is well known for having produced extraordinary advances in the arts and sciences, which helped to shake off the shackles of medieval Church dogma and social conformity. But it also gave birth to highly personalized cultural innovations, such as the self-portrait, the intimate diary, the genre of autobiography and the personal seal on letters. In doing so, it legitimized the idea of shaping your own identity and destiny.[6] We are the inheritors of this tradition of self-expression. Just as we seek to express our individuality in the clothes we wear or the music we listen to, so too we should search for work that enables us to express who we are, and who we want to be.

It is possible to find work that is life-enhancing and broadens our horizons.

Some people, especially those living on the social margins of poverty and discrimination, may have almost no opportunity to achieve this goal. That I recognize. If you are trying to support your family on the minimum wage or are queuing up at the local job centre during an economic downturn, the idea of a life-enhancing career might come across as a luxury.

For the majority living in the affluent West, however, there is nothing utopian about the idea of a fulfilling career. The hardships that existed in the past have eased. You are unlikely to wake up tomorrow with no other option than working a fourteen-hour day in a Lancashire textile mill or to find yourself picking cotton on a slave plantation in Mississippi. As we will discover, the landscape of career choice has opened up remarkably over the past century, offering a new vista of purposeful possibilities. Yes, the bar has been raised: we expect much more from our jobs than previous generations. But when somebody asks us the deadening question 'What do you do?', let us set our sights on giving an enlivening answer, which makes us feel that we are doing something truly worthwhile with our lives, rather than wasting away the years in a career that will leave the bitter taste of regret in our mouths.

Grin and bear it? Forget it. This is a book for those who are looking for a job that is big enough for their spirit, something more than a 'day job' whose main function is to pay the bills. It is a guide for helping you take your working life in new directions, and for bringing your career and who you are into closer alignment.

My approach is to interweave an exploration of two vital questions. First, what are the core elements of a fulfilling career? We need to know what we are actually searching for, and it turns out that there are three essential ingredients: meaning, flow and freedom. None of them are easy to attain, and their pursuit raises inevitable tensions. For instance, should we prefer a career that offers great pay and social status over working for a cause we believe in, with the prospect of making a difference? Should we aspire to be a high achiever in a specialized field, or a 'wide achiever' across several fields? And how can we balance our career ambitions with the demands of being a parent, or with a longing for more free time in our lives?

The second question threading its way through this book is: how do we go about changing career and making the best possible decisions along the way? Although I offer no blueprint strategy that will work for everyone, there are three steps we ought to take. A starting point is to understand the sources of our confusions and fears about leaving our old jobs behind us and embarking on a new career. The next step is to reject the myth that there is a single, perfect job out there waiting for us to discover it, and instead identify our 'multiple selves' – a range of potential careers that might suit the different sides of our character. Finally, we have to turn the standard model of career change on its head: rather than meticulously planning then taking action, we should act first and reflect later, doing experimental projects that test-run our various selves in the real world. Ever thought of treating yourself to a 'radical sabbatical'?

To help answer these questions we will seek inspiration in the lives of famous figures, amongst them Leonardo da Vinci, Marie Curie and Anita Roddick. We will look for insights in the writings of philosophers, psychologists, sociologists and historians, and encounter practical – yet intellectually imaginative – activities to help clarify our thinking and narrow down the career options, such as writing a Personal Job Advertisement. We will draw lessons from the surprising stories of everyday workers, including a Belgian woman whose thirtieth-birthday present to herself was to try out thirty different careers in one year, and an Australian former fridge mechanic who found fulfilment by becoming an embalmer. I will also touch on some of my own career experiences and experiments, which have ranged from journalist to gardener, academic to community worker, with a smattering of telephone sales, tennis coaching and caring for young twins.

In a moment we'll launch our odyssey by exploring why it is so hard to decide which career path to follow. But before we do so, spend a few minutes thinking about the following question – or even better, discuss it with a friend:

- *What is your current work doing to you as a person – to your mind, character and relationships?*

2. A Short History of Career Confusion

'Blue Poles'

I remember, aged 23, standing with my father in front of *Blue Poles*, a painting by Jackson Pollock. He told me that the poles made him think of the bars of a prison cell into which he was gazing. My interpretation was the opposite. I felt as if I was trapped inside a cell, looking out in frustration at the free world.

'But how could you possibly feel that?' he asked. 'You have so much freedom and so many opportunities before you.'

Of course he was right. After graduating from university in Britain, I had travelled around Australia and Indonesia, earned some money working in telephone call centres, and volunteered at Amnesty International. Finally, I had found a job as a financial journalist in London – although it was not nearly as fulfilling as I'd hoped it would be.

'I feel I've got too many choices. All those squiggles on the canvas are my confused thoughts about what to do next. And the bars, maybe, are my fears about making the wrong decision. I don't think journalism is my true vocation in life. But how am I supposed to discover what is?'

'You're only young, kiddo. You can try different careers. There's no point doing something you don't really enjoy.'

It was well-meaning but bland advice that brought out my frustrations.

'You don't realize how hard it is to be free,' I replied brusquely, recognizing how pathetic it sounded as I said it.

He couldn't really understand. It made no sense to him that someone in my position could feel trapped. My father had arrived in Australia as a refugee from Poland in 1951, and had little opportunity to pursue his talents as a mathematician, linguist and musician. After serving three years as an auxiliary nurse in a Sydney hospital – forced labour that was the price of his citizenship – he was lucky to find a job as an accountant at IBM, which gave him the security and stability he needed to construct a new life following years of wartime dislocation. He worked there for over fifty years.

I, on the other hand, had career possibilities that he could never have hoped to imagine. And yet there I was complaining, in the National Gallery in Canberra, feeling perplexed – almost paralysed – by the array of choices before me. Should I try another branch of journalism? Or perhaps train as an English teacher and find a tutoring job in Spain or Italy? Maybe do tennis coaching for a while? Or a postgraduate degree? No matter how hard I stared at *Blue Poles*, I could not see any answers.

I am not alone in having experienced such swirls of confusion. Indeed, very few people today are able to shift career without going through a turbulent period of uncertainty about what direction to follow, which can last months – or even several years. Yet before focusing on how to make the best choices to find fulfilling work, we need to address a critical question: why is it so difficult to decide which career path to take? We must understand the sources of our confusion prior to seeking a way out of the labyrinth.

On some level the problem is plain overload. We can walk into a bookshop and find dozens of inch-thick career guides, each profiling hundreds of different jobs. One website lists 12,000 careers, starting with 487 under the letter 'A' alone – able seaman, abrasive grinder, absorption operator, acetone-recovery worker . . .[7] How are we supposed to choose between so many options? But beneath the sheer number of possibilities lie three fundamental reasons why career choice is often such a conundrum: we are not psychologically equipped to deal with the expansion of choice in recent history; we are burdened by our own pasts, especially the legacy of our early educational choices; and because the popular science of personality testing rarely helps us pinpoint fulfilling careers. As we gradually grasp how these forces shape our lives, we will discover that being able to identify the causes of our career dilemmas is the beginning of moving beyond them.

The Inheritance of Choice

In 1716, the ten-year-old Benjamin Franklin began working with his father as a tallow chandler in Boston. But after two years, the young boy was sick of cutting wicks and filling moulds for candles, and began dreaming of running away to sea, so his father thought to find him another career. They walked together around the neighbouring streets, where Benjamin could see the available options, watching joiners, bricklayers and other tradesmen at their work. Although Benjamin was 'still hankering for the sea', his father finally decided that his bookish son was best suited to becoming a printer, and so secured him an apprenticeship that legally bound him to a print workshop for the next nine years.[8]

For most of history, people had little choice about the jobs they did. Work was a matter of fate and necessity rather than freedom and choice. As with Benjamin Franklin, the decision was often made by their parents, and they were typically expected to follow the family trade. The occupational surnames that so many of us still carry, such as Smith, Baker and Butcher, are remnants of this tradition (Krznaric means 'son of a furrier' in Croatian). Many had the misfortune to be born into slavery or serfdom, and women were generally confined to work in the home. Since the Industrial Revolution, however, the range of career opportunities has expanded beyond recognition. We need to understand not only the origins of our new era of choice, but how we have become psychologically tyrannized by our hard-won freedom.

Karl Marx, one of the first social thinkers to take the subject of career choice seriously, saw that the erosion of feudalism and the rise of wage labour in the eighteenth and nineteenth centuries offered some hope for change. Each worker had 'become a free seller of labour-power, who carries his commodity wherever he finds a market'.[9] That sounds like progress. But he also pointed out that this was an illusory freedom, because most of the possibilities on offer were back-breaking industrial jobs that turned people into slaves of the capitalist system, 'which, vampire-like, lives only by sucking living labour'. If you were a poor woman in Britain, France or Belgium, for instance, you might be working in the coal mines as a 'drawer', crawling down the shafts on your hands and knees, and hauling up loads of coal to the surface for twelve hours a day, through tunnels less than thirty inches high.[10]

Working life before the rise of career choice in the Western world: a young girl at a spinning machine in North Carolina, photographed by Lewis Hine in 1908.

The nineteenth century may have been the era of Dickensian poverty and hellish labouring in the mines and textile mills, but it simultaneously witnessed a revolution in career choice through the spread of public education and the invention of the career open to talent. It was increasingly common, especially in northern Europe, for job selection to be based on merit and qualification rather than bloodline or social connections. Here at last was a chance to scramble up the social hierarchy – though you were most likely to benefit if you were a middle-class man. The British civil service, for example, began making appointments through competitive examination, a development which infuriated the aristocracy, who wanted the cushy jobs for themselves. Few outsiders were able to break into esteemed professions such as law, medicine or the clergy, but if you were the clever and hard-working son – or even daughter – of an artisan or labourer, you might now be able to find your way into white-collar work as an office clerk, tax collector or teacher. By 1851, there were 76,000 men and women working as school teachers in Britain, with a further 20,000 governesses.[11]

If the expansion of public education was the main event in the story of career choice in the nineteenth century, in the twentieth it was the growing number of women who entered the paid workforce. In the US in 1950 around 30 per cent of women had jobs, but by the end of the century that figure had more than doubled, a pattern which was repeated throughout the West.[12] This change partly resulted from the struggle for the vote and the legitimacy gained from doing factory work in two World Wars. Perhaps more significant was the impact of the pill. Within just fifteen years of its invention in 1955, over twenty million women were using oral contraceptives, with more than ten million using the coil.[13] By gaining more control over their own bodies, women now had greater scope to pursue their chosen professions without the interruption of unwanted pregnancy and childrearing. However, this victory for women's liberation has been accompanied by severe dilemmas for both women and men as they attempt to find a balance between the demands of family life and their career ambitions – a subject I will come back to.

In the twenty-first century, we stand as the inheritors of this gradual shift from fate to choice that has filtered into most Western nations. This is not to say that we now live in an age of enlightenment where everyone can, like Sylvester Stallone's boxing hero Rocky Balboa, achieve the mythical American Dream and become whoever they want to be, even if they were born on the wrong side of the tracks. Just ask the migrant workers on the checkout till at your local supermarket, or professional women trying to break into the upper echelons of the corporate world. But looking at the big historical picture, there is little doubt that the majority of people searching for a job today are likely to have far more career opportunities than if they had been living only a century ago.

To get a personal feel for this historical transformation, it is worth pausing to draw a family tree going back a few generations, and including the occupations of each of your family members. Now ask yourself this question:

- *How much choice have you had over your working life compared with your parents or grandparents?*

As in my own case, this family tree is likely to show the career options dwindling away as you go back in time. Perhaps your grandfather was proud to be a factory foreman, but he did not have the education to climb further up the ladder, and his career was disrupted by the war. Maybe your mother was one of the brightest girls in her class at school and wanted to go to university, but she succumbed to family and social pressure to marry young, have children and become a housewife. In all probability, you will have had the good fortune to enjoy many more opportunities than your forebears.

Yet if we are so lucky, why does choosing a career and finding fulfilling work still feel like such a challenge? The answer, according to psychologist Barry Schwartz, is that we now have *too much* choice, and are not good at dealing with it. Although a life without choice is almost unbearable, says Schwartz, we can reach a tipping point where having an abundance of options becomes an overload. 'At this point, choice no longer liberates, but debilitates. It might even be said to tyrannize.'[14]

In his book *The Paradox of Choice*, Schwartz begins by discussing our excess of consumer choice, noting that his local supermarket offers its customers 285 varieties of biscuit and 175 kinds of salad dressing. Another example he gives is the telephone industry. Unlike only a few decades ago, most people in affluent Western nations now have a choice of dozens of private telephone providers for their homes. But it can be extremely difficult to choose between the various companies, since they all offer different pricing systems, special deals and contract rules. Researching and weighing up the options can take hours. 'One effect of having so many options,' argues Schwartz, 'is that it produces paralysis rather than liberation – with so many options to choose from, people find it very difficult to choose at all.' Hence we frequently give up and stick with the telephone company we've already got. A second effect is that 'even if we manage to overcome the paralysis and make a choice, we end up less satisfied with the result of the choice than we would be if we had fewer options'. His main explanation for this apparent paradox is that we can always imagine having made a better choice, so we will regret the decision we did make, and thus feel unhappy about it.[15]

Schwartz believes that similar effects can arise in the realm of career decision-making, since we now have so many more options than in the past, having left behind the days of Benjamin Franklin.[16] Of course, choosing a job is different from shopping around for the right phone company or stereo system: we can't simply select the most enticing offer, since we are limited by factors such as our educational qualifications and work experience. Still, we may face dozens of possible pathways. Do you try to switch out of insurance broking into management consultancy, or maybe law or teaching, or move to a smaller firm, or spend a year travelling to clear your head? Or if you are thinking of retraining as a psychotherapist, will you take a course that focuses on psychodymanic, behavioural or cognitive approaches, or perhaps humanistic, person-centred or integrative? Being confronted by so many options can be a bewildering experience, as I remember when standing in front of *Blue Poles*. The consequence is that we often become psychologically paralysed, like a rabbit caught in the headlights. We get so worried about regretting making a bad choice that we may end up making no decision at all, and remain frozen in our current unfulfilling career.

Are there any solutions for dealing with the choice overload that afflicts modern society? Schwartz makes two main suggestions.

First, we should try to limit our options. So when we go shopping for new clothes, we could make a personal rule that we only visit two shops, rather than endlessly hunting for a better design or a better bargain. Second, we should 'satisfice more and maximize less'. What he means is that instead of aiming to buy the perfect pair of jeans, we should buy a pair that is 'good enough'. In other words, by lowering our expectations, we can avoid much of the angst and time-wasting that arises from having excessive choice.[17]

The problem, though, is that while such strategies might be helpful when shopping, they are inappropriate for making career decisions. There are no easy ways to limit the options – should we just look under the letter 'A' of a career guide? Moreover, the work we do is such a significant part of our lives, that 'good enough' is just not good enough. We should be striving for greater satisfaction rather than settling for less. What we really need to do is narrow down the choices by thinking more deeply about the core elements of a fulfilling career, and then devise concrete ways of testing out which of them best suit our aspirations. And that is precisely what the remaining chapters of this book are about.

The Perils of Education

Although cursed by the tyranny of excessive choice, many people are subject to a second force that makes it difficult to escape their unfulfilling jobs: they are bound by their own pasts, especially the educational choices made in their youth. We find ourselves following the furrows of a career track with origins deep in our personal histories, which can prevent us veering off in more adventurous directions.

It often begins in our school days. At the age of 15 or 16 we may embark on educational pathways that affect our working lives for years. This is commonly the case in Britain, where 80 per cent of pupils choose their A-level subjects for the final two years of high school on the basis of them 'being useful for their career'.[18] If you are thinking of being a foreign-language teacher, you might opt to take French, Italian and History. But having steered clear of the sciences, you can forget about ever becoming a doctor or a vet. Yet equally, if you decide to study medicine at college and manage to get the required entry grades, after slogging away for five or six years to qualify, the chances of you then deciding to become a graphic designer or session musician instead are virtually nil. Doctors might complain about the long hours and high stress, but they rarely ever switch careers out of the health sector.

The way that education can lock us into careers, or at least substantially direct the route we travel, would not be so problematic if we were excellent judges of our future interests and characters. But we are not. When you were 16, or even in your early twenties, how much did you know about what kind of career would stimulate your mind and offer a meaningful vocation? Did you even know the range of jobs that were out there? Most of us lack the experience of life – and of ourselves – to make a wise decision at that age, even with the help of well-meaning careers advisers.

The result is that people so often find themselves stuck in careers that do not suit their personalities, ideals or expectations. Their educational choices and opportunities have come to haunt them.

That is what happened to Sameera Khan, who we heard from earlier, who eventually wrenched herself away from a full-time position as a lawyer to try her hand as a social entrepreneur:

> Looking back now, it's crazy. At 16 I wanted to become a lawyer. How on earth am I supposed to know that that is what I want to do for the rest of my life? I'm not going to be the same person I am at 16 as I am at 45. I'm going to have different values, opinions and motivations.

Family pressures and expectations can also shape our early educational and job decisions, especially for the children of immigrants or those with high-achieving parents. One quarter of British Asian graduates feel their parents significantly influenced their career choice, a figure that is just one in ten for non-Asians. And these parents have very clear ideas about what is an appropriate profession for their offspring: 24 per cent favour medicine, 19 per cent law and 14 per cent accountancy.[19] Sameera fits the pattern: she knew choosing a career in law would please her Pakistani father and Indian mother. Unsurprisingly, they found her decision to resign from a high-paying legal job utterly perplexing. 'It's very difficult for them to comprehend,' she says. 'They would understand if I was older and had paid off most of the mortgage, and had kids and sent them to school. But they think I've rashly walked away from security, from setting myself up with a comfortable future, without gaining the financial benefits. Though in a way they're right – it makes me feel sick every time I think about what I've done.'

Although family opinion might shape our choices as impressionable youths, as we get older this influence gradually fades away.

Disapproval from her parents was not going to stop Sameera handing in her notice to her company as a thirty-two-year-old. But something else was. And that was the idea that she had spent so long studying to become a lawyer that it would be an unforgivable waste of those years if she left the profession: 'I thought that there was no way I would or could quit only a short time after qualifying – I'd worked so hard to get there. I would be letting myself down.' This kind of thinking resembles what economists describe as a decision based on 'sunk costs': if you buy an expensive pair of shoes that turn out to be incredibly uncomfortable, you won't want to throw them out because they cost you so much.[20] Similarly, you will be reluctant to give up a legal career to which you've dedicated a decade of your life, even if you find it unfulfilling. The sunk costs are just too high to ignore.

This sense that we might be squandering everything we have struggled to achieve is one of the greatest psychological barriers facing those contemplating career change. If you have spent years working your way up the ladder in law, advertising or any other profession, and then realize you are miserable and want to leave, you will hardly be consoled by a friend who reassures you that it was 'all part of life's journey' or that 'nothing is ever wasted'. They could be right in the end – the skills gained in your former career might be successfully applied elsewhere – yet such clichés won't make you feel much better at the time. You may also be unwilling to relinquish a work identity that gives you a sense of status and belonging. As already mentioned, Sameera worried that losing her identity as a lawyer would 'make me feel naked and completely empty'.

The upshot is that we can find ourselves in a constant struggle with our pasts, unable to make a decision to try something new because of an allegiance to the person we have been, rather than to the person we hope to become.

A helpful way to think about this is that we are caught between two forms of regret. On the one hand, the regret of abandoning a career into which we've put years of time, energy and emotion. And on the other, the possibility of looking back on our lives in old age and regretting that we didn't leave a job that was not offering us fulfilment. So which kind of regret should we give the greatest weight to in our decisions? The latter, according to the latest psychology research: the most emotionally corrosive form of regret occurs when we fail to take action on something that matters deeply to us. As time goes on, the choice we didn't make looms larger and larger in our minds, and the thought 'if only I had . . .' casts a dark shadow over our lives.[21] The philosopher A.C. Grayling has come to a similar conclusion: 'If there is anything worth fearing in the world, it is living in such a way that gives one cause for regret in the end.'

We ought to recognize that our early educational and career choices could well have been made when we were very different people than we are today. Clinging onto a job that no longer suits your personality or aspirations can be like trying to hold onto a relationship that just isn't working because you've grown apart. There comes a point when splitting up is probably the healthiest option, painful though it may be. We all change: we learn more about ourselves, and shift our priorities and perspectives, under the challenging tutelage of human experience.

- *What were the key moments in your education that shaped the direction of your career?*

The Flawed Science of Personality Testing

Faced by an overload of job options, and a reluctance to let go of our old career, how we are supposed to find our way out of the confusion? Over the past hundred years, an intriguing new profession has emerged, designed specifically to help us with this task: the career counsellor. Within an extraordinarily short period of time they have become the high priests of the modern workplace, offering expert advice to everyone from school leavers and college graduates to those who have just been made redundant or are subsumed in a mid-life crisis.

There are many varieties of career counselling, some extremely subtle and penetrating, others less so. One form deserves special attention, both because of its ubiquity and its potential dangers: career advice based on personality testing. The idea that you can fill out a standardized questionnaire and find a perfect match between your personality type and a particular career is an enticing one. But there is strong evidence to suggest that it is an essentially flawed method, which, although having some benefits, raises expectations that are rarely met. An important reason why the search for a fulfilling career can feel so difficult is because this apparently 'scientific' approach to career advice seldom provides the answers we had hoped for. To explain exactly why this is so, we need to return to the roots of career advice itself.

The so-called 'father of vocational guidance' was a former engineer, lawyer and school teacher named Frank Parsons. In 1908 he established the Vocation Bureau in Boston, which offered one of the world's first career-counselling services.[22] His seminal book, *Choosing a Vocation*, was published the following year, and became the bible for early generations of professional advisers, especially in the United States. Parsons firmly believed that career guidance should be based on scientific principles. He developed an elaborate system designed to match his clients' personality traits with the desired characteristics for success in specific industries. Walk into his office and he would begin by asking you no less than 116 assessment questions. He wanted to know not only your personal ambitions, strengths and weaknesses, but also how often you bathed and whether you slept with the window open. This man was thorough.

There was just one more thing he had to do before offering his sage advice for your working future. 'I carefully observe the shape of the applicant's head.' Yes, his head. 'If the applicant's head is largely developed behind the ears, with big neck, low forehead, and small upper head, he is probably of the animal type,' wrote Parsons, 'and should be dealt with on that basis'.[23]

Parsons was an adherent of the now-defunct 'science' of phrenology, which taught that a person's character could be assessed by measuring their cranial prominences and depressions. A twenty-two-year-old department-store assistant who came to see Parsons was observed to have a 'narrow head not very well balanced', and was advised against pursuing his ambition to become a lawyer. Others were luckier – 'head large, splendidly shaped,' he declared of the bookish son of an engineer.[24] Parsons was not alone in his cranial obsessions. One of the darker secrets of the history of career counselling is that it originated in the vogue for phrenology in the US in the nineteenth century, which itself had roots in racial theories suggesting that the superiority of whites over other races was evident in their finely shaped skulls. From the 1820s, writes one historian, 'many

'The boy – what will he become?' In this 1820s cartoon, a phrenologist measures the bumps on a young gentleman's head. Hanging on the wall is a portrait of Franz Josef Gall (1757–1828), founder of the popular pseudo-science.

job advertisements asked applicants to submit a phrenological report along with their letter of reference', and thousands were issued with career guidance based on their head measurements.[25]

This dubious scientific approach to career advice underwent a transformation in the first half of the twentieth century. Instead of measuring the outside of the head, the new trend was to measure the inside using personality tests, which had become increasingly popular since the French psychologist Alfred Binet invented the IQ test in 1905. By the 1970s, the issuing of psychometric tests to determine personality type had become part of the standard repertoire for many career counsellors.

The obvious question is whether such tests are successful at helping people identify a fulfilling career. My discussions with job seekers revealed a multitude of sceptics. Lisa Gormley, for example, remembers her reaction, aged 15, at reading the response to the personality questionnaire run at her high school:

> The computer printout told me that the best career match was being a dental nurse. It was a ridiculous suggestion. Dentists – urgh! – writing down 'upper left 1, 2, 3, 4, 5, 6 not present, 7, 8' while the dentist counts across some punter's teeth – boring! Being stuck inside a blue examining room with dusty slatted blinds on a sunny day – not for me, baby! I'm down the riverbank with a book of poetry . . . It stopped me thinking about careers altogether.

Lisa took pleasure in ignoring the advice. She went on to study philosophy and French at Oxford University, worked with refugees in Guatemala and Jordan, and later became an international human-rights lawyer.

We should not, however, be too quick to dismiss personality tests. There is a whole industry of career advisers who take them very seriously. Yet even the most sophisticated tests have considerable flaws. Take the Myers–Briggs Type Indicator (MBTI), the world's most popular psychometric test, which is based on Jung's theory of personality types. Over two million are administered every year, and there is a good chance you will have done one in a career-guidance session, during a management course at work, or as part of a job-interview process. The MBTI places you in one of sixteen personality types, based on dichotomous categories such as whether you are an introvert or an extrovert, or have a disposition towards being logical or emotional (what it calls 'thinking' or 'feeling').

The interesting – and somewhat alarming – fact about the MBTI is that, despite its popularity, it has been subject to sustained criticism by professional psychologists for over three decades.[26] One problem is that it displays what statisticians call low 'test-retest reliability'. So if you retake the test after only a five-week gap, there is around a 50 per cent chance that you will fall into a different personality category compared to the first time you took the test.[27] A second criticism is that the MBTI mistakenly assumes that personality falls into mutually exclusive 'either/or' categories. You are *either* an extrovert *or* an introvert, but never a mix of the two. Yet in reality, most people fall somewhere in the middle on this and other dimensions of personality.[28] If the MBTI also measured height, you would be classified as either tall or short, even though the majority of people are within a band of medium height. The consequence is that the test score of two people labelled respectively 'introvert' and 'extrovert' may be almost exactly the same, but they are placed by the MBTI into different categories since they fall just on either side of an imaginary dividing line.[29]

One other thing. And this really matters for readers of this book. According to official Myers–Briggs documents, the test can 'give you an insight into what kinds of work you might enjoy and be successful doing'. So if you are, like me, classified as 'INTJ' (your dominant traits are being introverted, intuitive and having a preference for thinking and judging), the best-fit occupations include management consultant, IT professional and engineer.[30] Would a change to one of these careers make me more fulfilled? Unlikely, according to respected US psychologist David Pittenger, because there is 'no evidence to show a positive relation between MBTI type and success within an occupation . . . nor is there any data to suggest that specific types are more satisfied within specific occupations than are other types'. Then why is the MBTI so popular? Its success, he argues, is primarily due to 'the beguiling nature of the horoscope-like summaries of personality and steady marketing'.[31]

Personality tests have their uses, even if they do not reveal any scientific 'truth' about us. If we are in a state of confusion they can be a great emotional comfort, offering a clear diagnosis of why our current job may not be right, and suggesting others that might suit us better. They also raise interesting hypotheses that aid self-reflection: until I took the MBTI, I had certainly never considered that IT could offer me a bright future (by the way, I apparently have the wrong personality type to be a writer). Yet we should be wary about relying on them as a magic pill that enables us suddenly to hit upon a dream career. That is why wise career counsellors treat such tests with caution, using them as only one of many ways of exploring who you are. Human personality does not neatly reduce into sixteen or any other definitive number of categories: we are far more complex creatures than psychometric tests can ever reveal. And as we will shortly learn, there is compelling evidence that we are much more likely to find fulfilling work by conducting career experiments in the real world than by filling out any number of questionnaires.[32]

Where does this journey into career confusion leave us? It should now be clear that you are not alone in the uncertainties you may feel about which path to follow, nor are you personally to blame for them. History has bequeathed us an overload of options that few of us are psychologically equipped to handle. We might also be struggling against the legacies of educational and career decisions made in our immature youths or under family pressure. What is more, the promise of 'scientific' career advice, which maps our personalities onto specific jobs, has failed to materialize and offer an easy way out of our dilemmas.

You should also be in a better position to answer the central questions underlying your own career confusions. Give yourself ten minutes to consider them right now. On a sheet of paper, write down – or describe in pictures and diagrams – your responses to the following:

- *What are the three main reasons why you are feeling confused about where to go next?*
- *What are your three greatest fears about changing career?*
- *What are the three biggest practical challenges you face?*

I will be saying much more about how to confront our fears and other obstacles, but for the moment it is simply useful to think about these questions, identifying your worries and looking them in the eye.

We are now poised to move beyond the realm of uncertainties. We need to boldly go where most personality tests fail to take us, and explore exactly what kinds of fulfilment we wish to seek in our careers. Do we want to follow the glittering allure of money and status, or to be guided in our search for meaning by our values, talents and passions?

3. Giving Meaning to Work

The Five Dimensions of Meaning

The most terrible punishment for any human being, wrote Dostoyevsky, would be if they were condemned to a lifetime of work that was 'completely and utterly devoid of usefulness and meaning'. He was right that meaning matters. Along with flow and freedom, it is one of the three basic ingredients of a fulfilling career. But he leaves us wondering what meaning really *means*, and how to find it.

In this chapter I want to consider five different aspects of what can make a job meaningful: earning money, achieving status, making a difference, following our passions, and using our talents. We can think about these as the fundamental motivating forces that drive people in their careers. They are the psychological underpinnings of the work we do, and why we do it. Both money and status are known as 'extrinsic' motivating factors, since they are about approaching work as a means to an end, whereas the remaining three are 'intrinsic', with the work valued as an end in itself.[33]

The question we need to address is: Which of these motivations should be the principal guide in our career decisions? Should we, for instance, prefer a job with an excellent pay package over one with a lower salary but which provides greater scope for using our creative talents? Clarifying our thoughts on where our priorities lie can help us develop a personal vision of what meaningful work looks like, so we can narrow down the career possibilities and make the right choices.

As we explore each motivation in turn, we will discover not only their individual challenges and the tensions between them, but that there is no single blueprint for a meaningful career. Yet it will also become clear that pursuing a career mainly because it offers the tempting rewards of money and status is an unlikely route to the good life. With the help of a cosmetics tycoon, a professional athlete and a former space-flight engineer, we will learn that following our values, passions and talents is the most likely way to satisfy our hunger for fulfilment. At that point, we will be sufficiently primed to try three imaginative activities designed to generate concrete career options.

Money and the Good Life

Is one of the main reasons you're in your current job because the money is good? And is one of the main reasons you are reluctant to leave it because you can't imagine taking a substantial salary cut, or entering a profession with limited financial prospects? When I ask these questions in the classes I teach at The School of Life on 'How to Find a Job you Love', at least half the people in the room sheepishly raise their hands.

Their response is unsurprising, because choosing a career for its monetary rewards is the oldest and most powerful motivation in the world of work. In the nineteenth century, the German philosopher Arthur Schopenhauer suggested why this desire for money is so pervasive: 'Men are often criticized that money is the chief object of their wishes and is preferred above all else, but it is natural and even unavoidable. For money is an inexhaustible Proteus, ever ready to change itself into the present object of our changeable wishes and manifold needs . . . Money is human happiness in the abstract.' So does this mean we should place our hopes for career fulfilment in substantial salaries and big bonuses? The answer is no.

Schopenhauer may have been right that the desire for money is widespread, but he was wrong on the issue of equating money with happiness. Overwhelming evidence has emerged in the last two decades that the pursuit of wealth is an unlikely path to achieving personal wellbeing – the ancient Greek ideal of *eudaimonia* or 'the good life'. The lack of any clear positive relationship between rising income and rising happiness has become one of the most powerful findings in the modern social sciences. Once our income reaches an amount that covers our basic needs, further increases add little, if anything, to our levels of life satisfaction.[34]

This is because we typically get caught on what psychologist Martin Seligman calls a 'hedonic treadmill': as we get richer and accumulate more material possessions, our expectations rise, so we work even harder to earn money to buy more consumer goods to boost our wellbeing, but then our expectations rise once more, and on it goes.[35] We shift from a standard TV to widescreen, from one car to two, from renting a holiday home to owning a second home, and none of it does much to boost our sense of having a fulfilling and meaningful life, and may well contribute to higher levels of anxiety and depression since we are forever yearning for more. Few people have the conviction to avoid the hedonic treadmill, even those who promise themselves they will only stay in a soulless big-money job for a limited period such as five years before getting out: they almost always get caught on the treadmill and fail to keep their promise.

Amongst the wisest commentators on such matters is the psychotherapist Sue Gerhardt, who in her book *The Selfish Society* observes:

> In the West, we are trapped in these cycles of endless striving and dissatisfaction, trying to keep up with the ever-more elaborate displays of consumption we see on television and on the internet. This drive to accumulate material goods and services appears to have addictive qualities: it is a powerful appetite which has no inbuilt mechanism to alert us to when we have had enough; we want more and more – especially, it seems, just that little bit more than everyone else . . . Although we have relative material abundance, we do not in fact have emotional abundance. Many people are deprived of what really matters. Lacking emotional security, they seek security in material things.[36]

So we may be looking for fulfilment in the wrong places – in *having* rather than *being*, in accumulating possessions rather than in building nurturing, empathic relationships. It might be time to abandon the assumption that a career mainly driven by making money can buy us the purposeful, flourishing lives that we so dearly desire.

Furthermore, when people are asked about what gives them job satisfaction, they rarely place money at the top of the list. In the Mercer global-engagement scale – drawing on interviews with thousands of workers in Europe, the US, China, Japan and India – 'base pay' only comes in at number seven out of twelve key factors. What really seems to matter to people is the quality of their relationships in the workplace: both 'respect' and 'the people you work with' head up the list. Other polls similarly reveal that good relationships with colleagues, as well as issues such as work–life balance, job security and sense of autonomy trump pay as a source of satisfaction.[37]

Few people are likely to completely ignore money when making a career decision: we all have mortgages hanging over us, bills to pay, and families to care for. The real issue is how much weight we should assign to it. We don't need philosophers or spiritual gurus to tell us the answer. There is now abundant empirical evidence to suggest that if we truly aspire to live the good life, then we would be rash to allow money to be our primary goal.

- *What would you most like to change about your attitude to money?*

Status and the Secrets of Embalming

Apart from money, the other extrinsic reward people commonly seek is social status. This comes in two varieties. One is the status we get from having a prestigious job which is admired and revered by others, such as being a diplomat, television producer, barrister, surgeon, professional athlete, professor or writer. It's an alluring prospect: as one of my students recently told me, 'I've always wanted a job that sounded cool to my friends.' Like the ancient Romans, we still have a strong yearning for reputation and glory.

The second variety is status based on our position relative to others. This partly reveals itself in our income preferences. A famous study in behavioural economics showed that if given a choice between earning $50,000 a year with everyone else earning $25,000, or earning $100,000 while others earned $200,000, the majority of people would choose the former.[38] We also care about our relative position in career hierarchies. If you see all your peers climbing the ladder of success, becoming company directors or top managers, yet you remain languishing at the bottom of the ranks, then you may well feel something of a failure and have a desire to join them.

Status can be an important way to boost our self-esteem. But as the eighteenth-century philosopher Jean-Jacques Rousseau warned, 'this universal desire for reputation', in which we judge ourselves through other people's eyes, is fraught with dangers.[39] We can easily find ourselves pursuing a career that society considers prestigious, but which we are not intrinsically devoted to ourselves – one that does not fulfil us on a day-to-day basis. In my teaching, I am constantly meeting people who are deeply unhappy about their work despite having apparently enviable careers, such as being a photojournalist or neuroscientist. Others in the room can hardly believe that they are miserable in their outwardly impressive jobs.

There is a further problem. Once we achieve one status level, another often instantly appears above it. We may aspire, for instance, to be a successful TV producer. But having become the producer of a popular TV show, we might then want to be amongst those who have won coveted awards or who also make feature films. Our peer group shifts, and the status we seek is forever just beyond our grasp, much like the 'hedonic treadmill' that continually raises our expectations as consumers. The writer and spiritual thinker C.S. Lewis identified this problem when he said that most of us desire to be a member of an 'inner ring' of esteemed or important people, but we 'will reach no "inside" that is worth reaching' since there are always more rings within it.[40] The lesson may be the simple one that we should not be so concerned about what other people think about us.

- *Who do you imagine is judging your status – perhaps family, old friends or colleagues? Do you want to grant them that power?*

Of course, most of us do want recognition from others. But how can we gain it, if not through status? The answer lies in a funeral parlour.

Trevor Dean used to work as a refrigeration mechanic, and later as a shop assistant, in the Australian state of Victoria. One day, a friend mentioned that he was doing work experience at a local mortuary. Trevor, who was accustomed to seeing death, having spent years as a volunteer fire-fighter, found himself quizzing his friend about what sounded like a fascinating career:

> I wanted a job that had meaning, that was challenging, and that was interesting. So when a local ad appeared for a funeral assistant, I went for it and out of thirty applicants, I was the lucky one. Three years later I applied to do the embalmers course. I'm now fully qualified and have never looked back. The study made me realize how incredible this human body of ours is.
>
> What does the job mean to me? I look after loved ones on their last journey; I care for them as if they were my own. I have a folder full of thank-you letters from family members, which I think explain a lot about why I am an embalmer.

One letter says, 'his wife just kept saying how peaceful and beautiful he looked and wanted to pass on her thanks'. Another that, 'the family were absolutely rapt with the way she was presented and couldn't stop raving about how good she looked, so thank you for your work.' A third says, 'the friends of ___ have said that he looked "bloody fantastic", you've done a great job my friend!'

The sense of fulfilment that Trevor clearly derives from his work is not based on having a high-status job: being an embalmer is hardly a prestigious profession. As Trevor himself recognizes, 'The West fears death, and nine out of ten people really do freak out when I tell them I'm an embalmer.' What makes his job so worthwhile is that it gives him respect.

By respect I don't mean being treated with deference by others, like some big-time Mafia boss. What I mean is being appreciated for what we personally bring to a job, and being valued for our individual contribution. In Trevor's case, that sense of respect comes from family members of the deceased, who value his skills as an embalmer. More commonly, we might gain our respect from work colleagues who praise us for our creative intellect or organizational genius.

While most of us wish to enjoy a dose of social status, the feeling that we are respected by others for what we do and how we do it is one of the keys to having a meaningful career. As the sociologist of work Richard Sennett explains, respect enables us to feel like 'a full human being whose presence matters'.[41] No wonder it ranks so high in surveys of job satisfaction. The lesson is that in our quest for fulfilling work, we should seek a job that offers not just good status prospects, but good respect prospects. That may mean avoiding large bureaucratic organisations where individual efforts are barely acknowledged, and finding a workplace where employees feel treated as unique human beings and part of a community of equals. Who knows, you might even discover yourself working in a funeral home.

I Want to Make a Difference

'I want to make a difference' is a phrase that can be heard amongst recent graduates wandering the caverns of university careers offices, and equally amongst thirty-something professionals who feel frustrated that they spend most of their days dealing with tedious emails or marketing products they don't really care about. They want something more: to make a positive contribution to people and planet, and to put their values into practice. It is an increasingly common desire, even in our age of rampant hyper-individualism, and one that resembles the ancient Greeks' aspiration to perform some virtuous and noble deed that would give their lives a sense of purpose and ensure their immortality in historical memory.[42] We want to be able to look back in old age and feel that we have left our mark.

Most people intuitively know that making a difference is a promising path to a fulfilling career. And it's borne out by the evidence. A major study of ethical work by Howard Gardner, Mihaly Csikszentmihalyi and William Damon showed that those doing what they call 'good work' – defined as 'work of expert quality that benefits the broader society' – consistently exhibit high levels of job satisfaction.[43] The moral philosopher Peter Singer would agree. He argues that our greatest hope for personal fulfilment is dedicating our lives – and if possible our *working* lives – to a 'transcendent cause' that is larger than ourselves, especially an ethical one such as animal rights, poverty alleviation or environmental justice.[44] Such views build on deep traditions of religious thought that promote the idea that giving to others through our work is spiritually uplifting. As Martin Luther King said, 'Everybody can be great because everybody can serve.'

The question is how to go about it. People often assume that ethical careers are mainly found in charities or the public sector; say working at a homeless shelter or as a special-needs teacher in a state school. But one of the great revolutions of the modern workplace is that there are now so many more career opportunities for making a difference, as Clare Taylor discovered.

After graduating with a degree in engineering science, Clare found a job in an engineering consultancy in San Francisco, then moved to a better-paid position in a small software house. While busy working on building content-management systems for Sony, so people could get their soap-opera updates online, she began moonlighting for a media organisation called Internews, helping Palestinians use the internet to spread news of the violence they were experiencing. That's when she had a moment of political revelation, realizing that she cared much more about social justice than boosting Sony's corporate profits. 'I had an epiphany,' said Clare. 'I suddenly knew which side I was on.'

So she ditched her dotcom job and returned home to Ireland to start a new life. Appalled by the materialistic money-grabbing of the Celtic Tiger boom, she decided to take a risk and do something about it:

With no publishing experience, I used the last of my savings to start a magazine with the aim of changing the culture. It was called *YOKE: Free Thinking for the World Citizen.* It lasted two years, gained a fair bit of media attention and some great contributors, including Isabel Allende, Pico Iyer and Jeanette Winterson. I was living on the dole and in a bedsit, running the magazine from my office which was under the loft bed in the corner of the room. Although I was skint, I had a real sense that this was exactly what I was supposed to be doing.

Clare had to close the magazine when she became pregnant. Since then she has worked for an NGO on the economics of sustainability, for a government agency on renewable-energy policy, and has been a researcher for television programmes about sustainable development. Although not certain where she'll go next, Clare remains committed to the struggle against what she calls 'the death march of consumerism':

My career search has cost in financial terms but the experi-ence has enriched my life. Personally, I couldn't work for a cause that I didn't believe in – this is a very big part of meaningful work for me. I was once talking to a friend of my father's about life choices and the awkward translation of ideas into reality. He told me that life was short and I must use it to do the things I was born to do. The next day he died of a heart attack. Our time here is short and we must be willing to take risks and make fools of ourselves, but never give up hope of a better world. The stakes are so much higher than any of the status or money rewards of the rat race.

Clare's efforts to make a difference have taken her from online journalism and literary publishing to ecological campaigning, public-policy work and television. That's a lot more varied than would have been possible a century ago, when ethical careers were largely limited to missionary work and a few professions like nursing. But whichever paths we may choose to follow, there are two challenges that anybody hoping to make a difference will have to face.

The first concerns the impact of their actions. One of the greatest frustrations is that it is often difficult to see, in concrete terms, what difference your work is actually making. I know this from personal experience, having spent years as an academic and development consultant writing about poverty and human rights in Latin America. Were all those words I was churning out really helping to improve people's day-to-day lives? I felt much better when I made a major career change and started running a community project in my home town of Oxford, where the effects of my work were far more visible. But then I worried that I wasn't making a difference on a broad enough scale.

A second challenge is the tensions that can arise between making a difference and making money. In Clare Taylor's experience, doing work that embodies her values has involved a clear financial sacrifice. But the emergence of new economic sectors such as social enterprise raises the question of whether it might be possible to enjoy both the intrinsic rewards of being true to our beliefs and the extrinsic rewards of earning money. The career of Anita Roddick, founder of The Body Shop cosmetics chain, can help us dissect these issues.

By the time of her death in 2007, Roddick was one of the world's most successful and admired entrepreneurs, famous for having brought ethics into enterprise. But The Body Shop didn't start out

Anita Roddick in the early days of The Body Shop in the 1970s. She came to believe in 'the necessity of reinventing work by attaching a values system to it'.

as a values-driven business. When she founded the first store in Brighton in 1976 – after failed ventures running a bed & breakfast and a rock'n'roll burger bar – Roddick was merely trying to make enough money to survive on. She asked customers to return their bottles for refilling not for environmental reasons but for financial ones. 'Everything was determined by money, or rather a lack of it', she wrote in her memoirs.[45]

Gradually, however, values started filtering into the business, transforming The Body Shop into a company geared to making a difference as well as making face creams, and which earned profits while not intent on maximizing them. 'I am opposed to maximizing profits to satisfy investors,' Roddick stated bluntly. Instead, at the heart of the company's philosophy was 'the necessity of reinventing work by attaching a values system to it . . . we're a hair and skin company that works for positive social change'.

What did this mean in practice? An early initiative, working together with her husband Gordon, was to use their fleet of lorries to promote social causes, like pasting pictures of missing persons on the side of the trucks with a helpline number. Within weeks they had received 30,000 calls and several of the people were found. In 1988 they established Soapworks, a soap factory-cum-social enterprise in a deprived area of Glasgow, which funnelled profits back into the local community. In 1991, seed money from The Body Shop Foundation was used to start up the *Big Issue*, a magazine sold by homeless people, which now exists in eight nations and sells 300,000 copies a week. The Body Shop also pioneered fair-trade relationships, working with indigenous communities in Brazil and other countries to directly source ingredients for their products. Roddick later used the company as a political machine to campaign for the rights of the Ogoni people, whose lives were being destroyed by Shell's oil drilling in the Niger Delta.[46]

Throughout these decades, Roddick's sense of fulfilment in her job – and the fulfilment enjoyed by many of her employees – grew out of the company's radical socio-political agenda. So we might conclude that private enterprise offers enormous potential to those who seek a purposeful, values-based career. Not so fast. Even someone as brilliant and charismatic – and domineering – as Roddick could not survive without making serious ethical compromises.

'One of the biggest mistakes I made was to go public and on the stock market,' she admitted.[47] After doing so, growing obligations to shareholders, investors and corporate management began to eat away at the moral fibre of The Body Shop. The problems emerged in the early nineties when top management opposed her campaign against the Persian Gulf War, arguing that it would damage sales. Consultants were brought in to restructure the company and make it more profitable, reducing the scope for social initiatives.[48] Once Roddick stepped down from being CEO in the late nineties – some say she was pushed out – The Body Shop lost its ethical drive. Today, the company is part of the L'Oréal corporate group, and barely pays lip service to the values it once possessed.

It is a salutary tale, revealing the potential discord that can emerge when trying both to make money and to make a difference: enterprise and ethics do not easily mix.

Rather than hoping to create a harmonious union between the pursuit of money and values, we might have better luck trying to combine values with talents. This idea comes courtesy of Aristotle, who is attributed with saying, 'Where the needs of the world and your talents cross, there lies your vocation.' That may be the single most useful piece of career advice to have emerged in the past 3,000 years, and one with which Anita Roddick would probably have agreed. We might all contemplate turning our particular gifts and abilities towards the major social, political and ecological dilemmas of our age. Although we may believe that there are no ethical careers that can easily accommodate our talents or expertise, almost any professional skill can be applied in a job that makes a difference: we can use our marketing prowess working for a fast-food chain or for a cancer-research foundation; we can offer our accounting experience to an investment bank or a mental-health charity. Ultimately, the choice is ours.

- *Where do your talents meet the needs of the world?*

How to Cultivate Passions and Talents

While an ethical career is one intrinsically rewarding path to the good life, there is also the option of focusing on your passions and talents. Forget money, status or even making a difference: do what you love and what you're really good at. In all my years of talking to people about their jobs, I've never come across a better example of this than Wayne Davies.

For over two decades Wayne, who grew up in Australia, was a professional coach and player of the esoteric medieval sport of 'real tennis'. The forerunner of regular tennis, real tennis is played on an indoor court where the ball can ricochet off the walls and points are won by hitting targets. There are only forty-five courts and 5,000 players worldwide (I happen to be one of them). Wayne was so enamoured with real tennis when he first discovered it in 1978 that within months he resigned his job as a secondary-school science teacher, took a huge salary cut, and began a new career as an assistant coach in Melbourne. He had to travel for almost three hours each morning to arrive at work by 8 a.m. I once asked him what was the best thing about being a real tennis pro. 'Playing tennis,' he replied, as if I had asked a very stupid question. He immediately went on. 'What's the best thing about life? Playing tennis. That's what I think. Life is a tennis court. I'm never happier than when I'm playing a proper match – you can erase everything else in life.'

After becoming the head professional at the real tennis club in New York City, Wayne gave his whole life to the game, sleeping on a mattress at the club so he could get up and practise at dawn for four hours before his coaching work started for the day. He sometimes even practised in the middle of the night in his pyjamas. 'If you're going to get good at anything,' he told me, 'you've got to have tunnel vision.' This was a man obsessed, even possessed. The result? He became the sport's world champion in 1987, reigning undefeated for almost eight years.[49]

Two things made Wayne so fulfilled by his career, apart from the glory of his tournament victories. First, he felt he was realizing his potential as an athlete, stretching his talents as far as they would go. Second, he had merged his greatest passion with his work. Following the latter strategy, however, is a controversial choice. While some people swear that transforming their hobbies or interests into their jobs was the turning point on the road to fulfilment, others claim that it was a terrible mistake. You might love building model trains, but starting up a company selling them online, with all the stresses involved, could drain all the joy from your passion, and make you nostalgic for those rainy Sunday afternoons tinkering with engines, when you had no sales figures to worry about.

This is a subject I will address further when discussing freedom, but on balance I think mixing work and play is usually worth the risk of potential contamination. As the cultural critic Pat Kane argues, we should strive to develop a 'play ethic' in our lives, which places 'yourself, your passions and enthusiasms at the centre of your world'.[50] The French writer François-René de Chateaubriand made a similar point over a century ago:

> A master in the art of living draws no sharp distinction between his work and his play; his labour and his leisure; his mind and his body; his education and his recreation. He hardly knows which is which. He simply pursues his vision of excellence through whatever he is doing, and leaves others to determine whether he is working or playing. To himself, he always appears to be doing both.

There is a further dilemma awaiting those intent on pursuing their talents or passions in the workplace, which is whether we should aim to be specialists, directing ourselves towards a single profession, or aim to become generalists, developing our various talents and passions across several different fields. I think of this as the question of whether we should aspire to be high achievers or 'wide achievers'.

For over a century, Western culture has been telling us that the best way to use our talents and be successful is to specialize and become an expert in a narrow field, just like Wayne Davies. This ideology is to a significant extent rooted in the division of labour that emerged during the Industrial Revolution, which split most jobs into tiny segments in order to increase efficiency and production levels. So now many people find themselves funnelled into working in a limited field, for instance as a corporate-tax specialist, reference librarian or anaesthetist.[51] Specialization may be all very well if you happen to have skills particularly suited to these jobs, or if you are passionate about a niche area of work, and of course there is also the benefit of feeling pride in being considered an expert. But there is equally the danger of becoming dissatisfied by the repetition inherent in many specialist professions: studies of surgeons reveal that those who only perform operations on tonsils or appendices soon begin to feel the tedium and become unhappy in their lucrative jobs.[52]

Moreover, our culture of specialization conflicts with something most of us intuitively recognize, but which careers advisers are only beginning to understand: we each have multiple selves. According to Herminia Ibarra, one of the world's leading academic thinkers on career change:

> our working identity is not a hidden treasure waiting to be discovered at the very core of our being – rather, it is made up of many possibilities . . . we are many selves.[53]

Indeed, we need not think that being, say, a secondary-school English teacher is the only career that could bring us fulfilment. We have complex, multi-faceted experiences, interests, values and talents, which might mean that we could also find fulfilment as a web designer, or a community police officer, or running an organic cafe.

This is a potentially liberating idea with radical implications. It raises the possibility that we might discover career fulfilment by escaping the confines of specialization and cultivating ourselves as wide achievers. Only then may we be able to develop the many sides of who we are, allowing the various petals of our identity to fully unfold. There are two classic approaches to being a wide achiever: becoming a 'Renaissance generalist', who pursues several careers simultaneously, or a 'serial specialist', who does one after another.

The first option is modelled on the Renaissance ideal that to be fully human we should do all we can to foster the array of our individual talents and the many dimensions of our personality. Perhaps the greatest Renaissance generalist of them all was Leonardo da Vinci. He was not only a painter, but also an engineer, inventor, natural scientist, philosopher and musician. Open his notebooks and you will see jottings on an incredible variety of subjects: there are anatomical sketches of horses, plans for flying machines, investigations of human foetuses, astronomical observations, designs for theatrical costumes, fossil studies, to name but a few. As the art critic Kenneth Clark put it, Leonardo was 'the most relentlessly curious man in history'.[54] In terms of his working life, it meant that in the same week he might be creating a war machine for a power-hungry duke, doing a portrait for an artistic patron, and studying cloud movements on the side. History has never seen a more accomplished wide achiever.

Leonardo was an early example of what is today known as a 'portfolio worker', a term invented by management thinker Charles Handy.

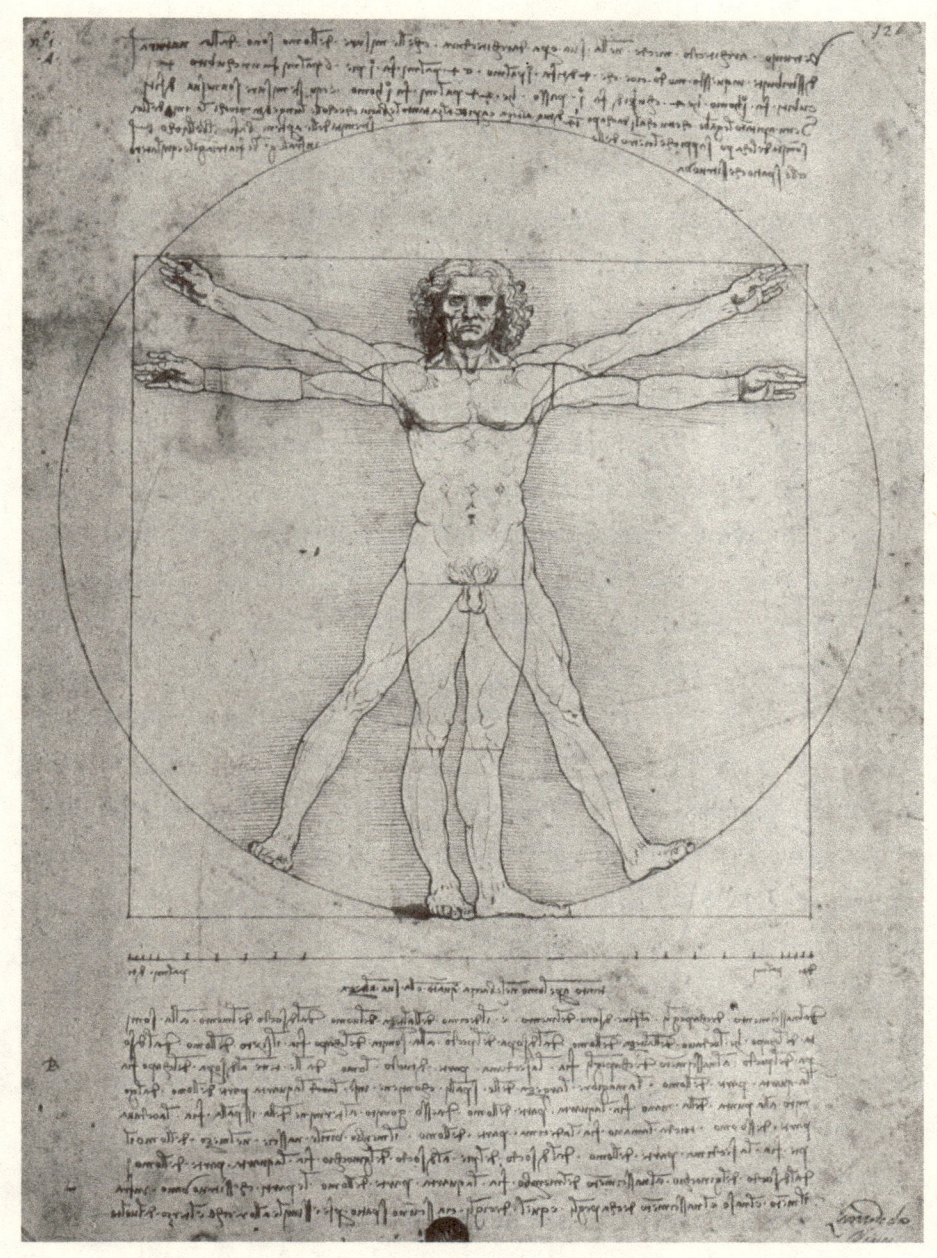

Leonardo's *Vitruvian Man*, arms stretched out wide, is the quintessential symbol of the Renaissance wide achiever.

A portfolio worker develops a range or 'portfolio' of careers, each of which they do part-time, and possibly on a freelance basis. So you might work as a development economist three days a week, then spend the rest of the week as a self-employed wedding photographer or online book dealer. Or you may wish to stretch both mind and body, dividing your time between being a software programmer and a ballet teacher. Handy believed that this was a smart survival strategy in turbulent economic times, reducing the risks of unemployment. But we need not think about portfolio working only in such negative terms. Adopting the more positive Renaissance perspective, pursuing several careers at the same time is a way of thriving and being true to our multiple selves.

Becoming a Renaissance generalist provides plenty of challenges, not least amongst them the prospect of financial insecurity if you are juggling freelance jobs – an issue I will return to. So you might feel more comfortable indulging your various talents and passions by becoming a serial specialist. Instead of pursuing several careers concurrently, we might imagine having three or four very different careers in succession – perhaps starting in public relations, followed by running a youth hostel, then becoming a self-employed gardener. This approach to being a wide achiever makes sense in a world where the retirement age keeps shifting back and working lives are getting longer: there is more space in which to fit several careers. Even making one substantial career change can free us from a profession that has lost its attractions and allow us to explore other sides of who we are.

Consider the example of Lisa Brideau, a former aerospace engineer who did contract work on design projects for NASA. A few years after discovering that space-flight engineering was not nearly as exciting as she thought it would be, and feeling that she wasn't particularly good at the job, Lisa was looking out for something new:

It turned out that the answer was all around me, in the horrifying suburbs of Wisconsin I had been living in: urban planning. The existence of soulless urban sprawl enraged me to such a degree that I had to do something about it. It was mostly a blind leap. I read some books on the subject, sat in on an urban-geography course at the local university, then applied to some graduate planning schools. After getting my Masters, I went to work in the planning department of a very progressive city. I've had to work my way up the ranks, but that's just given me more time to learn my craft. So far urban planning is awesome – it's endlessly fascinating.

I was lucky to have the financial resources to go back to studying, but what really made career change easy for me was that I never thought I'd have just one career. There are so many interesting things out there – why do just one forever? I think everyone should up and quit their job at least once in their life.

Lisa is a natural serial specialist. Her idea of shifting career at least once might be wise advice, especially because, as we have already discovered, our motivations and ambitions evolve throughout the course of our lives, and we are often poor judges of our future interests. The route of a serial specialist may be just what we need to nurture our many talents and passions, and to lead the many lives that lay dormant within us, like seeds beneath the snow.

- *What would being a wide achiever encompass for you?*

Imagining Your Many Selves

Having explored the various motivations that offer meaning, it seems that the prize of meaningful work goes to those who pursue intrinsically rewarding jobs that make a difference, use their talents or reflect their passions – or that involve some intoxicating combination of the three. Although we all desire money and status to some degree, a career decision driven primarily by these extrinsic motivations is unlikely to offer sublime depths of meaning to our lives.

Now we need to get practical, and use what we have learned about these five motivating factors to help generate concrete employment options that could provide a fulfilling, life-enhancing career. This is not a matter of finding that unique dream job which ticks all the boxes – that's a mythological ideal we would be wise to abandon. Rather, it is about identifying a range of possibilities reflecting our multiple selves, which we can later 'test out' in reality. Here are three activities, which build on one another, that I recommend you do to help with this task.

The Map of Choices

The first, called the Map of Choices, is designed to enable you to reflect on where you've come from, before you focus on where you're going. You start by spending ten minutes drawing a map of your career path so far. It can take any form – a zigzagging line, a branching tree or maybe a labyrinth. On this map you should indicate not only the jobs you have done, but the different motivations and forces that have shaped your route. If a major career decision was influenced by the prospect of more money or status, show it on your map – similarly if you were driven by your talents, passions or values. You should also add other factors that might have guided you, such as the role played by your educational choices, parental expectations, professional career advice or chance. Even if you've only ever held one job, try mapping out what drew you into it.

Having created your artwork, now spend another ten minutes looking at it and thinking about these three questions.

- *What does your map reveal about your overall approach to your working life so far? There may be general patterns you can see, such as the way you never stay in a position for more than a couple of years, or that you seem to have fallen into most jobs rather than really choosing them.*
- *Which of the following motivations have you given greatest priority to in your career choices: money, status, respect, passions, talents or making a difference? (rank them from greatest to least priority)*
- *Which two of the motivations mentioned above do you most want to shape your career choices in the future, and why?*

Make a note of your responses, ready for the next activity.

Imaginary Lives

Imaginary Lives is a thought experiment I have adapted from two important career-change thinkers, Julia Cameron and John Williams, which aims to take your ideas a stage closer towards specific job options.[55] It's simple but potentially powerful.

- *Imagine five parallel universes, in each of which you could have a whole year off to pursue absolutely any career your desired. Now think of five different jobs you might want to try out in each of these universes.*

Be bold in your thinking, have fun with your ideas and your multiple selves. Your five choices might be food photographer, member of parliament, tai chi instructor, social entrepreneur running a youth education project, and wide-achieving Renaissance generalist. One person I know who did this activity – a documentary film maker who was having doubts about her career – listed massage therapist, sculptor, cellist, screenplay writer, and owner of her own bar on a tiny, old-fashioned Canarian island.

Now come back down to earth and look hard at your five choices. Write down what it is about them that attracts you. Then look at them again, and think about this question:

- *How does each career measure up against the two motivations in the previous activity that you chose to prioritize in the future?*

If you decided, for instance, that you want a combination of making a difference and high status, check whether your five imaginary careers might provide them. The point is to help you think more deeply about exactly what you are looking for in a career, the kind of experiences that you truly desire.

The Personal Job Advertisement

These two activities are likely to have encouraged some clearer ideas about genuine career possibilities, but you should not assume that you are necessarily the best judge of what might offer you fulfilment. Writing a Personal Job Advertisement allows you to seek the advice of other people.

The concept behind this task is the opposite of a standard career search: imagine that newspapers didn't advertise jobs, but rather advertised people who were looking for jobs.

You do it in two steps. First, write a half-page job advertisement that tells the world who you are and what you care about in life. Put down your talents (e.g. you speak Mongolian, can play the bass guitar), your passions (e.g. ikebana, scuba diving), and the core values and causes you believe in (e.g. wildlife preservation, women's rights). Include your personal qualities (e.g. you are quick-witted, impatient, lacking self-confidence). And record anything else that is important to you – a minimum salary or that you want to work abroad. Make sure you *don't* include any particular job you are keen on, or your educational qualifications or career background. Keep it at the level of underlying motivations and interests.

Here comes the intriguing part. Make a list of ten people you know from different walks of life and who have a range of careers – maybe a policeman uncle or a cartoonist friend – and email them your Personal Job Advertisement, asking them to recommend two or three careers that might fit with what you have written. Tell them to be specific – for example, not replying 'you should work with children' but 'you should do charity work with street kids in Rio de Janeiro'.

You will probably end up with an eclectic list of careers, many of which you would never have thought of yourself. The purpose is not only to give you surprising ideas for future careers, but also to help you see your many possible selves.

After doing these three activities, and having explored the various dimensions of meaning, you should feel more confident about making a list of potential careers that offer the promise of meaningful work. What should you do next? Certainly not begin sending out your CV. Rather, as the following chapter explains, the key to finding a fulfilling career is to experiment with these possibilities in that rather frightening place called the real world. It's time to take a 'radical sabbatical'.

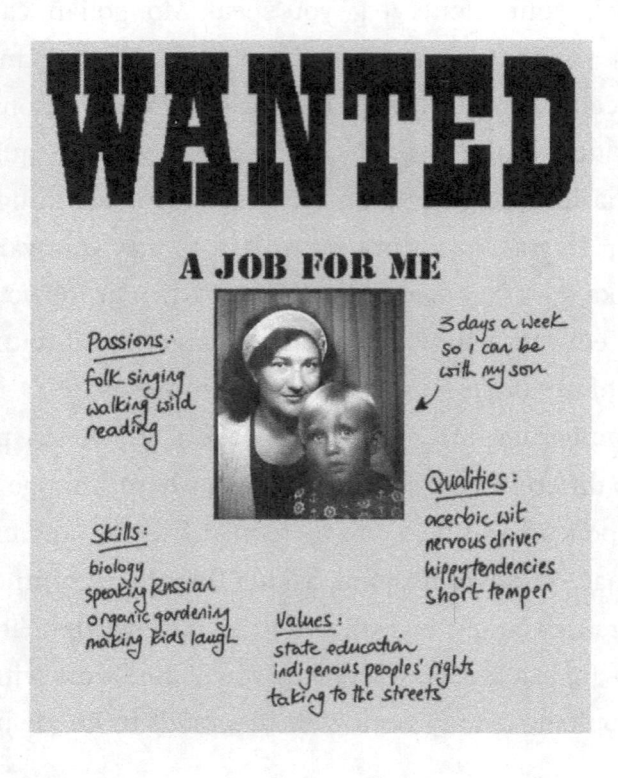

4. Act First, Reflect Later

In Search of Courage

In 1787, the pioneering feminist thinker Mary Wollstonecraft left her position as a governess for a wealthy family in Ireland and set out on a precarious career as a writer, at a moment in history when almost no women were professional authors. In 1882, Paul Gauguin gave up his steady and successful job as a stockbroker in Paris to become a full-time artist. At the age of 30, Albert Schweitzer left behind his glittering career as an organist and theological scholar in Strasbourg to retrain as a doctor, travelling to the African tropics in 1913 to establish a leper hospital.

While some people are inspired by such stories of bold career change, they may make others feel inadequate, even intimidated. Why? Because although we might dream of changing our jobs, we so often lack the courage to do so. Half the workforce in the Western world is dissatisfied with their careers, but around a quarter of them are too afraid to make any change, trapped by their fears and lack of self-confidence.[56] 'If the diver always thought of the shark, he would never lay hands on the pearl,' said Sa'di, a Persian poet from the thirteenth century. Fine words, but that shark can be constantly on our minds, preventing us from plunging into a different future.

We may have identified a range of careers, or 'possible selves', which offer the prospect of fulfilling work: perhaps starting a small business, retraining as a solicitor, or becoming a freelance translator. But how can we develop the courage to change – and make the right choices along the way? Taking those essential next steps into the unknown requires far more than pumping ourselves up with positive thinking. First, we need to understand the psychology of fear, and why the idea of changing profession can create such anxiety. Second, we must start testing our possible selves in reality by undertaking experimental projects such as 'radical sabbaticals', 'branching projects' and 'conversational research', which I will go on to discuss. Finally, we should explore the concept of 'flow', which is not only one of the three key components of fulfilling work – together with meaning and freedom – but which can help us choose effectively between the options.

It will gradually become clear that our greatest hope for overcoming our fear of change and finding a life-expanding career is to reject the traditional model of career change, which advises us to plan meticulously then take action, and replace it with the opposite strategy, which is to act now and reflect later. We must adopt Leonardo da Vinci's adventurous credo, 'experience will be my mistress'.

Why We Are Afraid of Change

Nearly everyone who contemplates changing career is deeply anxious about doing so. While there are a lucky few who possess the courage of mythical Greek heroes like Odysseus, most of us are haunted by fears that can prevent us from travelling in new directions. We worry that the job might not offer the satisfactions we had expected, or that we won't succeed in a new field, or that we are too old to change, or that we can't afford the financial risk with a big mortgage still to pay, or that we may be unable to return to our old job if our plan to become a puppeteer or perfumier doesn't work out.

Fear of failure is close to being a universal affliction. I have heard it expressed – in private – by everyone from burly army officers to millionaire CEOs, from government ministers to famous novelists. 'I tell very few people about my doubts – I'm outwardly confident but inside I'm not even sure I'm mediocre,' a prize-winning documentary maker told me. 'Can I really do it?' is a question carved into most of our souls.

It can be consoling to know that we are not alone in our uncertainties. When Anne Marie Graham decided, after twelve years, to leave her job as a project manager for a translation company and join a charity promoting foreign-language learning, she was anxious about succeeding in an area where she had little experience:

> Moving from something you know inside-out to something which you know nothing about is quite scary when you are over 30. There were times in that first year when I felt lost, convinced I was doing a rubbish job and was completely out of my depth. I would sit in meetings where everyone sounded so knowledgeable and I knew I was blagging it. Then one evening, as I shared my concerns over dinner, my partner pointed out that everyone else might be blagging it too. That suggestion started to lift the cloud of doubt in my own abilities. I also remembered that my old job was daunting at first too – it was just so long ago I had forgotten. It was a realization that made a huge difference to my confidence.

Yet even if we know that others share our fears, and are similarly riddled with doubts behind a carapace of outward self-confidence, we still need to understand why anxiety about career change looms so large in our lives. Why can't we just shake it off, send that resignation email and bound out of the door to do something new?

An answer lies in the peculiar attitude of human beings towards risk. In the 1970s psychologists Amos Tversky and Daniel Kahneman began a series of experiments that explored how we evaluate potential losses and gains, and discovered that we hate losing twice as much as we love winning, whether at the gaming table or when considering career change. According to Tversky, 'people are much more sensitive to negative than to positive stimuli . . . There are a few things that would make you feel better, but the number of things that would make you feel worse is unbounded'.[57] Evolutionary biologists have attempted to explain why we have this strong negative bias that means we focus much more on potential drawbacks than benefits. They speculate that it may be because early humans developed a high sensitivity to danger as a means of survival on the badlands of the African savannah: we are products of the primal terror experienced by our hominid ancestors. That hazy object in the distance could be a fruit-laden bush, but it might be a lion – best to steer well clear.

So when it comes to career change, we are psychologically disposed to magnify everything that could go wrong. Similarly, when thinking about whether a new job might suit us, we are more likely to highlight our personal weaknesses than our strengths. We find ourselves saying, 'I don't have the financial brain to run a social enterprise' more loudly than 'I'm great at generating creative ideas'. The result is that we tend to exhibit extreme caution, and remain in jobs that – at least in terms of fulfilment – are long past their sell-by date.[58]

'Without self-confidence we are as babes in the cradle,' wrote Virginia Woolf. She's right. The question, then, is how to let go of our fears, overcome our aversion to risk, and discover the courage we need to change.

Experimental Projects, or How to Have Thirty Jobs in One Year

Laura van Bouchout finally decided that she needed some professional advice. In her late twenties, and having already had five jobs – most of which involved organizing cultural events – she felt at a dead end, unable to find a career she loved. Luckily, in Belgium, where she lives, anybody who has worked for over twelve months is entitled to free sessions with a career coach. She booked an appointment, and after taking a standard personality test and being asked some probing questions, was told that she had been doing the wrong jobs for her personality. Now came the hard part: working out exactly what the right job might be. The coach told Laura to write down her dream careers, and the jobs of famous people she admired. But when Laura returned for the next session with a wildly long list covering several pages, the coach was as confused as she was. 'He didn't know where to start or what to advise me,' she recalls. 'I left the counselling sessions without an answer, but after moaning about it to my friends for a couple of months, I thought I'd take a risk and conduct an experiment.' This is what she did:

I decided to try out thirty different jobs in the year leading up to my thirtieth birthday, dedicating the whole year to my career struggle. So I'm working as a part-time programmer of music events to pay the bills, and in my leisure time I contact people who I think have dream jobs or interesting careers and ask if I can follow them or work with them for at least three days. So far I've 'been' a fashion photographer, a bed-and-breakfast review writer, a creative director at an advertising agency, an owner of a cat hotel, a member of the European parliament, a director of a recycling centre and a manager of a youth hostel.

The more jobs I try, the more I realize it's not a rational process of listing criteria and finding a job that matches them. It's a bit like dating. When I was single I had a mental list of qualities I thought my boyfriend should have. But some guys who met all the criteria on my list did nothing for me. And at one point you find someone who doesn't meet half your checklist but blows you away. I think that's what you have to look for in a job. I found it when following the advertising director; I was totally swept off my feet even though working in an advertising agency doesn't nearly match my ideals. So maybe it's not about thinking and planning, but about doing lots of job dating, trying things out until you feel a spark.

During the course of her thirty-job odyssey, Laura stumbled upon the most significant insight to have emerged in the last three decades of research into career change: act first, and reflect later.

Ever since Frank Parsons set up his Vocation Bureau in Boston over a century ago, the conventional wisdom for finding a new career has been to 'plan then implement'. This model typically starts with a deep internal exploration, drawing up lists of your personal strengths and weaknesses, and your skills, interests and ambitions, perhaps with the help of a psychometric test or a career advisor. This is followed by thorough research into various industries and professions to find out which best match your preferences and abilities. Having made a final decision, you create an action plan, and start sending out your CV and making job applications.

The problem with the 'plan then implement' model is simple: it rarely works. What generally happens is that we find ourselves in new jobs that don't suit us, because we haven't had any experience of what they are like in reality. As Laura would put it, the job matches our checklist, but we fail to fall in love. Alternatively, we spend so much time trying to work out what the perfect career would be, ceaselessly researching or getting lost in confused thoughts about the best option, that we end up doing nothing, overwhelmed by fears and procrastination, trapped by the paradox of choice I discussed earlier.

The art of career change requires turning the conventional approach on its head. We should wean ourselves off the rational-planning mentality and replace it by a philosophy of 'act first, reflect later'. Ruminating in an armchair or poring through files at a career centre is not what we need. We must enter a more playful and experimental way of being, where we *do then think*, not *think then do*.

The most recent research shows that successful change requires a substantial dose of experiential learning. Just like we can't learn carpentry from a book, we can't shift careers without taking practical action. First we should identify a range of 'possible selves' – careers that we believe might offer us purpose and meaning (the previous chapter should have helped with this). Then, like Laura, we have to trial them in reality by undertaking experimental projects. Following a period of job dating, we will be in a position to make better and more concrete decisions. As Herminia Ibarra argues:

> By far the biggest mistake people make when trying to change careers is to delay taking the first step until they have settled on a destination ... The only way to create change is to put our possible identities into practice, working and crafting them until they are sufficiently grounded in experience to guide more decisive steps ... We learn who we are by testing reality, not by looking inside ... Reflection best comes later, when we have some momentum and when there is something new to reflect on.[59]

Experimental projects take three main forms, which I will address in descending order of personal challenge: radical sabbaticals, branching projects and conversational research. They are designed to suit different kinds of people, with different career ambitions, at different stages of their journey. All of them, though, can help pinpoint which of our possible selves offers the greatest prospect for fulfilment.

We have already encountered the first and most demanding form, the radical sabbatical. This was Laura van Bouchout's approach, and involves granting yourself a dedicated period for action-based projects, such as shadowing or accompanying people in their work, or volunteering in an appealing organization. Laura gave herself the unusual birthday present of a whole year to flirt with thirty possible future selves. She had no clear destination, just a basketful of ideas, and made space in her life by working part-time to support herself, which left her plenty of time for experiential adventuring. But you might equally pursue a radical sabbatical – what I also think of as a 'job holiday' – by taking a few months of unpaid leave, or using a couple of weeks of your annual vacation. In fact, I think it would be a good idea if we all spent at least one week every year trying out a different career, even if we believe we are happy in our existing job. We may not even realize that we are unfulfilled until we immerse ourselves in an alternative world. Who knows – running a cat hotel might turn out to be unexpectedly rewarding.

A second and more common form of experimental project is the branching project, or what Ibarra calls a 'temporary assignment'. One of the most pervasive myths of career change is the belief that it requires a drastic shift to a completely new life, where we march into work on Monday morning and hand in our resignation, then boldly step into the unknown. That would put off almost anybody. But with branching projects, such a risky strategy is not necessary, because they are designed as short experiments pursued around the edge of our existing career, through which we test out our possible selves. Apart from options such as work shadowing or volunteering, we could do a training course that gives us a taste of a different career, or try out an initial, scaled-down version of a prospective job.

As an example of the latter, imagine that you felt stuck in your job as a literary agent and were thinking of becoming a yoga teacher. What should you do? Stop thinking about it and get into action by starting to teach yoga in your spare time, perhaps on a weekday evening or on the weekend, to discover whether it really does provide that spark of radical aliveness that you hoped for. If it does, you can gradually increase your teaching commitments until you feel confident about leaving your old career behind you.

In effect, you will have taken a number of small and relatively unrisky steps, but which have led to big results. With each step you take the more confident you will feel, making the journey easier as you go along, and circumventing your inbuilt evolutionary aversion to risk. You will no longer wonder whether you might enjoy being a yoga instructor: after just a few classes you will have a pretty good sense of whether it is right for you, since there is no better way of learning than direct experience. And if it doesn't feel right, then you can start on another branching project to test a different possible self, perhaps spending a month of Saturdays helping a friend who has an online vintage-clothing store. It may take some time to work your way through several selves, but there is compelling evidence that this is a necessary part of the process of successful change. 'We short-circuit it at our own peril,' warns Ibarra.[60]

I can personally endorse the idea of branching projects, having pursued one which took my career in a radically new direction. After several years as the project director at a small foundation, I had a yearning to leave and start running my own workshops on the art of living. But I was worried about the financial risks of doing so, and was equally anxious about whether they would be a success. After months of talking about it to my partner – should I stay or should I go? – she suggested I stop talking, take out my diary and choose a date for my first workshop. That's exactly what I did. I sent out an email to friends and recruited ten guinea pigs. Unable to find a venue, I ran the first session in my kitchen one Saturday, on how to rethink our attitudes to love and time. After a few more weekend courses around the kitchen table – and while still working at the foundation – I approached the QI Club in Oxford and asked if they would host an evening class on the art of living as part of their public events programme. It soon became a regular gig, the classes grew in popularity, and within a few months I felt assured enough to leave my day job, having overcome my primal fear of failure.

A final form of experimental project is conversational research. Perhaps less daunting than a radical sabbatical or a branching project, it can be just as effective. It simply requires talking to people from different walks of life who are engaged in the types of work you might imagine doing. That may strike you as an obvious strategy. But it is worth thinking about why conversation is such a vital component of almost any successful career change.

One of the greatest obstacles to change is that we get trapped by the strictures of our social circle and peers. If you are a lawyer, and spend most of your time with other lawyers or professionals, this is likely to condition your ideals and aspirations: you may feel that you need to have a relatively high salary, or a nice house and luxurious holidays, and that working sixty hours a week is quite normal. In other words, our social milieu strongly determines what the German sociologist Karl Mannheim called our *Weltanschauung* or 'worldview' – our underlying mental frame of reference and belief system. The problem is that we may rarely interact with those who see the world very differently. As Tolstoy noted, most people 'instinctively keep to the circle of those people who share their views of life and their own place in it'. When was the last time you spent an afternoon with a bee keeper or a shamanic healer?

The result is that our existing priorities and values are constantly reinforced. You might dream of leaving the law to become a teacher in a Steiner school, but you will probably conclude that it is a whimsical, unrealistic idea – and so will most of your friends. As I know from my own experience, our worldview is a psychological straitjacket that restricts us from pursuing new possibilities. When I was finishing university, the only job options I could think of were working in investment banking, joining the civil service or becoming a journalist. Why was my imagination so extraordinarily narrow? Because those were the standard career paths considered by most of my college peers. Like almost everyone else, I followed the crowd. (In case you are interested, I crashed out of my banking interviews because I kept talking about my bonsai-tree collection rather than currency trading; I failed the civil service exams; and so I became a journalist – but not for long.)

One of the best ways to escape the confines of our worldview is to shift our peer group and talk to people whose work experiences and daily lives are very different from our own. If you really want to ditch law, it might be wise to spend less time with your lawyer friends, good company though they may be. More specifically, you can learn an enormous amount by having conversations with people who have made career changes that match where you hope to be heading. If you really are drawn to teaching at a Steiner school, can you find a Steiner teacher who was once a lawyer or doctor, and take them out to lunch? If you are a jaded academic hoping to become a garden designer, you should do everything you can to find a fellow scholar who has made this same move, or some other radical change.

Conversational research is also a particularly good strategy for making discoveries about careers that are difficult to test out in branching projects. Imagine you are a yoga instructor who is considering becoming a literary agent. Unlike experimenting with teaching yoga, it's difficult to trial yourself as a literary agent: you can't exactly set up a mini agency in your spare time and try attracting a few client authors to see if you like it. A much more viable starting place is using every contact you have to arrange a meeting with a literary agent, where you can discuss the ups and downs of their everyday working life – and find out whether publishing lunches really are as long as is commonly believed.

Such conversations bring us closer to understanding the realities of career change, with all its pleasures and pains. Hearing first-hand stories from people, and asking them the questions that intrigue or concern us, is worth far more than reading about a profession in a glossy career guide, and can give us a vivid yet nuanced picture of a different life we might aspire to. Furthermore, studies of career change consistently show that most people find new jobs through personal contacts rather than official channels, and that shifting career requires developing new social networks.[61] Conversational research creates openings in both these realms.

Andy Bell knows just how powerful conversation can be. After dropping out of school at 16, he was offered work in a travel agency in a small English town, as part of a state-sponsored youth-training scheme. He hated it: they made him cut his punk hairdo and take out his earrings. Andy left after a couple of months and found a job on a building site. And that's where his conversational world exploded into life:

> I met some wonderful people who told me loads of stories about travelling. It was a real education. The crew were all

hippies who had travelled and become tradespeople – carpenters, plasterers, roofers, bricklayers. It was great fun, getting up in the morning and going to work and just having conversations with them. I found them inspiring partly because they were from a different social background than me – they were ordinary people, working people, they weren't from pampered backgrounds or spoilt brats. Hearing all these fantastic stories about driving to India, being at death's door with malaria, going to Morocco and staying with the Berber people. It all sounded so appealing – the only place I'd been abroad was when I went camping for two weeks in Spain.

It definitely influenced my life. My aspirations then were to save up some money and go travelling, which is what I did for the next six years. I went to work in Greece for about two years, doing farm work, digging graves, unloading the frozen-fish trucks, laying irrigation pipes. I did it in Israel too: digging graves, furniture removal, delivering tiles. I ended up in New Zealand, becoming a full-time farmhand. I've probably done twenty or thirty jobs in my life.

Eventually Andy returned to England and started a small business as an organic farmer, running a weekly vegetable-box scheme delivering his produce direct to people's homes. As he himself admits, he wouldn't be where he is today without those conversations on the building site, which did so much to broaden his imagination and shift his worldview.

So what will it be? A radical sabbatical, a branching project, or a conversational exploration? The moment has come to lay this book aside and take action. My advice at this point is as follows:

- *Brainstorm three possible selves, then think of three ways you could 'act now, and reflect later' to test each of these selves. Give yourself half an hour right now and get started. Phone an organization that interests you and ask if they take on volunteers. Register a domain name for a business idea you have. Order a prospectus for a training course you could take. Email a wide-achiever friend and ask if you could meet to discuss how they manage it.*

Even taking small steps such as these can give you an uplifting sense that you are making change and be catalysts for re-forging your future. No time? Too tired? Worried nobody will want to speak with you? Then allow Goethe to lead the way. He understood the wisdom of acting now, reflecting later:

> Then indecision brings its own delays,
> And days are lost lamenting o'er lost days.
> Are you in earnest? Seize this very minute;
> What you can do, or dream you can, begin it;
> Boldness has genius, power and magic in it.

I Flow, Therefore I Am

The quest to find fulfilling work begins with acting, but is resolved by reflecting. Because even when we have tested a selection of our possible selves, we still need to judge which is the best option (or combination of options, for wide achievers). How can we know which career is right for us at this time in our lives? We ought to ask ourselves some basic questions about the worlds of work we've dipped into through branching projects or other experiments:

- *How were the careers you explored different from what you had expected?*
- *Which kind of work did you find yourself talking to people about afterwards with most enthusiasm?*
- *Which best provides the kinds of meaning you're looking for in a career?*

The last question is vital, because meaning is the ballast of a fulfilling career. But we should recognize that meaning is not sufficient for human fulfilment: you might use your talents as a sculptor, but nevertheless feel lonely much of the time as you hack away at the stone. Most of us also want to enjoy our jobs on a day-to-day basis. That prompts another question about the jobs you tried:

- *Which gave you the best 'flow' experience?*

Flow has the potential to provide this sense of daily enjoyment. Never heard of it? Don't worry. Let me explain what this mysterious elixir of flow is, and how exactly it can help us choose a career.

The concept of flow dates from the 1970s, when it was first developed by the Hungarian-American psychologist Mihaly Csikszentmihalyi (and you thought Krznaric was difficult to pronounce). It is now widely accepted as one of the most fundamental indicators of 'life satisfaction' or 'happiness'. A flow experience is one in which we are completely and unselfconsciously absorbed in whatever we are doing, whether it is scaling a rock face, playing the piano, doing pilates, giving a conference presentation, or conducting a surgical operation. As Csikszentmihalyi puts it, we are 'so involved in an activity that nothing else seems to matter'. When this happens, we are 'in flow', a state that athletes often describe as being 'in the zone'. He says that we enjoy such activities because they are 'autotelic', or intrinsically motivating: the action is valuable in itself, not a means to an end. In a typical flow experience, we feel totally engaged in the present, and future and past tend to fade away – almost as if we were doing Buddhist meditation. In his renowned study of surgeons, Csikszentmihalyi found that when performing operations, 80 per cent of them lose track of time or feel that it passes much faster than usual. They're in the zone.[62]

One of the curious characteristics of flow, according to Csikszentmihalyi, is that it is not limited to 'high-end' professions like being a surgeon, but can equally be experienced by butchers, welders or farm workers. He would certainly recognize the presence of flow in the following scene from Tolstoy's *Anna Karenina*, when the shy aristocrat Levin joins the peasants on his country estate in a day of scything:

> Swath followed swath. They mowed long rows and short rows, good grass and poor grass. Levin lost all count of time and had no idea whether it was late or early. A change began to overcome his work which gave him intense satisfaction. There were moments when he forgot what he was doing, he moved without effort ... The longer Levin mowed, the oftener he experienced those moments of oblivion when it was not his arms which swung the scythe but the scythe

seemed to mow of itself ... These were the most blessed moments.

Perhaps an excessively romantic portrayal of life as a serf in nineteenth-century Russia, yet it is the kind of existential state that most of us have experienced. What kinds of activities typically give us flow? It most commonly occurs when we are using our skills to do a task that is challenging, but not so hard that we fear failing. That's why surgeons get a lot of it: the operations they perform are difficult and require immense concentration, but they are sufficiently trained that they feel confident of success. Flow is also enhanced when we are being creative and learning new skills, when we can see the immediate impact of our actions, and when we have clearly defined goals.[63] I am generally in flow while writing a chapter like this one, but not when answering administrative emails at the end of the day.

The implication of the flow theory is that we should aspire to be working in a career that offers us a high flow content. But this is the point at which it gets controversial. Csikszentmihalyi and many of his followers claim that almost any job can be altered so that 'its conditions are more conducive to flow'.[64] Even an apparently mundane job such as being a supermarket cashier, he says, can be approached in a way that makes it brimming with flow. So we may not need to change our career at all if we are feeling miserable in it: we just need to give ourselves more challenging tasks, or focus on the creative aspects of the work.

The problem is that the majority of jobs cannot be magically transformed to provide better flow experience. It might be possible if you are a fashion photographer, by deciding to shoot in more demanding

Jackson Pollock painting. What gives you flow experience?

locations or by playing around with new lighting techniques. But if you are deeply unhappy working as an IT project manager, you are unlikely to be able to recalibrate your daily tasks so they give you all the challenge, creativity and purpose you need to experience flow. Most workers, especially those in bureaucratic organizations or who do repetitive tasks, just don't have that much scope to alter their own jobs. I have consistently found that people who feel unfulfilled in their jobs are unable to adjust them sufficiently so that they can squeeze substantially more flow from them.

So instead of trying to *create* flow in our existing job, I believe that a more sensible path to pursue is to *find* work that gives us flow. Where can you discover that secret list of high-flow careers? It would be rash of me to offer one, because each of us experiences our work differently, depending on our skills, creative resources, fears and foibles. Which is precisely why it is so important to conduct branching projects: the best way to discover whether a career has high flow potential for you is to have a go at doing it. You can then choose between the options on the basis of which is most likely to put you in the zone.

The idea of flow can help us make career decisions in two other ways. First, through conversation. When talking to people whose jobs interest you, don't just ask vague questions such as 'What's it like being a taxidermist?'; ask them about flow – how often do they have that sense they are in the zone, and what precisely are they most likely to be doing when this occurs? A second strategy is to become a detective of flow in your own life by creating a Flow Diary. Spend a month keeping a daily note of the kinds of activities that give you flow – whether it is writing a tricky report at work, or cooking a Sunday lunch for a dozen people. You can then use this knowledge to help identify potentially fulfilling careers.

We must set our sights on finding a career that allows us to sing out to the world: I flow, therefore I am. But we should nevertheless beware becoming a flow junkie. Flow isn't everything. Necessary, yes. But sufficient on its own, no. We could be doing those challenging and creative flow tasks, yet still not find our work ultimately rewarding, because it does not embody our values or offer any of the other profound forms of meaning explored earlier. I used to experience flow when writing academic articles and lecturing, but I still didn't want to work as a university professor. What we need is both flow *and* meaning. Yet even this heady combination is not enough for the deepest forms of fulfilment. There is one more element we must consider, which is whether a job can offer us the liberating gift of freedom.

5. The Longing for Freedom

A Manifesto of Human Aspiration

In his book *Good Work*, the visionary economic thinker E.F. Schumacher lyrically describes the 'longing for freedom' that has become so widespread in Western society. This desire, he says, encapsulates a range of liberating ideas:

> I don't want to join the rat race.
> Not be enslaved by machines, bureaucracies, boredom, ugliness.
> I don't want to be a moron, robot, commuter.
> I don't want to become a fragment of a person.
>
> I want to do my own thing.
> I want to live (relatively) simply.
> I want to deal with people, not masks.
> People matter. Nature matters. Beauty matters. Wholeness matters.
> I want to be able to *care*.[65]

This poetic manifesto of human aspiration, written in the 1970s, is one that is likely to resonate with many people today who feel unfulfilled by their jobs. They may be suffering from chronic overwork

– one of the major causes of job dissatisfaction in the West – and typically arrive home exhausted after a stressful day and long commute, too tired to pursue their hobbies, go out with friends, or give their energies to family life.[66] They may enjoy aspects of their job, but dislike being told what to do all the time by haranguing bosses. They don't want their weekends to be constantly invaded by text messages and emails from the office. They talk about 'the rat race' or being a 'wage slave' or not having enough 'work–life balance'. They dream of more free time, more autonomy, more space in their lives for their relationships and to be themselves.

Not everybody feels these kinds of strictures: there are plenty of people who revel in hard work and long hours, passionately devoting themselves to careers they love. But if you have ever felt overburdened by work, and wished for more freedom and independence to live your life the way you want to, it may be worth considering this simple question: How can we satisfy a desire for greater freedom? The answer, however, is far from simple, and requires addressing three dilemmas. First, whether we should opt for the security and stability of a salaried job or embrace self-employment and invent our own job. Second, whether we ought to wean ourselves off the hard-work ethic by abandoning the goal of finding fulfilling work, and instead seek work for a fulfilling life. Third, the question of how we can balance our career ambitions with the desire to have a family, since trying to do both can not only create emotional strains, but put immense pressure on the limited hours at our disposal.

While exploring these issues we will meet an anarchist, a Wall Street analyst and a beekeeper. They will help us to recognize the virtues of idleness, to challenge the ideology of 'having it all', and to understand how freedom can be combined with meaning and flow to offer the most profound form of career fulfilment.

The Anarchist Alternative, or How to Invent Your Own Job

'Those who would give up essential liberty, to purchase a little temporary safety,' wrote Benjamin Franklin, 'deserve neither liberty nor safety.' Was he right? In deciding which career to pursue, we need to find a way to balance our twin desires for security and freedom. Most of us want some kind of stability in our working lives, especially in uncertain economic times: we need a regular income to repay the mortgage or hefty student loans, to support our children, and to ensure we have a pension for old age. At a deeper psychological level, from the moment the umbilical cord is cut and we are cast out into the loneliness of our individuality, we are in search of emotional and material security.[67] Although we may find it in a loving marriage or membership of a community, it can also be found in the workplace through a steady job that not only gives us a guaranteed pay check at the end of the month, but can also provide a network of friendships, a sense of identity and a feeling that we are valued. It was this overwhelming desire for security – rooted in a turbulent wartime childhood – that kept my father working at IBM for half a century.

While security may be at the foundation of our hierarchy of needs, human beings are equally driven by the quest for individual freedom. Throughout history, from the slave revolts under the Romans to the campaigns against apartheid in South Africa, social and political struggles have been fired by the yearning to escape oppression and enjoy personal liberty. This history is echoed in our attitude towards work. For decades, industrial psychologists have observed that job satisfaction is directly related to 'span of autonomy', meaning the amount of each day during which workers feel free to make their own decisions.[68] In nearly every class I teach, there are people whose dream is to enjoy more autonomy by leaving their jobs in large organizations and working for themselves, perhaps opening a small cafe or going freelance.

Their longing for freedom is perfectly understandable, according to Colin Ward, one of the most distinguished anarchist thinkers of the twentieth century. In his classic primer, *Anarchy in Action*, he asks the fascinating question of why a person will happily pick up a shovel and work in their garden after returning from a hard day at the factory or office:

> He enjoys going home and digging in his garden because there he is free from foremen, managers and bosses. He is free from the monotony and slavery of doing the same thing day in day out, and is in control of the whole job from start to finish. He is free to decide for himself how and when to set about it. He is responsible to himself and not to somebody else. He is working because he wants to and not because he has to. He is doing his own thing. He is his own man.
>
> The desire to 'be your own boss' is very common indeed. Think of all the people whose secret dream or cherished ambition is to run a small-holding or a little shop or to set up in trade on their own account, even though it may mean

working night and day with little prospect of solvency. Few of them are such optimists as to think they will make a fortune that way. What they want above all is the sense of independence and of controlling their own destinies.[69]

Ward offers a compelling vision of fulfilling work. Wouldn't you rather have that sense of independence and free choice than spend eight hours each day servicing the needs of your employer, whose bottom line is more likely to be quarterly profits than your personal wellbeing? It is also a realistic vision, recognizing that the freedom of self-employment may require hard graft. Ward belongs to an anarchist tradition that is not the media stereotype of black-masked youths throwing bottles at the police, but one reaching back to the eighteenth-century philosopher William Godwin, which argues that anarchism is about expanding the space in society for individual freedom and social cooperation, outside the realm of corporate business and authoritarian government institutions. His workplace heroes are precisely those people who start up their own cafe, or who work in a health-food cooperative where the employees jointly own the business. So if you've ever felt frustration at your lack of autonomy, and crave the independence of working for yourself, then you might have an anarchist lurking within you.

It may, however, be possible to feel freedom working in a big organization, especially if you are able to choose your daily tasks and targets, and are offered benefits such as flexitime. Many firms pride themselves on how much autonomy they give their workers. When I was an academic, I may have been employed by a large bureaucratic institution, but I also enjoyed considerable freedom to decide how and when I worked: I did my first two hours of work while lying in bed at home, before arriving at my department at eleven in the morning. Nobody seemed to mind, as long as I kept publishing research papers and performed my teaching duties.

But if you seek genuine autonomy, you are much more likely to find it by joining the 20 per cent of Europeans and North Americans who are self-employed. And the chances are that it will be good for you. 'Working for yourself makes you happy,' according to the UK's Work Foundation: 47 per cent of self-employed people say they are 'very satisfied' with their jobs, compared to only 17 per cent of those in regular employment.[70]

Fiona Robyn will tell you that such statistics mask a far more complex and challenging reality. After years working in customer services for a major corporation, she retrained as a counsellor to enjoy the liberation of self-employment. When her therapy client list grew thin after moving to a diferent part of Britain to live with her husband, she decided to try earning a living from her greatest love, which was writing. So she set up Writing Our Way Home, a small business inspired by her commitment to Buddhism, which offers month-long online courses to a global community of people who want to use writing to increase their engagement with the world. Would she recommend self-employment?

> Being self-employed is wonderful and awful. There's no holiday or sick pay, no security. No development opportunities are offered to me unless I pay for them myself, and there's nobody to tell me I'm doing a good job or even notice how hard I'm working. Work easily bleeds into before breakfast,

after dinner and weekends if I'm not careful. If things go wrong, there's no one else to blame or to discuss things with.

Having said that, I wouldn't have it any other way. I love being able to manage my own diary, build relationships with the people I want to build relationships with, and know that I'm forging my own way through the world of work. I love knowing that what I'm doing is making a real difference to people – they tell me so.

It's helpful to remember that the security I think I'm missing out on by not working for a corporation is non-existent anyway. People are made redundant, people get ill. There's never any guarantee that life will continue in the way we want it to for any length of time.

It is quite possible that Fiona's experience will convince you that self-employment – what some call a 'freestyle' career – is a crazy option. Who needs all that insecurity, stress and the prospect of no weekends? She could be right that ultimately nobody is safe in their job: the recent financial crisis has shown that we are all expendable when the markets demand it. Yet it may seem far too risky to forgo a regular wage during a recession or if you are anxious about whether your new independent career will be a success.

On the other hand, Fiona offers a profound insight into the value of freedom for the art of living. Almost everyone I've spoken to who has switched to self-employment has reached the same conclusion as Fiona: despite all the uncertainties, responsibilities and frustrations, they would still not give it up to return to being employed in a nine-to-five job. Once they have tasted freedom, it is almost impossible to turn back. That is a remarkable fact that should be a lesson to us all.

Fiona also provides an example of the most radical form of self-employment, which is to invent your own job – a bespoke career. This is an aspiration with origins in the Renaissance ideal of expressing individuality and uniqueness, but which has been more recently promoted by the management expert Charles Handy:

> For the first time in the human experience, we have a chance to shape our work to suit the way we live instead of our lives to fit our work . . . We would be mad to miss the chance.[71]

A bespoke career, sometimes described as a 'customized job', is one which you design yourself to suit your particular interests, talents and priorities. Typically they cannot be found in a standard career guide, such as Fiona's job of running online writing courses with a Buddhist twist. They also usually involve being self-employed, so you can decide exactly when and how you work. Inventing your own job is becoming increasingly common: there are people who earn their daily bread working as professional whistlers and travelling pizza chefs. Needless to say, these are not professions featured at any careers fair.

The internet has revolutionized the possibilities for custom-designed jobs, especially for those with a little entrepreneurial flair. I know of a woman who lives in a village in rural Mexico while teaching English as a foreign language to students in Italy and Japan. How does she do it? Using Skype, which allows her to have low-cost, face-to-face conversations with them. I find this technological advance extraordinary, having memories of teaching English to Spanish engineers in the mid-nineties, when I had to get up at five each morning and travel by bus to a remote industrial estate north of Madrid. Today you can also set up and launch a business for free in a single day by opening an account on eBay and offering a few homemade craft items for sale. Eventually you may become one of the estimated half a million people whose main income comes from selling on the site.[72] Niche products now have access to global markets: your online crossbow magazine can reach archery addicts from Beijing to Buenos Aires. Further opportunity has emerged from large companies and organizations farming out a huge portion of their work to freelance consultants, following years of downsizing. So you might be able to work from home for multiple employers, perhaps from several countries, and take a midday bubble bath without anybody knowing. This all leaves us with a question to ponder:

- *If you could create a bespoke career, what would it look like, and what branching projects would help transform it into reality?*

Inventing our own job might be too much of a gamble if we are running behind with mortgage repayments or bringing up a child alone. But if we wish to experience career fulfilment in its most sublime form, we ought to do everything we can to work in a way that suits who we are, with all our quirks and qualities. If we have a choice between security and freedom, I say choose freedom. This was a credo shared by the American hobo and explorer Chris McCandless, subject of the film and book *Into the Wild*, who died in the Alaskan wilderness in 1992:

> So many people live with unhappy circumstances and yet will not take the initiative to change their situation because they are conditioned to a life of security, conformity, and conservatism, all of which may appear to give one peace of mind, but in reality nothing is more damaging to the adventurous spirit within a man than a secure future.[73]

What if our ideal of freedom is not feeling free and independent *within* our job, but feeling free *from* our job? As we are about to see, that may require weaning ourselves off the work ethic, and developing a philosophy of idleness.

Weaning Yourself Off the Work Ethic

'All work is a form of voluntary enslavement.' Karl Marx? No, James Lam, an English-Chinese IT analyst. He works for a software company and has spent the last ten years in a series of IT posts. The pay is good but the hours are long and the stress is high. In one job he was regularly woken by his BlackBerry at two in the morning to fix urgent software problems. 'When I was 15, I was thinking of going on the road, leading a bohemian life like Jack Kerouac,' James told me. All these years he has retained his dream of greater freedom.

Why is it that so many people, like James, find themselves working too hard and too much in jobs they don't particularly enjoy? It may be that they consider it a price worth paying for a position that offers them an attractive financial package – the classic Faustian bargain of the modern workplace. Sociologists might alternatively suggest they are the unlucky inheritors of the Protestant work ethic, an ideology that emerged in seventeenth-century Europe, promoting the belief that hard work was good for you and would bring you closer to God. The legacy today is that we feel guilty if we are not putting in long days with our nose to the grindstone.

A third possibility is that they have succumbed to the current epidemic of work addiction. Over one million Britons say they are workaholics and voluntarily do extra hours. In Japan, 10 per cent of male deaths are job-related; they even have a special word for it, *karōshi*, death by overwork.[74] Those who end up as addicts tend to be initially lured by the benefits of working hard, such as the satisfactions of being a perfectionist, or the kudos of being last to leave the office. Eventually, however, their work obsession gets out of control. According to psychotherapist Bryan Robinson, we should be asking ourselves questions like 'Do I find myself doing two or three things at once, such as eating lunch and writing a memo?' and 'Do I put more time and energy into my work than into my relationships with loved ones and friends?' Answering yes could mean we are sliding into addiction, especially if we are regularly putting in a lot of 'voluntary hours' beyond official duties.[75] Of course, working a twelve-hour day does not necessarily mean we are workaholics: it might be a reflection of the fact that we have found a stimulating and absorbing vocation.

Assuming, however, that we are feeling overworked – whether we consider ourselves addicts or not – what might be the cure? To work less, obviously. Not particularly helpful advice, I'll admit. To make sense of it, we need to think about what it would take to wean ourselves off the work ethic, and what the implications might be for finding a job we love, as well as for our pockets. In the end, we may decide to shift our priorities: instead of thinking that the goal must be to find fulfilling work, our ambition could be to seek work for a fulfilling life.

The philosopher Bertrand Russell can help us explore the issues. In his scintillating 1932 essay 'In Praise of Idleness', Russell shocked the establishment by arguing that 'there is far too much work done in the world' and that 'immense harm is caused by the belief that work is virtuous'. He saw no good reason why people should be sweating away producing so many consumer goods that added little to quality of life. Like many progressive thinkers of his era, including the economist John Maynard Keynes, he was convinced that economic growth and technological advances had made it possible for most people in wealthy countries to enjoy a decent standard of living by working no more than four hours a day. Russell also thought we should recognize the virtues of leisure. By 'leisure' he didn't mean passive pastimes, but rather activities that could expand our human potential:

> In a world where no one is compelled to work more than four hours a day, every person possessed of scientific curiosity will be able to indulge it, and every painter will be able to paint without starving, however excellent his pictures may be ... There will be happiness and joy of life, instead of frayed nerves, weariness and dyspepsia.[76]

If a four-hour day seems a little too ambitious, we might more realistically consider the possible benefits – and costs – of shifting to a four-day week, a popular aspiration since the 1970s, and one that

The philosopher Bertrand Russell (sitting on the right) believed we should all work a four-hour day. He used his 'leisure time' to co-found Britain's Campaign for Nuclear Disarmament.

employers are increasingly willing to accept. Or at the very least, imagine reducing your time at work by just one hour a day. Clearly, you would be left with more time for family and friends, which is exactly what 70 per cent of people say that excessive work is depriving them of.[77] Do you think your children would prefer to play with you for an extra hour each evening, or that you regularly stay late at the office so you can earn enough to afford a bigger home? As one friend of mine put it, 'I think my kids would rather have more father than more garden.'

A second benefit is that it might provide, as Russell suggests, the freedom to pursue life-enhancing projects outside official working hours. Take the case of the American poet Wallace Stevens. By day he worked in an insurance company, eventually becoming vice-president of an established firm in Connecticut. But he was no workaholic: he returned home each evening to write verse, and was considered one of the great modernist poets of the early twentieth century. Stevens kept these two lives separate: he always felt something of an imposter in his day job; it was 'like playing a part', he wrote. He regarded poetry as his 'real work' – even if he wasn't paid for it – and never wanted to commercialize his art by becoming a 'professional' poet. After winning the Pulitzer Prize in 1955 he was offered a faculty position at Harvard that would have allowed him to write poetry for a living, but he turned it down to stay in his insurance job.

In effect, Stevens opted not to make his daytime career the main project of his life, but used it as a foundation to pursue his wider ambitions as a human being. That's what I mean by 'seeking work for a fulfilling life'. It's a common strategy for the art of living: you hold down a job that leaves you sufficient time and energy for a serious free-time pursuit such as playing the fiddle, doing landscape photography, or being a community activist.

Does this imply giving up on the possibility of having a fulfilling career? Not necessarily. For a start, a meaningful job need not be one that completely consumes your whole life. I was once lucky enough to have a wonderful job organizing 'conversation meals' between strangers, but by agreeing with my boss that I'd work from noon until six, I could spend my mornings writing a novel. Moreover, fulfilment remains possible if we are willing to break down the conceptual barrier between work and leisure. So-called 'leisure activities' may not offer us hard cash, but they can provide many of the other benefits of a fulfilling career if we pursue them with dedication. Through his poetry, Wallace Stevens was able to obtain social status, respect from fellow poets, and a sense that he was using his talents and following his calling. So let's not be so hung up on the traditional idea that a career necessarily involves earning money.

But we can't just forget about money. Indeed, anxiety about money is the major factor preventing most people from following Bertrand Russell's advice and reducing their working hours so they have enough time for creative idling. Just imagine you convinced your employer to let you work four days a week instead of five. Could you survive the 20 per cent drop in salary?

The most effective way to meet this challenge is to become an adherent of simple living, one of the fastest-growing religions of our post-industrial age. By doing so, you would be joining a venerable tradition of individuals who have voluntarily turned against materialism and consumerism in pursuit of a more meaningful – and cheaper – existence. Think of the nineteenth-century American naturalist

Henry David Thoreau, who spent two years conducting an experiment in self-sufficiency in the 1840s. Thoreau lived in a log cabin he built with his own hands for less than $30, and kept his costs down by growing most of his own food. Devoting himself to reading, writing and observing nature, he famously declared in *Walden*, 'a man is rich in proportion to the number of things he can afford to let alone'.

Someone who followed his example was Joe Dominguez, a founder of the modern simple-living movement in the United States and co-author of *Your Money or Your Life*, one of its most influential manifestos. The son of poor Cuban immigrants, in the 1960s Dominguez climbed out of the ghetto and into a job as a financial analyst on Wall Street. 'When I worked on Wall Street,' he said, 'I saw that most people were not making a living, they were making a dying. They would come home from work a little deader than when they started out in the morning. I was determined not to make the same mistake.'[78] So he came up with a plan. He saved every cent he could, living cheaply in Harlem, making his own furniture and buying second-hand clothes. By the age of thirty he had put away enough money to be able to survive, if he was careful, on the annual interest of $6,000 a year. He resigned his job, bought a camper van, and headed out west into a new life of frugal freedom.

Thoreau and Dominguez approached simple living as an extreme sport, and few people are ready to make such a radical change in lifestyle. But if you doubt that you could get by on even 20 per cent less than you currently earn, or think that it wouldn't be worth the material sacrifices involved, let me share with you one of the great secrets of the art of living. You've probably experienced the phenomenon whereby an increase in your salary fails to lead to any increase in your savings, because your spending mysteriously expands to fill the space of your available income. Well, the reverse also applies. When your income goes down from working less (or maybe from taking a salary cut to do a more fulfilling job), as a general rule your daily living expenses – on things like food, clothing and entertainment – will naturally contract to fit your new financial circumstances, and yet you will not feel any worse off. In fact, it is quite likely that you will feel life is better than ever, since you will be luxuriating in an abundance of that most precious commodity, time.

Don't believe me? When Sameera Khan left her job as a corporate lawyer in London and took up working on social enterprise projects and doing sporadic legal work on a freelance basis, she and her husband had to adjust to a significant reduction in their joint income. I asked her how they were managing.

> We are thousands of pounds a month down. How on earth did we used to spend that money? I am ashamed to say that I have no idea what I spent it on. When you take it away you can live fine. And my quality of life has improved. I'm at home more, I see more of my friends, my family. I cook nice evening meals whilst being frugal as I can shop in the greengrocers or farmer's market rather than having to shop in Sainsbury's. I can go to the fishmonger and buy locally caught fish that is cheaper because it's from our shores. I'm finally applying the 'waste not, want not' ethos of my parents' generation, but I really wish I'd had the sense to apply this when I was earning a full salary. I get so much pleasure in not spending money. I've also had time to take hula-hoop lessons

and teach myself how to knit on YouTube. I'm being creative – I didn't even know I was creative!

Sure, we've had to make changes, we've taken a long hard look at how we spent money and why we spent it. I guess before I just wasn't focused on what I needed versus what I wanted. We can't as easily go out to expensive restaurant meals with friends because it's harder for us to justify the cost. When I want to treat myself, I try to earn some extra money through selling things I no longer need on eBay – it's quite addictive. Overall, the whole experience has taught me to be incredibly more reflective, and to value everything I've got.

Making a transition towards simpler living requires embracing Picasso's philosophy: 'art is the elimination of the unnecessary'. One worthwhile experiment is to keep detailed accounts for a month of all your expenses, labelling each item as a 'need' or a 'want', and in the following month trying to halve the spending on your 'wants'. Did your quality of life plummet, or was it surprisingly liberating? Another option is to cultivate yourself as a connoisseur of flea markets and second-hand shops, and sign up to online communities such as Freecycle, where people give away unwanted consumer goods, from tricycles to sofas. At the same time, it is important to recognize that our jobs can actually cost us money: think how much you spend on what Joe Dominguez called your 'work uniform' (suits, dresses, shoes, bags), on commuting to the office, daily snacks, and on luxury vacations to help you recover from the stress. Should you really be paying so much to be in work?

Simple living also has more general applications to career change. If you decide to take a radical sabbatical like Laura van Bouchout, an ability to live relatively cheaply may extend the amount of time you can give to your work experiments. And a knowledge that you are able to live lightly could make it easier to shift to a job with less pay but more meaning.

In a culture obsessed with hard work and career success, it can be difficult to wean ourselves off the work ethic. And we may not want to if we are engrossed in a career that is making us feel fully alive. But if we do seek the advantages of a four-day week, and the space to nurture other parts of who we are, then we might be wise to put our hopes in the virtues of simple living, discovering beauty in the ideal that less truly is more.

While we may be able to find a gratifying job which also leaves us with an abundance of idle hours for enriching projects, what will happen to our prospects for career fulfilment when we take on the ultimate project of having a family?

How to Think About 'Having it All'

It is eight o'clock on a Wednesday morning and I'm arguing with my partner about who will stay home to look after our three-year-old twins, who are too ill to go to nursery today. She's an economist at a development-aid agency, busy writing a report on alternatives to economic growth, and trying to hold down a demanding professional job on just three days a week. I'm struggling to meet my deadline to finish a book on how to find fulfilling work, within the confines of my four-day week. We love our children, but are also both immersed in our careers. Neither of us really wants to make what we each think of as a 'sacrifice' to do an unscheduled day of childcare.

This kind of dilemma is typical for anybody trying to 'have it all' – to pursue a fulfilling career while also being a dedicated parent. Unless you are one of the lucky few who have grandparents on call or can afford expensive childminders, there can be just too many demands on our time, especially when children are below school age. The result is not only lack of sleep and lack of space for ourselves. Under so much pressure, relationships can crumble, career ambitions fall by the wayside, and freedom of choice disappear.

Despite these challenging realities, having it all has become a widespread aspiration in Western society, especially since the 1980s when the phrase was popularized and became associated with the ideal of the 'superwoman' who had well-adjusted children, a great marriage and a top-flight job. But is it really possible – for both women and men – to combine a thriving career with an enriching family life? The best way to approach this question is not to answer it directly, but to demystify it. I want to suggest four ways of rethinking the issue of how to have it all.

Don't think of it as your dilemma, it's society's dilemma

If you are finding it hard to have an enjoyable and successful career while also bringing up children, remember this: it's not your fault. The time strictures and emotional strains you face are in large part a consequence of social and cultural factors that make it extraordinarily difficult, particularly for women, to have it all. This is not your work crisis, it's society's crisis.

One aspect of the problem is that men's attitudes towards family life have not changed sufficiently to keep pace with women's emancipation. The French philosopher and feminist Simone de Beauvoir recognized this back in the 1940s. When discussing the significant increase of women entering the paid workforce during the early twentieth century, she pointed out that 'it is through gainful employment that woman has traversed most of the distance that separated her from the male; and nothing else can guarantee her liberty in practice'. Yet she saw that the majority 'do not escape from the traditional feminine world' of childcare and housework, even if they have a job.[79]

De Beauvoir highlighted what has become known as the 'double burden': women doing paid work often face a 'second shift' of domestic work when they get back home, since they tend to do a far greater proportion of the household tasks than men, from cooking the evening meal to getting up in the night to comfort a crying baby. No wonder Erica Jong declared that liberated women 'have won the right to be terminally exhausted'. A revealing recent study by psychologist Paula Nicolson showed that first-time mothers who believed the father would be an equal partner in infant care were almost always wrong in their prediction.[80] Soon after the baby arrived, the men tended to step back into the traditional breadwinner role, and were unwilling to give up their old social life to take on domestic responsibilities. And don't be fooled by all those magazine articles about superdads: stay-at-home dads may be on the rise, but in countries like Britain only one in twenty fathers is the primary carer.[81] We continue to live in cultures that typically expect women to take on most of the childcare, and that assume it is the mother, more than the father, who should be adjusting her career to have a family.

A second factor compounding the problem is that the way work is structured is out of kilter with the realities of raising children. For instance, even when fathers want to get involved in childcare, employment laws in many countries only grant them a few weeks of paternity leave. If only we all lived in Norway, where couples can choose how to divide their forty-six weeks of paid parental leave between them, with the result that 90 per cent of fathers take at least three months of paternity leave.[82] Some countries, though, are beginning to catch up: new legislation in the UK will allow fathers to take six months of leave. A further barrier is that in most countries employees are given around four weeks of annual holiday, yet school children are on holiday for some twelve weeks. How are parents supposed to close the gap without at least one of them putting their work in the background? Similarly, schools tend to finish two hours earlier than the office day, with only a minority of workers enjoying flexitime that allows them to leave early to pick up the kids. In such a crazy system, so desperately in need of reform, you should hardly blame yourself for your frustrations when trying to balance career ambitions and family obligations.

'Can women have it all?' is the wrong question

An underlying assumption in most books and news articles about how to have it all is that this is primarily an issue for and about women. It is standard practice to interview a variety of mothers, some of whom manage the superhuman feat of being both a corporate CEO and a domestic goddess, while others struggle with the challenge. What is the great secret of those who have it all? We might meet one human dynamo who gets up at five each morning and is a genius at time management, and another who is a brilliant multitasker, able to negotiate a deal before whipping up a gourmet meal. An implicit message is often that women who aren't able to shine in both their job and as mothers are somehow inadequate and haven't quite got what it takes. As superwoman commentator Shirley Conran made clear two decades ago, this message has had a real impact:

> I had noticed a growing anxiety and depression among ordinary women as the result of media propaganda about females who effortlessly organize a career (not a 'job'), home, husband, children and social life, while simultaneously retaining a twenty-four-hour perfect hairstyle and doing something esoteric, such as learning Japanese in their spare time.[83]

But what about the men? While women are put under the spotlight, the men in their lives are usually left standing quietly in the background. Yet we can't fully understand the possibilities for working mothers unless we know what the men around them are doing. In traditional two-parent households, the factor that might make it possible for a woman to maintain a demanding career while spending quality time with her children is the support of a husband who cooks half the meals and works part-time from home. Equally, what might make it impossible for some women is not any personal failing, but the fact that their husbands barely lift a finger to help with domestic chores.

Focusing on women while neglecting the role of men also reinforces the cultural norm that it is mothers, rather than fathers, who should be adjusting their lives to the complexities of managing both a career and a family, and making compromises where necessary. If we want to live in a more equal society, where both men and women can enjoy fulfilling careers, we need to challenge this bias. The dilemmas of having it all ought to be faced by both sexes, and be negotiated by them together. Iain King, for instance, knew that his wife 'wanted some mental stimulation beyond juggling nappy changes with meal planning', so they decided that he would give up his peacekeeping job in Afghanistan and become a full-time househusband caring for their son, enabling her to return to her diplomatic career. Men should not presume that they can automatically continue working as they always have done once they have children, just as women need not assume that they are the ones who have to put their careers on hold to manage the household economy. Instead of asking 'Can women have it all?', the real question should be 'How can parents support each other so they can *both* have some of it all?'

Having it all does not mean you must have it all at once

Across Europe and North America, the most common strategy for reconciling the demands of work and family is for one parent — usually the mother — to shift to working part-time while the children are small. Yet the strictures of doing so can turn the idea of career fulfilment into a fantasy. Is it really possible to flourish in your chosen profession on a three-day week? Unlike your colleagues, you may, for example, be unable to go that extra distance and stay late at the office, because the kids need to be picked up from nursery. Many part-timers end up worrying that while they aren't able to do their jobs well, neither are they giving enough time to their children. 'I feel like I'm being good at nothing,' admits a child psychologist who juggles consulting work with caring for her three-year-old son.

An alternative approach is to avoid the juggling act by adopting the philosophy that having it all does not mean you must have it all at the same time. This requires stepping back to take the long view. Imagine your life as a series of phases, each expressing a different dimension of who you are – something like Shakespeare's Seven Ages of Man. The idea is to have a fully committed career phase, where you throw yourself into work, then switch to a phase of dedicated parenting, and perhaps return to work again at a later stage. In effect, stretching your ambition to 'have it all' over an extended time span. In pursuit of this strategy, professional women frequently choose to put off motherhood until their late thirties, to give themselves sufficient years to experience a feeling of career achievement.[84]

Like all strategies, this one has its risks, as Helena Fosh can tell you. She traded in her top job in advertising, where she was in charge of several multi-million-dollar accounts, to have a family. 'But two children later, I was secretly envious of the women I knew who were still working,' she remembers. 'They seemed to have a sense of purpose I lacked – I didn't think my contribution to my family's and husband's life was valued.' Helena discovered how difficult it can be to make the identity transition from 'successful professional' to 'full-time parent', which is not helped by the fact that being a parent is unpaid and has no promotion prospects. Helena's eventual solution was to try to return to the workplace. But she found not only that her CV and skills were out of date, but that her extended career break had eroded her self-esteem: 'A huge challenge has been to overcome my feelings of inadequacy and loss of self-confidence.' So now she believes that 'leaving a professional career is the worst mistake that a woman can make; women should always try to keep a foot in the door, at any cost, while raising a family'.

Not everyone would agree with this. There are many people who thrive on full-time parenting and think about it as the most fulfilling career they could imagine. They approach bringing up their children as a vocation that provides their life with a sense of meaning and direction. Unlike their previous paid work, where they may have felt expendable, they commonly feel that as a parent they are irreplaceable, the only person who can be mother or father to their own child. This idea of acknowledging that childcare is a job in itself is one promoted by feminist economists such as Nancy Folbre, who point out the huge social contribution and economic value of unpaid work such as childcare and housework. In Britain, for example, the average value of unpaid work by a mother in the home is estimated to be worth £30,000 a year, yet it remains invisible in the national accounts.[85]

Brian Campbell, a Canadian father who had to give up a promising career as a scholar of Chinese poetry to bring up four boys himself after he split up with his partner, adopted the attitude that child-rearing was a worthwhile form of work, albeit unpaid. 'I approached single parenting as a job,' he told me, describing how he even home-schooled his children for a couple of years. Although he regrets losing his chance of an academic career, 'I discovered that raising my kids, imparting to them my values, my passion for learning, for problem-solving and supporting them in every way possible, was a sacrifice worth making.' The rewards of working as a parent lie not in money or status, but in human relationships.

Raising children is an opportunity to go in new career directions

There is more to the story of Brian Campbell. When his kids were little, he thought it would be interesting if they all developed their botanical minds by learning about the bees buzzing around their garden. Soon he was drawn to keeping bees himself to earn some money on the side. Fifteen years later, with his children almost all grown up, Brian now leases a small farm, has hives all over the city, and teaches courses on urban beekeeping. 'I enjoy bees and sharing my passion for them with others,' he says. 'It took me a while to realize that this has become a career, alongside being a stay-at-home dad. It definitely wasn't planned; it just evolved slowly out of a need to support myself and my family. I suppose jobs become careers when they take on a life of their own.'

A final way of rethinking the problem of balancing work and family is to recognize that raising children can create unexpected opportunities for taking your career in different directions. Like Brian, many parents develop new interests and skills that grow out of their engagement in family life, which often sends them into startlingly unfamiliar territory. Tom Burrough, who became a full-time father after losing his job in the advertising industry, was appalled by the second-rate baby food on offer for his infant. So he started up a small business producing gourmet meals for babies, like Moroccan lamb stew and cod-and-pea mornay, while caring for his daughter. Keira O'Mara, an enterprising mother who was made redundant from her marketing job while on maternity leave, told me how she was tired of getting disapproving stares when trying to feed her baby in public, and so she invented Mamascarf, a new kind of breastfeeding scarf, which is now sold in retail outlets across Britain.

Rather than being the end of our career, or an extended pause, becoming a parent can signal a fresh beginning. A radical new experience like having children might leave us utterly exhausted at the end of each day, but it can also free our minds, encourage our creativity, and stir us to experiment with the worker bee buzzing in our souls.

The Captive Slave

Michelangelo's sculpture *The Captive Slave*, seemingly half-finished, shows a figure attempting to free himself from the stone. Some art historians interpret it as a metaphysical vision of the soul endeavouring to escape from matter. Others consider it a metaphor for how we need to discover our true selves and destinies, which lie hidden within us, like a figure within a block of stone. For me, this work of art is about the struggle for freedom in everyday life.

How much should freedom matter to us? I am not saying that we should all become self-employed fire jugglers, for there are times in life when job security is essential. I don't believe we should all

Michelangelo's captive slave, struggling to free himself from the stone.

join the revolution of idleness, since there are some people who will thrive on committing their entire being to their work. And of course compromise is sometimes a necessary part of life, especially when it comes to balancing career ambitions with tending to our children.

Yet I also believe it is a worthy aspiration to try to break free from the stone, to liberate ourselves from the personal fears, social conventions and myths that might be holding us back from releasing our adventurous spirit. There are many ways to free that spirit, from inventing our own job to unchaining ourselves from the culture of overwork by living a simpler life with more space for pursuing our passions. In the affluent nations of the modern world, there is no need for most of us to be captive slaves, to 'be enslaved by machines, bureaucracies, boredom, ugliness', as Schumacher put it. We have the ability, the obligation, to escape the stone by carving out new possibilities in our lives.

- *What is the kind of freedom that you most desire for your working life?*

6. How to Grow a Vocation

The Prize of Soulful Work

'Without work, all life goes rotten, but when work is soulless, life stifles and dies,' wrote Albert Camus. Finding work with a soul has become one of the great aspirations of our age. While the 'grin and bear it' school of thought still has its followers, there is a growing movement of people in the Western world and beyond who are asking more of their jobs, who seek work that reflects who they are and makes them feel more human. Those who wish to join this movement, and be successful in their quest for a life-expanding career, need to consider two final questions.

In this book I've tried to distil the very essence of a fulfilling career, and discovered that there are three essential ingredients: meaning, flow and freedom. People who are fulfilled have some combination of them, while also being wary of an excessive allegiance to the desire for money or status. Yet even those with all three elements in their working lives can feel there is a greater prize, what we might think of as the Holy Grail of soulful work: a career that is not just fulfilling, but that additionally feels like a 'calling' or 'vocation'. This raises the first question: how can we discover our true vocation in life?

There is another unresolved issue, which concerns how we complete the task of turning our ideal of fulfilment into the reality of a new career. We now know the fundamentals of this process.

Once we have narrowed down the options to a range of jobs that express our multiple selves, we need to test them out with radical sabbaticals, branching projects and conversational research. We must adopt the revolutionary philosophy of 'act now, reflect later', and become what Leonardo da Vinci called a *discepolo di esperienza*, a disciple of experience.

Yet even if we have followed this experimental pathway and identified a potentially fulfilling career, we still may find ourselves frozen in indecision, because we are too afraid to take that final – and unavoidable – step into the unknown that allows us to break with our past and reinvent ourselves. Thus emerges the second question: how can we overcome this barrier to change?

To answer these two questions, we must travel first to a scientific laboratory in Paris, then to small island off the coast of Greece.

Marie Curie and the Meaning of Life

In the classes I teach, I regularly hear people lament that they are 'still searching for their vocation' or envying others who have 'found their ultimate calling'. What they seem to be looking for is a career that offers them an all-embracing sense of mission or purpose. Their search, however, is almost certain to be unsuccessful. Not because vocations do not exist. But because we have to realize that a vocation is not something we *find*, it's something we *grow* – and grow into. Before revealing the secret of how to grow one, we need to be clear about what a vocation really means, and why it matters.

It is common to think of a vocation as a career that you somehow feel you were 'meant to do'. I prefer a different definition, one closer to the historical origins of the concept: a vocation is a career that not only gives you fulfilment – meaning, flow, freedom – but that also has a definitive goal or clear purpose to strive for attached to it, which drives your life and motivates you to get up in the morning. The goal or purpose for a medical researcher might be to discover a cure for motor neurone disease; for an environmental activist it could be to promote the ideal of low-carbon living; for a painter, to break traditional conventions and replace them with a new vision of the objectives of art. You shouldn't worry at all if you don't feel you have a vocation. However, while they are relatively rare, with the right approach it is quite possible for a vocation to emerge in your life.

Amongst the most important discoveries in the history of Western thought is that having this kind of clear goal or purpose to pursue is one of the surest routes to a deeply satisfying life. In fact, if there is any answer to the question of the meaning of life, this is a major contender. Aristotle was the first thinker to recognize it explicitly, writing that every person should have 'some object for the good life to aim at . . . with reference to which he will then do all his acts, since not to have one's life organized in view of some end is a mark of much folly.'[86]

The idea of having a meaningful goal re-emerged in the sixteenth-century Protestant concept of a 'calling'. This was the belief that each of us should follow the preordained path or 'calling' determined for us by God: so a farmer should grow his crops to the best of his abilities, and a magistrate should dedicate himself completely to his profession. Doing so, wrote the theologian John Calvin in 1536, would cure us of the 'great restlessness' that we often feel, and prevent our lives from being 'topsy-turvy'.[87] Calvin's views reflected the rigid social hierarchies of his time – we should be satisfied with the career we were born into – so bad luck if you happened to be a serf. But underlying this was the goal of striving to do God's bidding on earth.

The German philosopher Friedrich Nietzsche similarly stressed the beneficial effects of having a mission to guide us: 'He who has a *why* to live for can bear with almost any *how*.' This thought found its way out of philosophy and into twentieth-century psychology. In the 1940s, the Austrian psychotherapist Victor Frankl suggested: 'What man actually needs is not some tension-less state but rather the striving and struggling for some goal worthy of him.' Each of us should pursue a 'concrete assignment', which is our 'specific vocation or mission in life'.[88] This long tradition of thought is today reflected in the writings of psychologist Mihaly Csikszentmihalyi, who believes that 'wherever it comes from, a unified purpose is what gives meaning to life'. What people require is 'a goal that like a magnetic field attracts their psychic energy, a goal upon which all lesser goals depend'.[89] Aristotle would have thoroughly approved.

Let's leave the theory for a moment and examine the realities of a working life driven by this kind of missionary purpose: the career of Marie Curie, whose overriding goal was to discover the secrets of radiation.

Born into a studious but impoverished family of Polish intellectuals in 1867, Marie Curie – then known as Manya Skłodowska – was a gifted student. She dreamed of studying medicine in Paris, but lack of funds prevented this, and she was condemned to working as a governess in rural Poland for five years, saving her pennies and reading maths and anatomy books alone deep into the night. Finally arriving in Paris in 1891, aged 24, she commenced her medical studies, and gradually found herself drawn to doing research in chemistry and physics, an interest she had partly inherited from her father.

It was the beginning of an extraordinarily intensive life of scientific endeavour that would last over forty years. Curie normally worked twelve to fourteen hours a day, continuing at home until two in the morning after returning from the lab. In 1897 she began her study of radiation, in collaboration with her husband Pierre, which led to the discovery of radium a year later. This was followed by four years working in a draughty old shed to further explore the properties of radium, and another new element she discovered, polonium. Her brilliance and dedication were rewarded with a Nobel Prize in Physics in 1903, and another in Chemistry in 1911. She became France's first female university professor, and one of the world's most famous scientists.

Curie was absolutely committed to her career. She lived an almost monastic lifestyle in her early years in Paris, surviving on nothing but buttered bread and tea for weeks at a time, which left her anaemic and regularly fainting from hunger. She shunned her growing fame, and had no interest in material comforts, preferring to live in a virtually unfurnished home: status and money mattered little to her. When a relative offered to buy her a wedding dress, she insisted that 'if you are going to be kind enough to give me one, please let it be practical and dark, so that I can put it on afterwards to go to the laboratory'.[90] Before her death in 1934, aged 67, she summed up her philosophy of work. 'Life is not easy for any of us,' she said. 'But what of that? We must have perseverance and above all confidence in ourselves. We must believe that we are gifted for something, and that this thing, at whatever cost, must be attained.'[91]

What conclusions can we draw from Marie Curie's career? Certainly it had all the qualities of a vocation. Her work offered the fundamental elements of meaning: it used her intellectual talents, embodied her great passion for science, and allowed her to feel she was making a difference – especially in the potential uses of radiation therapy for cancer treatment. But she also had that Aristotelian sense of purpose, embodied in her goal, or 'concrete assignment', to make discoveries about the nature of radiation.

A more important point concerns where that goal actually came from. What everyone in the career doldrums really wants to know is: 'How can I find a vocation?' And the answer that emerges from Marie Curie's experience is that vocations are grown, and grown into, rather than found.

There is a widespread – and mistaken – assumption that a vocation usually comes to people in a flash of enlightenment or moment of epiphany. We're lying in bed and suddenly we know exactly what we're supposed to do with our life. It's as if the voice of God has called to us: 'Go forth and write Chinese-cookery books!' Alternatively we put ourselves through a process of intense self-reflection which, at some point, is supposed to give us a blinding insight into our future: 'My task in life is to set up an otter sanctuary!' It's an enticing thought, which, in effect, takes the responsibility away from us: someone or something will tell us what to do with our lives.

But Marie Curie never had such a miraculous moment of insight, when she knew that she must dedicate her working life to researching the properties of radioactive materials. What really occurred was that this goal quietly crept up on her during years of sustained scientific research. After an initial desire to become a doctor like her elder

Marie Curie didn't find her vocation. She grew it.

sister, she did research on the magnetization of tempered steel. Only at the age of 30 did she begin studying uranium rays for her doctoral thesis, building on recent work done by Henri Becquerel. Following her discovery of radium, several more years of experiments were required to prove its existence to an incredulous scientific establishment.[92] Her obsession grew in stages, without any Tannoy announcement from the heavens that issued her a calling. That's the way it typically happens: although people occasionally have those explosive epiphanies, more commonly a vocation crystallizes slowly, almost without us realizing it.[93]

So there is no great mystery behind it all. If we want a job that is also a vocation, we should not passively wait around for it to appear out of thin air. Instead we should take action and endeavour to grow it like Marie Curie. How? Simply by devoting ourselves to work that gives us deep fulfilment through meaning, flow and freedom (though a fourteen-hour day might be overdoing it a little). Over time, a tangible and inspiring goal may quietly germinate, grow larger, and eventually flower into life.

A Message from Zorba

Many people baulk at the final hurdle of making a career change. They've done months of thinking through the options, perhaps undertaken a few branching projects, tried some conversational research, and eventually realized what the best career choice would be. And then they stop, faced by a paralysing fear. Doubts start running through their head. What if I've made a terrible mistake and the job ends up a disaster rather than a source of fulfilment? Wouldn't it be safer just to hold back on handing in my notice, and wait until I'm absolutely certain that I've found the right career to move into?

This kind of anxiety is perfectly normal. There is no escape from the fact that, in the end, changing career is a risk. It is full of uncertainties and unknowns, no matter how much we prepare ourselves for it.

How can we make that final leap into the darkness?

While researching this book, I asked many people this question. And they all gave me a similar answer. Sameera Khan, who resigned from her full-time corporate law job and is now working in the social enterprise sector and as a freelance lawyer, told me what she had learned from her own experience:

> I went to an amazing career coach. I couldn't believe I was seeing a career coach, it was embarrassing to admit to friends, embarrassing to admit to myself. After a couple of sessions she said, 'Well, you know you've got to quit your job, otherwise you'll be stuck in this despair forever. Once you quit, some of the fog will be lifted. So we've got to set a date.' So we set a date of July 1 and this was in the middle of May! I said that was really soon, and she replied, 'Well, you're not going to do it otherwise.' And of course I wasn't going to. So I did quit on July 1. Ultimately, when you want to quit your job you just have to do it.

Indeed, the inconvenient truth is that there comes a point when you need to stop thinking and just do it. This is one of the most ancient pieces of wisdom for the art of living. Like the idea of having a purposeful goal in life, it has been articulated in many forms over the centuries. Its most famous expression, in Western culture, appears in the *Odes* of the Roman poet Horace: *carpe diem*, he advised, seize the day – before time runs out on you. In the Rabbinical tradition there is a saying attributed to the sage Hillel the Elder: 'And if not now, when?' The Danish philosopher Søren Kierkegaard gave us the idea of a 'leap of faith'. For a literary version try George Eliot's *Middlemarch*: 'I would not creep along the coast but steer out in mid-sea, by guidance of the stars.'

The ubiquity of this ideal reveals an adventurous spirit in humanity, one fired by a knowledge that life is preciously short, and that to make the most of it – to 'suck out all the marrow of life', as Thoreau put it – we have no choice but to take risks that promise us the gift of a more profound and vibrant existence.

There are, without doubt, ways of making that final step towards change easier. By ensuring we have some financial safety net – perhaps a few months of savings stashed away – we can allay our fear of destitution if our new job fails to work out. We can also put our faith in the power of public declarations: by openly telling friends and family that we are about to change career, we may begin to shift our own expectations and give ourselves more courage to act. And don't forget the power of the written word: try writing your own obituary. Imagine yourself in the future, looking back over your life, and write the story of what you did, or hoped you had done. It is up to you to decide whether or not, at the age of 36, you left your job in financial services to work for a local community theatre, or to become a freelancing wide achiever. Writing your obituary is a startlingly effective way to help avoid a corrosive feeling of regret that you did not take your life in new directions when you had the chance.

There is one last way to break with your past and begin a new stage of your career journey, which is to take some advice that appears at the end of the 1964 film *Zorba the Greek*.

Zorba, the great lover of life, is sitting on the beach with the repressed and bookish Basil, an Englishman who has come to a tiny Greek island with the hope of setting up a small business. The elaborate cable system that Zorba has designed and built for Basil to bring logs down the mountainside has just collapsed on its very first trial. Their whole entrepreneurial venture is in complete ruins, a failure before it has even begun. And that is the moment when Zorba unveils his philosophy of life to Basil:

ZORBA: Damn it boss, I like you too much not to say it. You've got everything except one thing: madness! A man needs a little madness, or else . . .
BASIL: Or else?
ZORBA: . . . he never dares cut the rope and be free.

Basil then stands up and, completely out of character, asks Zorba to teach him how to dance. The Englishman has finally learned that life is there to be lived with passion, that risks are there to be taken, the day is there to be seized. To do otherwise is a disservice to life itself.

Zorba's words are one of the great messages for the human quest in search of the good life. Most of us live bound by our fears and inhibitions. Yet if we are to move beyond them, if we are to cut the rope and be free, we need to treat life as an experiment and discover the little bit of madness that lies within us all.

Are you ready to take that final step to be free?

Homework

If you are hungry for more ideas on the art of working, the following books, films and websites will provide the necessary sustenance. All of them, in different ways, helped to inspire the thoughts that appear in this book.

1. The Age of Fulfilment

A good starting place to explore the possibilities for a fulfilling career is Studs Terkel's extraordinary oral history *Working*, in which everyday workers, from bank tellers to barbers, talk about what their jobs mean to them. Also treat yourself to Po Bronson's *What Should I Do With My Life?*, a compilation of real-life stories describing the challenges and fears involved in changing career. *Salesman* (1968) is a riveting documentary about four door-to-door salesmen selling very expensive Bibles to low-income families in the United States. The way they deal with constant rejection, homesickness and burnout provides lessons for anyone in search of a fulfilling job.

2. A Short History of Career Confusion

On the history of work, the best overview is Richard Donkin's *Blood, Sweat and Tears: The Evolution of Work*. Theodore Zeldin's remarkable *An Intimate History of Humanity* is a history of human relationships from the earliest times and across all cultures, chronicling how the past has shaped the way we approach work and other areas of life such as love and time. *The Paradox of Choice* by psychologist Barry Schwartz provides useful insights into why we get so confused about career choice. There is a witty and wise TED talk by philosopher Alain de Botton on our inherited cultural ideas about success and failure at: www.ted.com/talks/lang/eng/alain_de_botton_a_kinder_gentler_philosophy_of_success.html. For a critique of the Myers–Briggs Type Indicator, read David Pittenger's article 'Measuring the MBTI . . . And Coming Up Short' at www.indiana.edu/~jobtalk/articles/develop/mbti.pdf.

3. Giving Meaning to Work

The temptations of a big salary are analysed in Oliver James's *Affluenza*, in which he argues that we place an excessively high value on acquiring money and possessions, and wanting to look good in the eyes of others. Oliver Stone's film *Wall Street* (1987) delves further into this theme in his parable of the 1980s corporate raider Gordon Gekko. The story of Anita Roddick's attempts to bring her ethics into the workplace appear in her autobiography *Business as Unusual*. If you are keen to cultivate your talents and experiment with being a wide achiever rather than a high achiever, get yourself a copy of Charles's Nicholl's biography *Leonardo da Vinci: The Flights of the Mind*.

4. Act First, Reflect Later

The psychology and sociology of risk are discussed in Richard Sennett's profound and beautifully written meditation on modern work, *The Corrosion of Character*. In *Working Identity*, professor of organizational behaviour Herminia Ibarra outlines principles for career reinvention, busting several myths about career change in the process. Solidly grounded in analysis of countless case studies, this is one of the finest academic books on what it takes to find fulfilling work. Out of psychologist Mihaly Csikszentmihalyi's numerous works on flow experience, the best is *Flow: The Classic Work on How to Achieve Happiness*. The film *American Beauty* (1999) examines a family whose members make some life-changing choices, including a father who gives up his career in advertising in search of a more meaningful existence. Political writer George Monbiot offers some timeless and inspiring advice on how to make career choices at www.monbiot.com/archives/2000/06/09/choose-life/.

5. The Longing for Freedom

Colin Ward's *Anarchy in Action* is the ultimate handbook for those in search of greater freedom in their working lives. *Screw Work, Let's Play* by John Williams offers useful practical tips on how to make it in the freelance world. One of the best ways to wean yourself off the work ethic is by reading Bertrand Russell's essay *In Praise of Idleness*. In *Walden*, the nineteenth-century naturalist Henry David Thoreau offers a compelling and poetic vision of simple living, while a programme for turning it into reality can be found in *Your Money or Your Life* by Joe Dominguez and Vicki Robin. Illuminating on women's role as workers are Rosalind Miles's scintillating *The Women's History of the World* and Simone de Beauvoir's feminist blockbuster *The Second Sex*. The tensions between career aspirations and family life are exposed in the tear-inducing film *Kramer vs. Kramer* (1979).

6. How to Grow a Vocation

Follow the career story and scientific discoveries of Marie Curie in *Madame Curie*, the biography by her daughter Eve Curie. Join the immortal Alexis Zorba (Anthony Quinn) and the staid Englishman Basil (Alan Bates) on an isolated Greek Island in the film *Zorba the Greek* (1964). Zorba teaches Basil about the art of taking risks and going in new directions in working life, and delivers his famous line: 'A man needs a little madness, or else he never dares cut the rope and be free.' In my book *The Wonderbox: Curious Histories of How to Live*, I reveal what history can teach us about finding a job we love and becoming more adventurous in the way we make decisions about our careers and other realms of everyday life.

A comprehensive bibliography is available online at: www.panmacmillan.com/theschooloflife

Notes

1. The Age of Fulfilment

1. Thomas, Keith, *The Ends of Life: Roads to Fulfilment in Early Modern England*, Oxford: Oxford University Press, 2009, p.8.
2. www.opp.eu.com/SiteCollectionDocuments/pdfs/dream-research.pdf; http://news.bbc.co.uk/1/hi/world/americas/8440630.stm
3. www.statistics.gov.uk/articles/labour_market_trends/jobmobility_nov03.pdf , p.543.
4. Svendsen, Lars, *Work*, Stocksfield: Acumen, 2008, p.5.
5. Batchelor, Stephen, *Buddhism Without Beliefs: A Contemporary Guide to Awakening*, London: Bloomsbury, 1998, p.25.
6. Burckhardt, Jacob, *The Civilization of the Renaissance in Italy*, Oxford and London: Phaidon, 1945, p.81; Greenblatt, Stephen, *Renaissance Self-Fashioning: From More to Shakespeare*, Chicago: University of Chicago Press, 2005, p.2; Krznaric, Roman, *The First Beautiful Game: Stories of Obsession in Real Tennis*, Oxford: Ronaldson Publications, 2006, chapter 11.

2. A Short History of Career Confusion

7. www.careerplanner.com/ListOfCareers.cfm.
8. Franklin, Benjamin, *Autobiography and Other Writings*, Oxford: Oxford University Press, 1998, pp.9–14.
9. Marx, Karl, *The Marxist Reader*, ed. Emile Burns, New York: Avenel Books, 1982, pp.273–274.
10. Miles, Rosalind, *The Women's History of the World*, London: Paladin, 1989, p.191.

11 Hobsbawm, Eric, *The Age of Revolution 1789–1848*, New York: Vintage, 1996, pp.189–194.
12 www.bls.gov/mlr/1999/12/art1full.pdf; www.voxeu.org/index/php?q=node/3946.
13 Miles, Rosalind, *The Women's History of the World*, p.271.
14 Schwartz, Barry, *The Paradox of Choice: Why Less Is More*, New York: Harper Perennial, 2005, pp.2, 9–10, 221.
15 Ibid. pp.9–10, 24–25; http://www.ted.com/talks/barry_schwartz_on_the_paradox_of_choice.html.
16 Ibid. pp.118–119, 140–141.
17 Ibid. pp.221–227.
18 www.cambridgeassessment.org.uk.
19 world-countries.net/archives/2218.
20 Schwartz, Barry, *The Paradox of Choice: Why Less Is More*, pp. 72–73.
21 Ibid. 149–150.
22 Pope, Mark, 'A Brief History of Career Counselling in the United States', *The Career Development Quarterly*, Vol.48, No.3, 2000, p.196.
23 Parsons, Frank, *Choosing a Vocation*, Boston, Houghton Mifflin, 1909, pp.21–22, 27–31.
24 Ibid. pp.133–136.
25 Hershenson, David B., 'A Head of Its Time: Career Counselling's Roots in Phrenology', *Career Development Quarterly*, Vol.57, No.2, 2008, pp.181–190; Lindqvist, Sven, *The Skull Measurer's Mistake*, New York: New Press, 1997; www.archive.org/stream/systemofphrenoloo0combuoft#page/n7/mode/2up.
26 Bjork, Robert A. and Daniel Druckman, *In the Mind's Eye: Enhancing Human Performance*, Washington: National Academies Press, 1991, pp.99–100; Gregory, Robert J., *Psychological Testing: History, Principles, Applications*, 4th edn, Boston: Pearson, p.524; Hunsley, John, Catherine M. Lee and James M. Wood, 'Controversial and Questionable Assessment Techniques' in Scott O. Lilienfield, Steven Jay Lynn and Jeffrey M. Lohr (eds), *Science and Pseudoscience in Clinical Psychology*, New York: The Guilford Press, 2003, pp.61–64; Boyle, Gregory, 'Myers–Briggs Type Indicator (MBTI): Some Psychometric Limitations', Bond University Humanities and Social Sciences Papers, No.26, 1995; McCrae, Robert and Paul Costa Jr, 'Reinterpreting the Myers–Briggs Type Indicator From

the Perspective of the Five-Factor Model of Personality', *Journal of Personality*, Vol.57, No.1, 1989, pp.17–40.
27 Pittenger, David, 'Cautionary Comments Regarding the Myers–Briggs Type Indicator', *Consulting Psychology Journal: Practice and Research*, Vol.57, No.3, 2005, p.214.
28 Ibid; Boyle, Gregory, 'Myers–Briggs Type Indicator (MBTI): Some Psychometric Limitations', Bond University Humanities and Social Sciences Papers, No.26.
29 Hunsley, John, Catherine M. Lee and James M. Wood, 'Controversial and Questionable Assessment Techniques' in Scott O. Lilienfield, Steven Jay Lynn and Jeffrey M. Lohr (eds), *Science and Pseudoscience in Clinical Psychology*, p.62; McCrae, Robert and Paul Costa Jr, 'Reinterpreting the Myers–Briggs Type Indicator From the Perspective of the Five-Factor Model of Personality', *Journal of Personality*, Vol.57, No.1, 1989, p.20.
30 OPP Unlocking Potential, *MBTI Step 1 Question Book*, European English edn, Oxford: OPP, 1998, p.1; OPP Unlocking Potential, *Introduction to Type and Careers*, European English edn, Oxford: OPP, 2000, p.26.
31 Pittenger, David, 'Measuring the MBTI ... And Coming Up Short', *Journal of Career Planning and Placement*, Vol.54, pp.48–53; Pittenger, David, 'Cautionary Comments Regarding the Myers–Briggs Type Indicator', *Consulting Psychology Journal: Practice and Research*, Vol.57, No.3, pp. 211, 217; personal communication with David Pittenger, 5/9/11. See also Hunsley, John, Catherine M. Lee and James M. Wood, 'Controversial and Questionable Assessment Techniques' in Scott O. Lilienfield, Steven Jay Lynn and Jeffrey M. Lohr (eds), *Science and Pseudoscience in Clinical Psychology*, p.63; Bjork, Robert A. and Daniel Druckman, *In the Mind's Eye: Enhancing Human Performance*, pp.99–101.
32 Ibarra, Herminia, *Working Identity: Unconventional Strategies for Reinventing Your Career*, Boston: Harvard Business School Press, 2004, pp.35–37.

3. Giving Meaning to Work

33 Argyle, Michael, *The Social Psychology of Work*, London: Penguin, 1989, pp. 99–101.

34 Layard, Richard, *Happiness: Lessons from a New Science*, London: Allen Lane, 2005, pp.32–33; for more recent research, see www.pnas.org/content/107/38/16489.full.pdf+html?sid=aac48a0b-d009-4ce6-8c14-7f97c5310e15.
35 Seligman, Martin, *Authentic Happiness: Using the New Positive Psychology to Realize Your Potential for Lasting Fulfillment*, Nicholas Brealey, 2002, p.49; James, Oliver, *Affluenza: How to be Successful and Stay Sane*, London: Vermilion, 2007, p.52.
36 Gerhardt, Sue, *The Selfish Society: How We All Forgot to Love One Another and Made Money Instead*, London: Simon & Schuster, 2010, pp.32–33.
37 www.guardian.co.uk/money/2011/jul/15/happiness-work-why-counts; www.theworkfoundation.com/assets/docs/publications/162_newwork_goodwork.pdf.
38 Schwartz, Barry, *The Paradox of Choice: Why Less Is More*, p.190.
39 Rousseau, Jean-Jacques, *A Discourse Upon The Origin And The Foundation Of The Inequality Among Mankind*, 1754, http://www.gutenberg.org/files/11136/11136.txt.
40 Lewis, Clive Staples, 'The Inner Ring', 1944, www.lewissociety.org/innerring.php.
41 Sennett, Richard, *The Corrosion of Character: The Personal Consequences of Work in the New Capitalism*, New York: Norton, 2003, p.3.
42 Arendt, Hannah, *The Human Condition*, Chicago: University of Chicago Press, 1989, p.18–19; Csikszentmihalyi, Mihaly, *Flow: The Classic Work on How to Achieve Happiness*, London: Rider, 2002, p.218.
43 Gardner, Howard, Mihaly Csikszentmihalyi and William Damon, *Good Work: When Excellence and Ethics Meet*, New York: Basic Books, 2001, pp.ix, 5.
44 Singer, Peter, *How Are We To Live? Ethics in an Age of Self-interest*, Oxford: Oxford University Press, 1997, pp.255–258.
45 Roddick, Anita, *Business As Unusual: My Entrepreneurial Journey, Profits With Principles*, Chichester: Anita Roddick Books, 2005, p.37.
46 Ibid. pp.83, 96, 122, 157, 179, 205.
47 www.satyamag.com/jan05/roddick.html.
48 Roddick, Anita, *Business As Unusual: My Entrepreneurial Journey, Profits With Principles*, pp.18, 92, 246.
49 Krznaric, Roman, *The First Beautiful Game: Stories of Obsession in Real Tennis*, pp.72–84.

50 Quoted in Williams, John, *Screw Work, Let's Play: How to do what you love and get paid for it*, Harlow: Prentice Hall, 2010, p.3.
51 Saul, John Ralston, *Voltaire's Bastards: The Dictatorship of Reason in the West*, London: Sinclair Stevenson, 1992, p.474; Zeldin, Theodore, *An Intimate History of Humanity*, London: Minerva, 1995, pp.197–198.
52 Csikszentmihalyi, Mihaly, *Flow: The Classic Work on How to Achieve Happiness*, p.155.
53 Ibarra, Herminia, *Working Identity: Unconventional Strategies for Reinventing Your Career*, p.xi.
54 Quoted in Nicholl, Charles, *Leonardo da Vinci: The Flights of the Mind*, London: Penguin, 2005, p.7.
55 Cameron, Julia, *The Artist's Way: A Course in Discovering and Recovering Your Creative Self*, London: Pan, 1995, p.39; Williams, John, *Screw Work, Let's Play: How to do what you love and get paid for it*, p.37.

4. Act First, Reflect Later

56 www.opp.eu.com/SiteCollectionDocuments/pdfs/dream-research.pdf.
57 Quoted in Sennett, Richard, *The Corrosion of Character: The Personal Consequences of Work in the New Capitalism*, p.82.
58 Seligman, Martin, *Authentic Happiness: Using the New Positive Psychology to Realize Your Potential for Lasting Fulfilment*, pp.30–31; Csikszentmihalyi, Mihaly, *Flow: The Classic Work on How to Achieve Happiness*, p.169. Special thanks to Rob Archer for helping me think about this issue.
59 Ibarra, Herminia, *Working Identity: Unconventional Strategies for Reinventing Your Career*, pp.xii, 16, 18, 91.
60 Ibid. p.45.
61 Ibid. p.113–120.
62 Csikszentmihalyi, Mihaly, *Beyond Boredom and Anxiety: Experiencing Flow in Work and Play*, San Francisco: Jossey-Bass, 2000, pp.35–36, 132, 137; Csikszentmihalyi, Mihaly, *Flow: The Classic Work on How to Achieve Happiness*, p.4.
63 Ibid. pp.48–67.
64 Ibid. p.152.

5. The Longing for Freedom

65 Schumacher, E.F., *Good Work*, London: Abacus, 1980, p.50.
66 www.theworkfoundation.com/assets/docs/publications/162_newwork_goodwork.pdf, p.29.
67 Fromm, Erich, *Fear of Freedom*, London: Routledge, 1960, pp.19–20, 85.
68 Ward, Colin, *Anarchism: A Very Short Introduction*, Oxford: Oxford University Press, 2004, p.49; www.guardian.co.uk/money/2011/jul/15/happiness-work-why-counts.
69 Ward, Colin, *Anarchy in Action*, London: Freedom Press, 1996, pp.94–5.
70 www.fsb.org.uk/policy/images/2011%2004%20self%20employment%20one%20page%20briefing.pdf; www.theworkfoundation.com/assets/docs/publications/145_Joy_of_Work.pdf, p.14.
71 Quoted in, Williams, John, *Screw Work, Let's Play: How to do what you love and get paid for it*, p.1.
72 http://www.thedailybeast.com/newsweek/2008/05/21/my-ebay-job.html.
73 Krakauer, Jon, *Into the Wild*, London: Pan Books, 2007.
74 www.guardian.co.uk/money/2000/oct/01/workandcareers.madeleinebunting2.
75 Robinson, Bryan, *Chained to the Desk: A Guidebook for Workaholics, Their Partners and Children, and the Clinicians Who Treat Them*, New York: New York University Press, 2001.
76 Russell, Bertrand, *In Praise of Idleness and Other Essays*, London: Unwin, 1976.
77 www.workfoundation.com/assets/docs/publications/177_About%20time%20for%20change.pdf, p.5–6.
78 Lerner, Steve, *Eco-Pioneers: Practical Visionaries Solving Today's Environmental Problems*, Boston: MIT Press, 1998, pp.71–72; Dominguez, Joe and Vicki Robin, *Your Money or Your Life: Transforming Your Relationship with Money and Achieving Financial Independence*, New York: Penguin, 1999.
79 De Beauvoir, Simone, *The Second Sex*, Harmondsworth: Penguin, 1972, pp.689–690, 703.
80 Nicolson, Paula, *Having It All? Choices for Today's Superwoman*, Chichester: John Wiley, 2002, pp.19, 155.

81 www.stayathomedads.co.uk/news.html
82 www.guardian.co.uk/money/2011/jul/19-norway-dads-paternity-leave-chemin
83 Quoted in Nicolson, Paula, *Having It All? Choices for Today's Superwoman* Nicolson, pp.12–13.
84 Ibid. pp.140, 142.
85 Folbre, Nancy, *Who Pays for the Kids? Gender and the Structures of Constraint*, London: Routledge, 1994, pp.2–3; http://www.legalandgeneralgroup.com/media-centre/press-releases/2011/group-news-release-876.html; www.sociology.leeds.ac.uk/assets/files/research/circle/valuing-carers.pdf.

6. How to Grow a Vocation

86 Quoted in Thomas, Keith, *The Ends of Life: Roads to Fulfilment in Early Modern England*, p.vii.
87 Quoted in Meilaender, Gilbert C., *Working: Its Meaning and Its Limits*, Notre Dame: University of Notre Dame Press, 2000, p.107.
88 Frankl, Victor, *Man's Search for Meaning: An Introduction to Logotherapy*, London: Hodder and Stoughton, 1987, pp.107, 110.
89 Csikszentmihalyi, Mihaly, *Flow: The Classic Work on How to Achieve Happiness*, pp.217–218.
90 Curie, Eve, *Madam Curie*, London: William Heinemann, 1938, p.134.
91 Ibid. p.113.
92 Ibid. pp.150–151, 162–163.
93 Bronson, Po, *What Should I Do With My Life: The True Story of People Who Answered the Ultimate Question*, London: Vintage, 2004, pp.291–292.

Acknowledgements

It has been a great pleasure working with Alain de Botton, the series editor, who has provided excellent ideas and advice throughout the course of creating this book. Thanks to Liz Gough, Dusty Miller, Tania Adams, Katie James, Kate Hewson and everyone at Pan Macmillan for all their backing and encouragement. My agent, Margaret Hanbury, has been tremendously supportive as always, offering wise counsel and inventive thoughts, as has Henry de Rougemont at the Hanbury Agency.

The origins of my interest in work go back to my years working with the historian and thinker Theodore Zeldin at The Oxford Muse, which gave me the opportunity to talk to people from every walk of life about their struggles to find a fulfilling career, from warehouse workers to CEOs, from pole dancers to Buddhist monks. I was later inspired by my involvement with The School of Life, where I teach and helped design the courses on work. Thanks to everyone there, including Morgwn Rimel, Caroline Brimmer, Harriet Warden and Mark Brickman, and to Sophie Howarth, the founding director. My ideas have also benefited from conversations with friends in the Relational Politics group in Oxford: Sue Gerhardt, Adam Swift, Jean Knox, Sarah Stewart-Brown and Sue Weaver. Thanks too to David Pittenger at Marshall University.

I could not have written this book without people from many countries generously sharing their career stories with me. I learned a huge amount from their experiences and insights. They include: Amanda Beckles, Andy Bell, Andy Kwok, Annalise Moser, Anne Marie Graham, Brian Campbell, Cathy O'Neil, Chris Dean, Clare Taylor, Esther Freeman, Fiona Robyn, Fiona Sanson, Flutra Qatja, George Marshall, Helena Fosh, Iain King, James Attlee, Jonty Olliff-Cooper, Karen Byrne, Karen Macmillan, Keira O'Mara, Kirsten Puls, Laura van Bouchout, Lee Rotbart, Lisa Brideau, Lisa Gormley, Meike Brunkhorst, Paula Ligo, Rob Archer, Rupert Denyer, Sam Lewis, Sameera Khan, Sarah Best, Sharon Harvey, Tom Burrough, Trevor Dean, Wayne Davies and Yvonne Braeunlich. Please note that I have changed the names of some people I quote in the text.

Special thanks to my parents, Anna and Peter Krznaric, for all their support while completing this book, to my children Casimir and Siri for tolerating my long absences, and to Kate Raworth for more than I can say.

I dedicate this book to another book, which has done so much to shape how I think about work: Studs Terkel's superb oral history *Working: People Talk About What They Do All Day and How They Feel About What They Do.*

Picture and Text Acknowledgements

Every effort has been made to contact the copyright holders of the material reproduced in this book. If any have been inadvertently overlooked the publisher will be pleased to make restitution at the earliest opportunity.

Page 48 extract is taken from *The Selfish Society*, Sue Gerhardt (Simon & Schuster/RCW Literary Agency, 2010); Page 99 extract is taken from *Good Work*, E.F. Schumacher (Jonathan Cape, 1979) and reproduced courtesy of the Estate of E.F. Schumacher; Page 102 extract is taken from *Anarchy in Action*, Colin Ward (Freedom Press, 1973); Page 110 extract is taken from 'In Praise of Idleness', *In Praise of Idleness and other Essays* (Allen and Unwin, 1935).

The author and publisher would like to thank the following for permission to reproduce the images used in this book:

Page 15 Aerial silks artist © Thomas Barwick / Getty Images; Page 25 Girl at a spinning machine © Corbis; Page 37 Phrenology cartoon © Heritage Images / Corbis; Page 57 Anita Roddick © The Roddick Foundation; Page 65 *Vitruvian Man*, Leonardo da Vinci. Photograph © Garry Gay / Getty Images; Page 93 Jackson Pollock at work © Time & Life Pictures / Getty Images; Page 111 Bertrand Russell © Mary Evans Picture Library / Marx Memorial Library; Page 127 *The Captive Slave*, Michelangelo. Photograph © Time & Life Pictures / Getty Images; Page 137 Marie Curie © Time & Life Pictures / Getty Images; Page 142 Zorba the Greek © Moviestore Collection Ltd / Alamy.

All other images provided courtesy of the author.

How to
Stay Sane
Philippa Perry

By the same author:

Couch Fiction

Contents

Introduction 161

1. Self-Observation 173
2. Relating to Others 189
3. Stress 215
4. What's the Story? 229

Conclusion 253

Exercises 257

Notes 285
Homework 289
Acknowledgements 291

For Mark Fairclough (Dad)

Introduction

In the *Diagnostic and Statistical Manual of Mental Disorders*, the handbook that most psychiatrists and many psychotherapists use to define the types and shades of insanity, you will find numerous personality disorders described. Despite this huge variety, and despite the proliferation of defined disorders in successive editions, these definitions fall into just two main groups.[1] In one group are the people who have strayed into chaos and whose lives lurch from crisis to crisis; in the other are those who have got themselves into a rut and operate from a limited set of outdated, rigid responses. Some of us manage to belong to both groups at once. So what is the solution to the problem of responding to the world in an over-rigid fashion, or being so affected by it that we exist in a continual state of chaos? I see it as a very broad path, with many forks and diversions, and no single 'right' way. From time to time we may stray too far to the over-rigid side, and feel stuck; few of us, on the other hand, will get through life without occasionally going too far to the other side, and experiencing ourselves as chaotic and out of control. This book is about how to stay on the path between those two extremes, how to remain stable and yet flexible, coherent and yet able to embrace complexity. In other words, this book is about How to Stay Sane.

I cannot pretend that there is a simple set of instructions that can guarantee sanity. Each of us is the product of a distinctive combination of genes, and has experienced a unique set of formative relationships. For every one of us who needs to take the risk of being more open, there is another who needs to practise self-containment. For each person who needs to learn to trust more, there is another who needs to experiment with more discernment. What makes me happy might make you miserable; what I find useful you might find harmful. Specific instructions about how to think, feel and behave thus offer few answers. So instead I want to suggest a way of thinking about what goes on in our brains, how they have developed and continue to develop. I believe that if we can picture how our minds form, we will be better able to re-form the way we live. This practice of thinking about the brain has helped me and some of my clients to become more in charge of our lives; there is a chance, therefore, that it may resonate with you too.

Plato compares the soul to a chariot being pulled by two horses. The driver is Reason, one horse is Spirit, the other horse is Appetite. The metaphors we have used throughout the ages to think about the mind have more or less followed this model. My approach is just such another version, and is influenced by neuroscience in conjunction with other therapeutic approaches.

Three Brains in One

In recent years, scientists have developed a new theory of the brain. They have begun to understand that it is not composed of one single structure but of three different structures, which, over time, come to operate together but yet remain distinct.

The first of these structures is the brain stem, sometimes referred to as the reptilian brain. It is operational at birth and is responsible for our reflexes and involuntary muscles, such as the heart. At certain moments, it can save our lives. When we absentmindedly step into the path of a bus, it is our brain stem that makes us jump back onto the pavement before we have had time to realize what is going on. It is the brain stem that makes us blink our eyes when fingers are flicked in front of them. The brain stem will not help you do Sudoku but at a basic, essential level, it keeps you alive, allows you to function and keeps you safe from many kinds of danger.

The other two structures of the brain are the mammalian, or right, brain and the neo-mammalian, or left, brain. Although they continue to develop throughout our lives, both of these structures do most of their developing in our first five years. An individual brain cell does not work on its own. It needs to link with other brain cells in order to function. Our brain develops by linking individual brain cells to make neural pathways. This linking happens as a result of interaction with others, so how our brain develops has more to do with our earliest relationships than with genetics; with nurture rather than nature.

This means that many of the differences between us can be explained by what regularly happened to us when we were very little. Our experiences actually shape our brain matter. To cite an extreme case from legend, if we do not have a relationship with another person in the first years of life but are nurtured by, say, a wolf instead, then our behavioural patterns will be more wolf-like than human.

In our first two years, the right brain is very active while the left is quiescent and shows less activity. However, in the following few years development switches; the right brain's development slows and

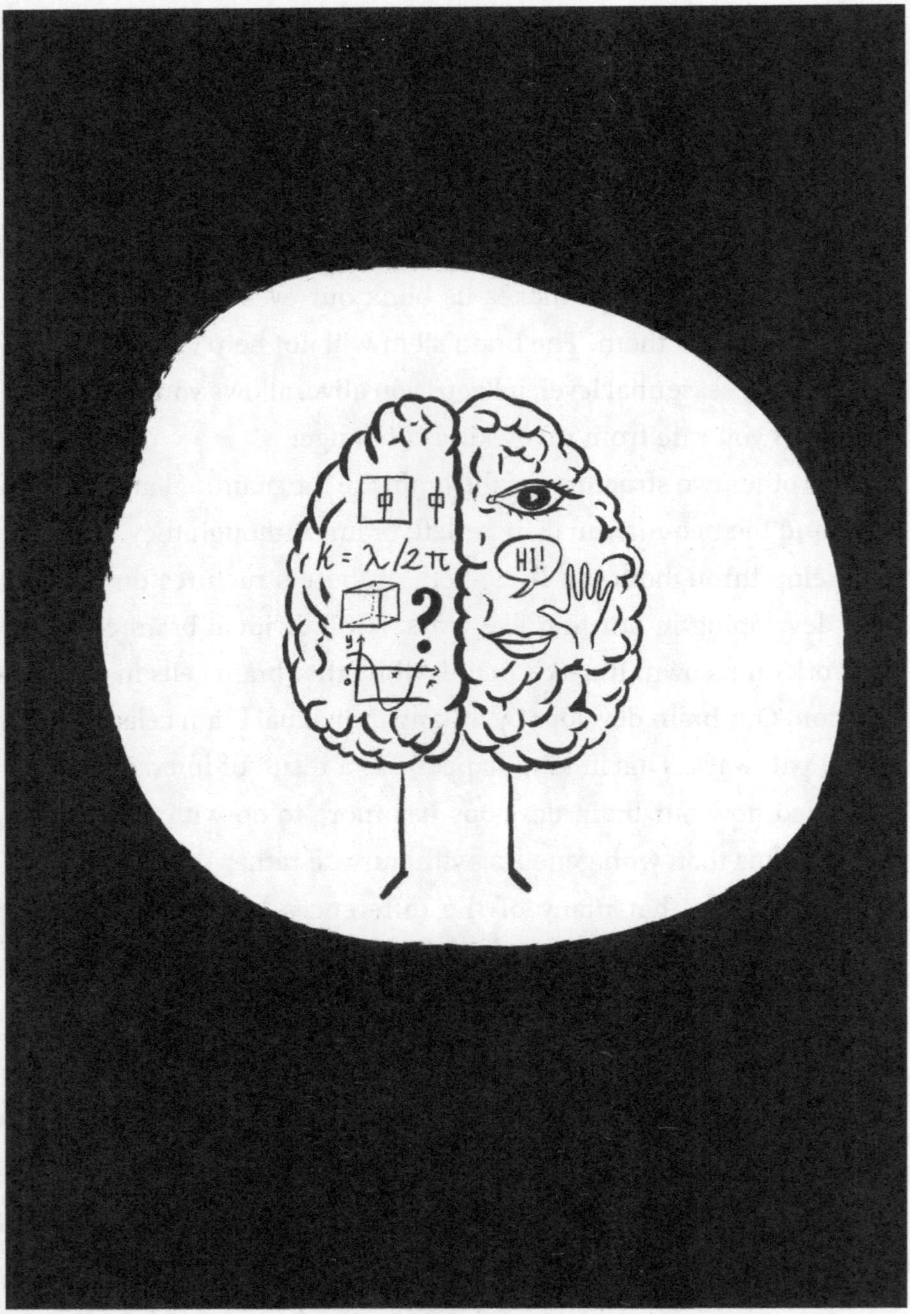
k = λ/2π
HI!

the left begins a period of remarkable activity. Our ways of bonding to others; how we trust; how comfortable we generally feel with ourselves; how quickly or slowly we can soothe ourselves after an upset have a firm foundation in the neural pathways laid down in the mammalian right brain in our early years. The right brain can therefore be thought of as the primary seat of most of our emotions and our instincts. It is the structure that in large part empathizes with, attunes to and relates to others. The right brain not only develops first, it also remains in charge. With one glance, one sniff, the right brain takes in and makes an assessment of any situation. As the Duke of Gloucester says in Shakespeare's *King Lear*, when he looks about him: 'I see it feelingly.'

What we call the left brain can be thought of as the primary language, logic and reasoning structure of our brain. We use our left brain for processing experience into language, to articulate our thoughts and ideas to ourselves and others and to carry out plans. Evidence-based science has been developed using the skills of the left brain, as have the sorting-and-ordering disciplines of taxonomy, philosophy and philology.

As I have said, in the first two years of life, left-brain development is much slower than in the right brain, which is why the foundations for our personalities are already laid down before the left brain, with its capacity for language and logic, has the ability to influence them. This could be why the right brain tends to remain dominant. You may be aware of the influence of both what I am calling the left and the right brains when you experience the familiar dilemma of having very good reasons to do the sensible thing, but find yourself doing the other thing all the same. The apparently sensible part of you (your left brain) has the language, but the other part (your right brain) often appears to have the power.

When we are babies our brains develop in relationship with our earliest caregivers. Whatever feelings and thought processes they give to us are mirrored, reacted to and laid down in our growing brains. When things go well, our parents and caregivers also mirror and validate our moods and mental states, acknowledging and responding to what we are feeling. So around about the time we are two, our brains will already have distinct and individual patterns. It is then that our left brains mature sufficiently to be able to understand language. This dual development enables us to integrate our two brains, to some extent. We become able to begin to use the left brain to put into language the feelings of the right.

However, if our caregivers ignore some of our moods, or knowingly or unknowingly punish us for them, we can have trouble later, because we will be less able to process these same feelings when they arise and less able to make sense of them with language.

So if our relationships with early caregivers were less than ideal, or we later experienced trauma so severe that it undid the security established in our infancy, we may find ourselves experiencing emotional difficulties later in life. But although it is too late to have a happier childhood, or avoid a trauma that has already happened, it is possible to change course.

Psychotherapists use the term 'introjection' to describe the unconscious incorporation of the characteristics of a person or culture into one's own psyche. We tend to introject the parenting we received and carry on where our earliest caregivers left off – so patterns of feeling, thinking, reacting and doing deepen and stick.

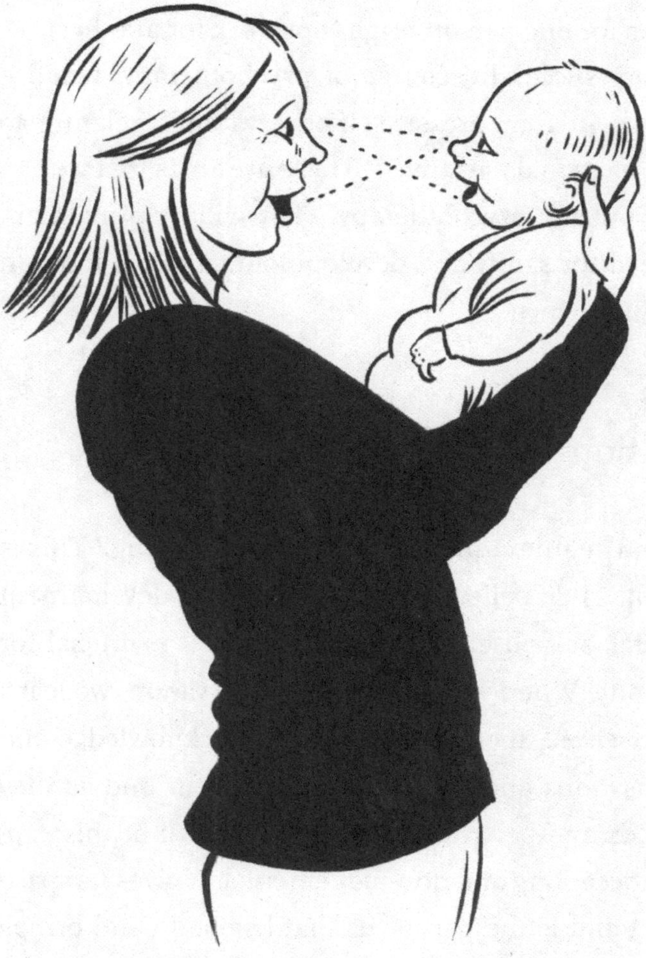

This may not be a bad thing: our parents may have done a good job. However, if we find ourselves depressed or otherwise dissatisfied, we may want to modify patterns in order to become saner and happier.

How do we do that? There is no foolproof prescription. If we are falling deeper into a rut, and/or deeper into chaos, we need to interrupt our fall – either with medication, or with a different set of behaviours: we may want a new focus in life; we may benefit from new ideas – or from something else entirely (I am being vague on purpose; what works for one person might not work for another).

However in every successful course of psychotherapy, I notice that change happens in four areas: 'self-observation', 'relating to others', 'stress' and 'personal narrative'.[2] These are areas that we can work on ourselves, outside psychotherapy. They will help maintain the flexibility we need for sanity and development, and it is to them that we are now going to turn.

1. Self-Observation

Socrates stated that 'The unexamined life is not worth living.' This is an extreme stance, but I do believe that the continuing development of a non-judgemental, self-observing part of ourselves is crucial for our wisdom and sanity. When we practise self-observation, we learn to stand outside ourselves, in order to experience, acknowledge and assess feelings, sensations and thoughts as they occur and as they determine our moods and behaviour. The development of this capacity allows us to be accepting and non-judgemental. It gives us space to decide how to act and is the part of us that listens to and brings together our emotions and logic. In order to maximize our sanity we need to develop self-observation to increase self-awareness. This is a job that is never finished.

2. Relating to Others

We all need safe, trusting, reliable, nourishing relationships. These might include a romantic relationship. Contrary to some people's belief, romance is not necessarily a prerequisite for happiness; but some of our relationships do need to be nurturing ones: a nurturing relationship might be with a therapist, a teacher, a lover, a friend, or our children – someone who not only listens but reads between the lines and perhaps even gently challenges us. We are formed in relationship, and we develop and change as a result of subsequent relationships.

3. Stress

The right kind of stress creates positive stimulation. It will push us to learn new things and to be creative, but it will not be so overwhelming that it tips us over into panic. Good stress causes new neural connections. It is what we need for personal development and growth.

4. What's the Story? (Personal Narrative)

If we get to know the stories we live by, we will be able to edit and change them if we need to. Because so much of our self is formed pre-verbally, the beliefs that guide us can be hidden from us. We may have beliefs that start with 'I'm the sort of person who . . .' or 'That's not me; I don't do that . . .' If we focus on such stories and see them from fresh angles, we can find new, more flexible ways of defining ourselves, others and everything around us.

Although the content of our lives and the methods we use to process that content will be different for all of us, these areas of our psyche are the cornerstones of our sanity. In the pages that follow I've examined these four key areas in more detail.

1. Self-Observation

When I advocate self-observation people sometimes assume that it's just another form of self-absorbed navel gazing. Self-observation is not *self-obsession*, however. On the contrary, it is a tool that enables us to become *less* self-absorbed, because it teaches us not to be taken over by obsessive thoughts and feelings. With self-observation we develop more internal clarity and can become more open to the emotional lives of those around us. This new receptiveness and understanding will greatly improve our lives and relationships.

Self-observation is an ancient practice and it has been called many different things. It was advocated by Buddha, Socrates, George Gurdjieff and Sigmund Freud among others. When we become practised self-observers we are less likely to trip ourselves up by acting out our hidden feelings, less likely to repeat self-sabotaging patterns and more likely to have compassion for ourselves and therefore for others.

The ability to observe and listen to feelings and bodily sensations is essential to staying sane. We need to be able to use our feelings but not be used by them. If we *are* our emotions, rather than an *observer* of them, we will veer into a chaotic state. If, on the other hand, we repress our feelings altogether, we can swing the other way, into rigidity. There is a difference between saying 'I am angry' and saying 'I feel angry'. The first statement is a description that appears closed. The second is an *acknowledgement* of a feeling, and does not define the whole self. In the same way that it is useful to be able to separate ourselves from our feelings, it is also necessary to be able to observe our thoughts. Then we can notice the different kinds of thoughts we have, and can examine them, rather than *be* them. This allows us to notice which thoughts work well for us, and whether any of our internal mind chatter is self-defeating.

To help explain the theory, let's look at this example: how a mother observes her infant in order to understand him or her. She mirrors back to the baby its expressions, its inner states and from what she observes she learns to understand its needs from moment to moment. Being observed, understood and met in this way is vital for the formation of our personality and, indeed, our survival. The practice of self-observation mirrors the way in which a mother observes and attunes to her baby. Self-observation is a method of re-parenting ourselves. When we self-observe it helps us to form and re-form.

It may help to think of our self-observing part as a distinct component of ourselves. It is self-accepting and non-judgemental. It acknowledges what is, not what should be, and does not assign values such as 'right' or 'wrong'. It notices emotions and thoughts but gives us space to decide how to act on them. It is the part of us that listens both to our emotions and our logic and is aware of sensory information.

To begin self-observing, ask yourself these questions:

What am I feeling now?
What am I thinking now?
What am I doing at this moment?
How am I breathing?

These simple questions are important because when we have answered them, we are in a better position to proceed to the next question:

What do I want for myself in this new moment?[3]

You may have made instantaneous changes just by reading the questions. For example, when we bring our attention to our breathing we become aware of how we are inhibiting it, and while we remain aware of it we tend to breathe more slowly. Change happens, if it needs to, when we become aware of what we are, not when we try to become what we are not.

I call these questions the 'Grounding Exercise'. If we do this, or something similar, at odd moments during the day and get into the habit of doing so, we can create a space for self-observation. Then if we are going off course we have the opportunity to re-direct ourselves.

When I did the Grounding Exercise myself yesterday, I noticed that, when I asked myself the questions, I felt dissatisfied. I found I was dreaming of replacing all my furniture. What was I doing? I was reading an interior-design magazine and I was breathing shallowly. After I had answered the first four questions I was in a better position to answer the last. What did I want for myself? What I wanted for myself, at that moment, was to exhale, put the magazine down and turn my attention to something different; and so I went for a swim to switch my focus.

Doing the Grounding Exercise helps us to place ourselves in our internal experience. People can be loosely put into two groups, those who *externally* reference and those who *internally* reference. Externally referenced people are more concerned with the impression they make on other people: *What do I look like? What does this look like?* Internally referenced people are more concerned with what something feels like: *Do I like the feel of this or that better?* Externally referenced people want to get it right for others (so they will be accepted, impress them or be envied by them) but internally referenced people want to get it right for themselves (so they feel comfortable with themselves).

I'm not saying that one way of self-referencing is always superior to the other but I do want to stress the desirability of increasing our awareness of how we reference ourselves, so that we can work out how we place ourselves on the internal–external scale. Too far on the externally referenced side and we lose a sense of ourselves and become off-balance. If, on the other hand, we swing too far the other way, towards internally referencing, we may find it necessary to adapt to society a little more, in order to be a part of it. We can ask ourselves whether the way we manage our emotions is prompted by what we imagine other people are thinking about us, or by what we know will make us feel comfortable.

Let's take an example: two people are sailing in identical boats. One is fantasizing, 'Look at me in my fabulous yacht; I bet everyone thinks I look cool and envies me', while the other is simply enjoying mastering the skill of sailing, feeling the breeze on his face and noticing the feelings that the open seas evoke in him. Two people doing the same thing but enjoying themselves in quite different ways. Many of us are a mixture of these two types; but if we often feel dissatisfied with life, it can be useful to understand how we are referencing ourselves; this in turn will allow us to experiment with change.

Internal or external referencing is one of the things to hold in mind while doing the Grounding Exercise. The Grounding Exercise is about finding out how we are functioning at any one moment. We can adapt the exercise for ourselves. For example, when I do the exercise I check how much tension I am holding in my shoulders, giving myself the opportunity to notice if I am tense, so I can loosen up if necessary.

When I am practising self-observation I also take time to notice what I call post-rationalization, which could also be called self-justification. This describes the way we have of mentally 'tidying up' what is going on inside and outside of ourselves, often coming up with convenient explanations which may be actually be nonsense, to justify our behaviour.

Experiments carried out by the neuropsychologist Roger Sperry have thrown into question the notion that we are rational beings led by our reason and intellect. In the 1960s, Sperry and his colleagues carried out some experiments on people who had had the connective tissue (called the corpus callosum) between the right and left hemispheres of their brain cut, in order to treat severe epilepsy. That meant the two sides of their brains could no longer connect or interact.

When the experimenters flashed the command 'WALK' into the visual field of the subject's right brain (bypassing the left brain completely) the subject got up and walked as directed. When asked why they walked, a question to which the left brain (responsible for language, reasons, labels and explanations) responded, they never said 'Because your sign told me to' or 'I don't know, I just felt an inexplicable urge to do so', which would have been the truth (as the action was triggered by their emotional right brains). Instead, they invariably said something like 'I wanted to get a drink of water' or 'I wanted to stretch my legs'. In other words, their rational left brain made sense of their action in a way that bore no relation to the real reason for it.

Considering this alongside further experiments that have been done on left-brain, right-brain splits[4] we have no reason to think that the patient's left hemisphere is behaving any differently from our own, as we make sense of the inclinations coming from our right brain. In other words, our 'reasons' for doing anything could be a *post*-rationalization, even when our corpus callosum has not been cut.

Even after our left brains have developed to give us the powers of language and logic, reasoning and mathematics, we continue to be ruled by the mammalian right brain. It turns out that we are unable to make any decision without our emotions. The neurologist Antonio Damasio had a patient called Elliot who, after an operation to remove a brain tumour, was unable to feel. His IQ remained excellent but he had no feelings even when shown terrible pictures of human suffering. We might think that, with his reasoning intact, Elliot could still decide where to go for lunch or what to invest his money in, but he was unable to make these decisions. He could imagine the probable outcomes of his choices, he could calmly weigh up the advantages and disadvantages, but he could not come to a decision. Damasio wrote up his findings about Elliot and other patients like him in his book *Descartes' Error: Emotion, Reason and the Human Brain*. This book concluded that, contrary to our expectations, a lack of emotion does not lead to logical, reasoned choices but to chaos. This is because we rely on feelings to navigate our way through our lives. This is true whether or not we are aware of our emotions.

In order to understand our motivation better, it can be helpful to spend more time with our feelings, which is where self-observation comes in. We will not be able to fathom all our feelings; and we should not cling to the reasons we so speedily come up with – some of these may only be a mechanism for self-soothing or justifying what the right brain has already decided upon. Instead we can increase our tolerance for uncertainty, nurture our curiosity and continue to learn. There is a danger when we prematurely reach a judgement about something that we stop ourselves from learning anything further about it. I do not advocate dithering about everyday decisions (such as what to have for lunch), but the re-examination of our beliefs and opinions from time to time is beneficial. As the psychoanalyst Peter Lomas suggested, 'Hold your beliefs lightly.' Certainty is not necessarily a friend of sanity, although it is often mistaken for it.

We live in a so-called 'age of reason', and yet, research such as Sperry's and Damasio's demonstrate, many of our ideas, feelings and actions come from the right brain, while the left brain makes up reasons for those ideas, feelings and actions retrospectively. Every war might only be the playing out of an old dispute that happened in the nursery, for which the leader concerned is still trying to find a resolution.[5] A lone gunman's killing spree results from a lack of empathy for others, more than from his particular ideology.[6] 'Ideology' is merely the reason he applies to his feelings – of, say, bitterness or hatred. When we argue vehemently against something, we do so not on account of the reasons we generate, but on account of the *feelings* that the reasons are created to support. They may be the 'wrong' reasons but our feeling is never the wrong feeling – our feelings just are. A feeling cannot be 'right' or 'wrong'. It is how we act out our feelings that is moral or immoral. A feeling on its own is no more right or wrong than a needle on a gauge, pointing to how much fuel you have in your tank. We might feel like annihilating someone but it is only the acting out of that feeling that is indicative of dubious morality.

A psychotherapist once told me when he was training that, previously, he had been sure that all his angry feelings were brought forth by the person in front of him, but as he learnt more about the psyche in general – and his in particular – he changed from pointing the finger and saying 'You, you, you'; instead the finger went round in a circle until he was pointing at himself, and saying far more quietly, 'Me, me, me'. As I have said, self-observation is the very opposite of self-indulgence. It makes self-responsibility possible.

Our post-rationalizing capacity – or what I am calling the left brain – means that we may come up with reasons not to self-examine. So if you decide to skip the self-observation exercises in this book, try to be more interested in the feelings that dictate that behaviour than in the reasons you apply to those feelings. You are being 'run' by those feelings, so rather than brush them off with your left brain, spend some time exploring them.

A psychotherapist is practised in hunting down the feelings behind justifications and fixed patterns of behaving and helping his or her client to see them. If you have the inclination and means, I recommend psychotherapy or psychoanalysis as a way of discovering more about the unconscious and how we integrate the unconscious with our logical side. However, it can be difficult to find the right therapist, and therapy tends to cost a good deal. There are other means and exercises that can help us develop the art of self-observation. There

words for how I
layer I can feel, they tak
ach other and to me, I can be thi
f having a bath and then I'm
emembering primary school. And yet
also keeping a bit in my head of the
day and sort of sticking to it. Wh
I woke up this morning I was st
dreaming after I woke up and
me a few seconds to w
as dream and what

isn't a right way to practise self-observation because one size does not fit all. I am an advocate of using whatever works. But however we get there, I believe that being able to self-observe is an essential part of staying sane. As well as using a focused attention technique like the Grounding Exercise, regularly keeping a journal can be a useful tool to aid self-observation.

A study in which half the participants kept a diary and half did not demonstrated the positive effects of writing something down about yourself each day. Diarists reported better moods and fewer moments of distress than non-diarists. Those, in the same study, who kept a journal following trauma or bereavement also reported fewer flashbacks, nightmares and unexpected difficult memories. Writing can itself be an act of emotional processing so it can help in many situations of danger, extremity and loss of control. People who keep diaries are admitted to hospital less often and spend fewer days there than those who do not. Research shows that liver function and blood pressure are improved in diarists. All personality types are shown to benefit from keeping a diary. I am particularly fascinated by the way that diary-keeping has been shown to positively affect several aspects of the immune system – including T-cell growth[7] and certain antibody responses. Studies have also shown that people who regularly keep daily 'gratitude' diaries, in which they list things for which they are grateful, report increased satisfaction with their lives and relationships.[8] However, these benefits are not the main reasons I recommend diary-keeping. I'm keen on it because it is a useful tool for developing self-observation.

A few hints for starting a diary: be honest and keep it simple; it is just for you. Try not to start with a flourish and then tail off after a few days: persevere! What you write is up to you. I am a fan of random memories, as well as what you are thinking and feeling at the moment of writing. I also like dreams. Dreams fascinate therapists because they dramatize experiences and parts of our psyches that we may not have processed into language. I recommend writing down your dreams and your reactions to them in your diary.

If you cannot think what to write just keep writing to see what emerges. In fact, stream-of-consciousness writing, done first thing in the morning just after waking, has been found to be effective in raising self-awareness. Write in longhand, and record anything and everything that comes into your head for a couple of sheets of paper.[9]

If you read your diary back to yourself you may identify some of your behavioural and emotional habits. For example, can you spot how much justification or reasoning you are using, or how much compassion you show yourself, or how much of what you write is fantasy?

Whatever method you find works best, keeping a diary is a way of processing your feelings, and getting to know yourself better.

Learning and practising focused attention is a key tool in the development of self-observation. Focused attention improves our ability to observe and experience body and mind in the present and without criticism. There are many names for this practice: prayer, meditation, contemplative practice and self-directed neuroplasticity. Learning to focus our attention is also a key part of the practice of mindfulness. This focusing of the individual's attention is a feature of many cultures and religions. Rituals as apparently different as Christian prayer and Sufi whirling are both forms of focused attention, but we can practise it whether we believe in a god or not. Practising focused attention boosts our concentration, helps with stress, anxiety, depression and addictive behaviours, and can even have a positive effect on physical problems like hypertension, heart disease and chronic pain.[10]

The practice of focused attention has further benefits. Studies have shown that the brains of those who regularly meditate or practise similar behaviours show permanent, beneficial changes. New neural pathways and connections proliferate. The pre-frontal cortex, which is the part of the brain associated with concentration, measurably thickens. The insula, the part of the brain that tracks the interior state of the body, as well as the emotional states of other people, also grows. Thus the practice of focusing attention for the purpose of self-observation literally strengthens and grows the brain. That in turn makes us more self-aware and thus better able to soothe ourselves, and it also means that we are able to empathize better with others. Practising self-observation helps to keep our brains flexible. Using it, we can become more aware of mental processes, without being taken over by those processes. It allows us to develop emotional resilience without repressing or denying our feelings. You'll find some exercises for promoting focused attention and self-observation in the exercise section in the back of this book.

One of the things we become more aware of when we develop self-observation is what I call 'toxic chatter'. Our heads are always full of chatter, littered with phrases, images, repeated messages, running commentaries on our actions and thoughts. Much may be harmless, but some can be toxic: hateful thoughts about ourselves or others; unconstructive self-scoldings; pointless pessimism. These types of thoughts can go round in circles; they get us nowhere and can cause depression. Self-observation allows us to impartially notice our mind-chatter and distance ourselves from that which is toxic. In this way the neural pathways that promote toxicity will be used less and will gradually shrink, while those that promote awareness and empathy will grow.

Using self-observation we can give ourselves the same sort of close attention that good parents give their children. As we saw earlier, such mirroring is the way children learn who they are and how to acknowledge, soothe and regulate themselves. Throughout our lives we have a desire and a need to be acknowledged and understood. Although this is most productively achieved in conjunction with another person, contemplative practice is one way we can achieve this on our own.

There is no limit to the number of ways we can develop self-observation. We may choose one-to-one therapy with a psychotherapist, analyst or other practitioner, or join a therapy or yoga group. One of my biggest increases in self-awareness came when I trained for and completed the London Marathon. Using focused attention techniques such as meditating whilst running as part of a transformative physical project, I improved my concentration, self-confidence and self-awareness more than I could have imagined when I began training a year before the event.

In conclusion, practising self-observation can give us more insight into the emotions that play such a large part in our behaviour. When we become more sensitive towards ourselves and more knowledgeable about our own feelings, we are more able to attune to, and empathize with, the feelings of other people. In short, self-awareness improves our relationships. Relationships are the second cornerstone of our sanity, and we will now look at their role and importance.

2. Relating to Others

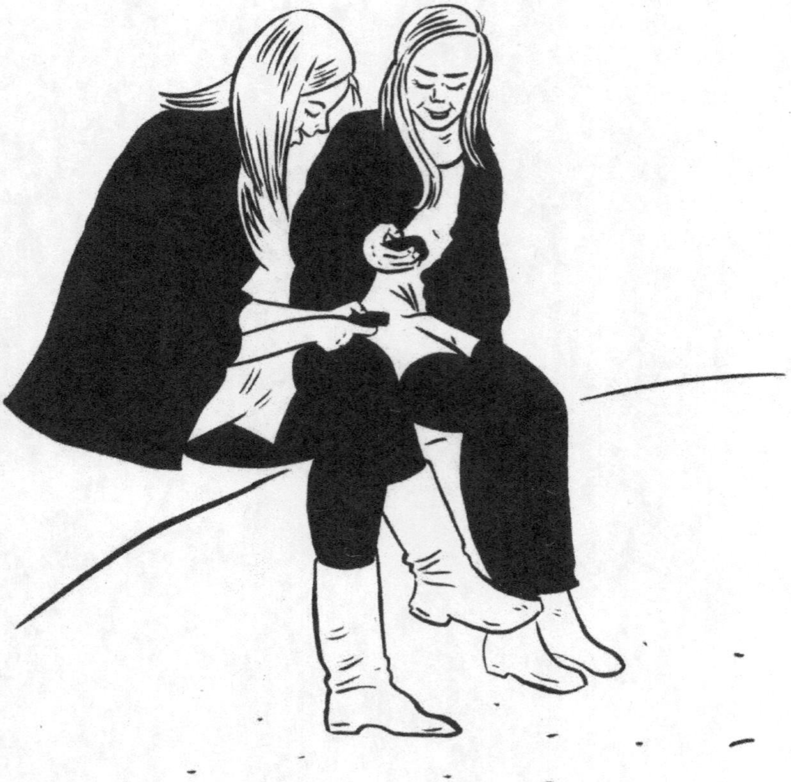

A brain, like a neuron, is not much use on its own. Our brains need other brains – or, as we more often put it, people need people. We may think of ourselves as an 'I', and the notion of the isolated self takes up a lot of space in Western civilization, but we are in fact creatures of the group, like starlings in a flock that appears as one body against the sky, with each bird affecting and being affected by the movements of the birds closest to it. Our brains are linked together and grow together in relationship with each other.

We understand that the quality of the formative relationships we had as infants determines our initial place in the spectrum of mental health. However, it is also known that other people continue to be our best resource for staying sane. Any mutually impactful, mutually open relationship can reactivate neuroplastic processes[II] and actually change the structure of the brain at any stage of our lives.

I have seen such changes time and time again in many years of practice as a psychotherapist. I have witnessed clients become more fully themselves, more at ease and less neurotic. I believe that it is the *relationship* with the therapist, as much as any brilliant intervention, that brings these changes about. I learnt from Irvin Yalom, an American psychiatrist, that as a therapist you need to assess how clients feel about the therapeutic relationship, and ask them what was useful and what did not work in each session. As a young therapist I was often surprised that it was not new insight that was the most powerful catalyst for change, but the moment when the client saw that they had moved me; or when they felt accepted because I patted their arm; or when they saw that, even if I did not say anything at that point, I understood. But that is only half of it. I was changed by my clients too: they helped me to grow. In a relationship in which we are ourselves without a social mask and fully present, our brains are continually shaped. Seeing the world from another's viewpoint as well as our own can allow us both to expand. If we get too 'set in our ways', we are less able to be touched, moved or enlightened by another and we lose vitality. And we need to allow ourselves to be open to the impact of the other if we are to impact upon them.

Dialogue

The philosopher Martin Buber said, 'All real living is meeting.' He realized that only in relationships can we fully open ourselves to the world and to each other. Buber wrote that 'genuine dialogue', whether spoken or silent, occurs only when each of the participants really has in mind the other or others, in their 'present and particular being and turns to them with the intention of establishing a living mutual relation between himself and them'. I would add that in order to meaningfully connect to another person, one has to be open. This means being not who we *think* we should be, but allowing ourselves to be who we really *are*. This usually involves risking feeling vulnerable. Being open, and therefore vulnerable, does not guarantee that we will connect

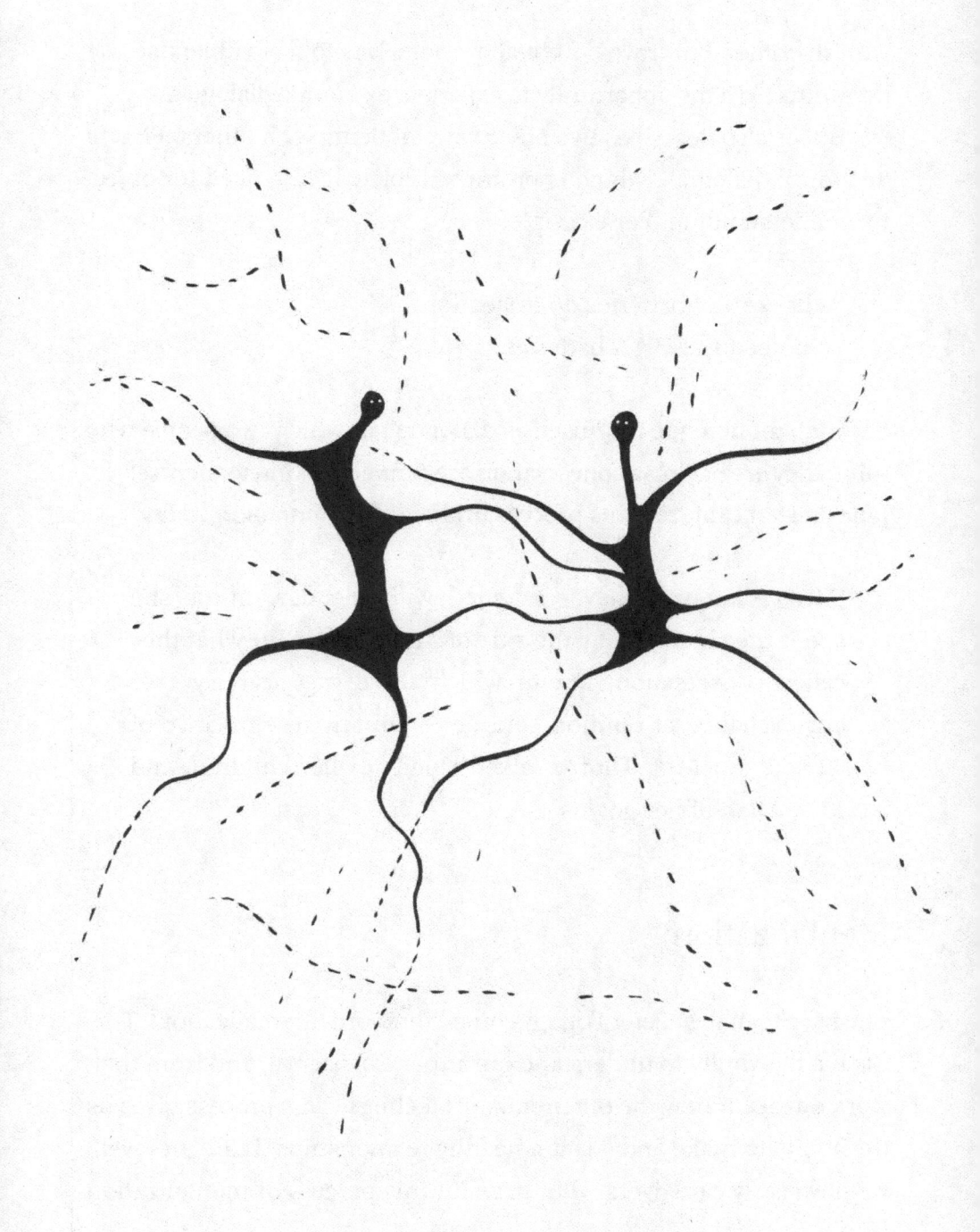

with the other, but if we do not allow ourselves to feel vulnerable, we deny ourselves the opportunity to experience genuine dialogue.

Buber also describes two other ways of being with others. First is 'technical dialogue', which is prompted solely by the need for objective understanding. For example:

'What sort of batteries do I need for this?'
'You need size AAA batteries.'

Second, 'monologue disguised as dialogue', in which two people who think they are having a conversation are actually talking to themselves. Jane Austen captured this process brilliantly in *Northanger Abbey*:

[Mrs. Allen was] never satisfied with the day unless she spent the chief of it by the side of Mrs. Thorpe, in what they called conversation, but in which there was scarcely ever any exchange of opinion, and not often any resemblance of subject, for Mrs. Thorpe talked chiefly of her children, and Mrs. Allen of her gowns.

Mentalization

The psychoanalyst Peter Fonagy coined the word 'mentalization'. This means the ability to understand our inner experience, and from that, work out accurately the other person's feelings. This process gives us the ability to make and sustain healthy relationships. If all goes well, we have early caregivers who carry out this process of mentalization naturally, and we pick it up unconsciously from them. This process is aided by self-observation, because as we develop and become more sensitive to our own feelings we also become more sensitive to what other people are feeling. This does not mean projecting our own thoughts onto them, but understanding, on the level of feeling, that the way they feel and think might be different from the way we do.

If we find people so unpredictable that we are unable to relate to anyone, then it is probable that it is the process of mentalization that is letting us down. There is so much that is unspoken and unconscious in the process of relating to another that the only way to learn it is in relationship with someone else. If our earliest caregiver was unable to provide a model for mentalization we will not have learnt it from them. But the brain is plastic. We can learn it later in life with a psychotherapist or in other close relationships. When we begin to understand what it really feels like to be deeply understood, we can begin to understand others and have satisfying relationships.

When psychotherapy began it was about the practitioner listening to a patient and interpreting what the patient said, in order to afford the patient insights about his or her psyche. But now we understand that the main curative part of psychotherapy is the relationship itself. It appears not to be relevant whether the practitioner is an analytic Freudian or a counselling Rogerian[12], a transactional analyst or a life coach, or from an eclectic school. What matters is the quality of the relationship and the practitioner's belief in what he or she is offering. In the same way, our sanity and our happiness will have more to do with our interpersonal relationships than with what the weather is like, or what job we do, or our hobbies. We run about, earning a living, achieving things and making a decent show of it all (or not), but what affects us most are the people around us: our parents, our children, our lovers, our colleagues, our neighbours and our friends. As the psychotherapist Louis Cozolino says, 'From birth until death, each of us needs others who seek us out, show interest in discovering who we are and help us feel safe.' A trauma consultant puts it more starkly, 'Everyone should walk through an Emergency Room at least once in their life. Because it makes you realize what your priorities are. It's not the rush, rush, rush and the money, money, money; it's the people you love and the fact that one minute they might be there and one minute they might be gone.'[13]

Staying connected with others is a vital – the vital – part of staying sane.

How to Have Good Relationships

This is a 'how-to' book and at this point I wish it was not, because as soon as we start to legislate for how to have relationships, we are already in danger of getting it wrong. This is because if we attempt to manipulate a relationship, there is a danger of treating the other as an 'it' rather than as an equal; of seeing him or her as an object to be steered rather than another subject to meet. Nor can we have a simple rule: 'be empathetic' – since empathy is only part of a process, not a rigid set of behaviours.

My friend Astrid had a rule she applied to relationships. When she was working out how she felt about someone she would say, for instance, '. . . And he asked me no questions about myself at all' – as

if she was seeking to prove something; but as I come from a different background I was not sure what it was she was trying to tell me. She explained that in her originating culture it was polite to ask questions when you meet a new person. If the other person does not return the compliment by showing curiosity in return then the suspicion is that they are self-absorbed and selfish. I thought that, as well as sounding like a post-rationalization for Astrid's not taking to a particular person, this way of looking at the world did not take into account the 'negative politeness' rule[14] which is an unspoken part of the rituals of my culture. Gross generalization coming up. Basically there are two sorts of cultures. In crowded countries such as Japan and Britain we tend to have 'negative-politeness'. This means that people are aware of others' need for privacy, and their desire not to be intruded upon. In countries where there is more space, like the USA, people are more inclined to practise 'positive politeness', where the emphasis is on inclusion and openness. The anthropologist Kate Fox says that what looks like stand-offishness in a negative-politeness culture is really a sort of consideration for people's privacy. So you see, for every overarching rule about how to have relationships, there will always be another that contradicts it. You may *act* in a caring way towards somebody, but if you have not absorbed the rules of that person's family of origin or culture you can still get it wrong.

Our codes about manners differ from family to family and culture to culture. Manners are a societal attempt to regulate the way we treat one another. If we follow manners strictly, we may turn into a 'super-charmer', and other people may doubt our sincerity. If we become extra sincere, we may appear over-earnest in a way that might be acceptable in, say, America but not in Britain. It is difficult to formulate guidelines about other people's feelings because they vary so much, from culture to culture, from family to family, from person to person, and from moment to moment. We are either good at picking up on people's feelings and attuning to them, or we are not. The way to learn how to be with someone is by being with them; if we cannot get that far we are a bit stuck. In trying to please one group of people we can end up offending another. Asking people what we are doing wrong will either upset us (when we get the answer), or will only tell us what we are doing wrong *in their eyes* – and it might not be us who is 'wrong' anyway. Adhering to strict guidelines about how to behave around others is a form of rigidity. Not being mindful of your impact upon others is a form of chaos. What we are seeking is a middle way, which can be defined as 'flexibility'; this allows us to reach out and respond to others with attunement. This flexibility is something we can aim for but we should not expect to achieve it in every encounter. However, if we find forming any relationship at all difficult, we may need to invest in consulting a relationship expert, a psychotherapist or another kind of mental-health worker.

Very often we begin a relationship or an encounter with another person by engaging in small talk about the weather, or by playing out the sort of rituals that the transactional analyst Eric Berne identified in the Sixties as 'games'. In developed countries, for instance, men may play a competitive game by arguing about whose car is best – 'You've got the X5 M? Oh dear, not enough power. You have to have the X6 M model like mine.' Women in such cultures, on the other hand, often practise competitive self-deprecation – 'You say you like this dress? But it's so old; I got it from a charity shop ten years ago.' That game might be called the 'Mine is Smaller than Yours' game.

For me, small talk and 'games' like these can, at times, feel far more appropriate than 'big talk', especially before I have formed a bond with the other person. I once attended a counselling course in which students were encouraged to abandon their comfortable rituals and games and express the feelings that lay underneath them. I found this hard, because I am uncomfortable with the type of 'real' talk that involves saying things like, 'I notice I am experiencing feelings of envy toward you' before I have even taken off my coat. However, some people prefer this way of relating to preliminary chit-chat. I remember saying to some of my fellow students, 'Does anyone want a coffee?' They all shook their heads and asked me to rephrase my question to reflect my real feelings. So I had to feel and think and then I came up with, 'I want coffee and I want you to come with me.' Having tried it, I found I really liked this process of turning a ritualized question into a statement, and I still try to do this when I remember. Although it is more of a risk (making a statement about myself rather than asking a question of another makes me feel more vulnerable), I find expressing an invitation like this gives me more of a chance of connecting to others. However, saying 'I want a coffee and I want you to come with me' with the old crowd of ex-students has become so ritualized that it is now no different to saying 'Does anyone want a coffee?' If you try to bring meaning to every single word it becomes exhausting (for me, anyway) and if the once meaningful utterance gets repeated it too becomes like ritual, just as those exchanges about the weather have become ritualized. Being real and open is a way to make real connections with others, but connections are made in more ways than simply exchanging meaningful words, and I would never rule out the significance of small talk. We need it in order to bond, and to pave the way for 'big talk'. It is the equivalent of monkey grooming[15] or the mutual sniffing that dogs do, and we need it. (I would not actually fancy doing what dogs do, nor do I want to look for your fleas, so I will continue to find out what you think of this weather we've been having . . .)

In *Watching the English*, the anthropologist Kate Fox has observed that rules exist about how to talk about the weather, and as this is a how-to book, I will share one with you. The point is that when I tell you we have had a lot of rain recently, what I am really wondering is not whether you know how many inches of rainfall we have had but whether you are an agreeable sort of person. I am more likely to form a favourable opinion of you if you agree with me. This is the rule of reciprocity. Remarks about the weather are phrased as questions not because we care about the weather but because we want a response. You may not be particularly interested in the weather but that does not mean you do not care about your relationship with the person you are talking to. It does not matter that the words we use for this 'nice-day-isn't-it?' ritual are empty. Such exchanges are not about what we say but how we acknowledge each other as we say it.

Unfortunately, whether we are adept at following such rules or not, we often trip ourselves up on the way to forming relationships, and sometimes stop ourselves from having them at all. There are many ingenious ways in which we unwittingly limit our contact with others and thus deprive ourselves of their potentially beneficial influence on us. Sometimes we assume we are having a relationship with another person when that relationship in fact exists mostly in our heads, because we are unknowingly misreading that person. Misreading can happen in several different ways:

- We can project ourselves onto the other person, so instead of having an 'I–You' relationship, we have an 'I–I' relationship; 'She will respond just as I would respond.'
- We can objectify the other person and have an 'I–It' relationship: 'If I phrase it like this, she will think of me like that.'
- We can also blur the boundaries between the person with us in the present with people we have known before, and transfer our experience of people from the past onto this person in the present, and have 'I–Ghost' relationships: 'If I do this, other people always respond like that.'

We tend to trust people in ways that are derived from past conditioning and experience. For example, we will have beliefs about how trustworthy a person is. Some people learn to trust no one, and this causes them to lead lonely and often isolated lives that restrict the possibility of full mental health. In contrast, there are those who trust too much and are therefore too vulnerable. Trust is just an example. To a lesser and greater extent we all view people through the lens of our past experiences, and we need to do this. For instance, it is not appropriate to ask the bus driver to show us his driving licence; we have to take it on trust that he knows what he is doing. The key, though, is to be aware of the patterns we fall into when summing people up, and to learn to hold our views lightly and be more open to finding out about the people in front of us.

A group of people I find I always learn from are children, as they can offer us fresh eyes on the world and a new perspective. A schoolboy chatting to me recently said that he thought sanity is not about how knowledgeable you are, or how 'realistic'. He knows some clever people with first-class degrees and doctorates who have loads of facts at their fingertips; nevertheless, he experiences some of them as less than sane because they cannot relate to others. He also knows some people who believe in things he personally finds odd (like God or homeopathy) and, although he finds their beliefs unrealistic, he finds some of them appear saner than some members of the former group. He thought this was because sanity has more to do with openness and emotional honesty than with leak-proof logic.

The Daily Temperature Reading

Here is an exercise that may help you get more emotional honesty into your relationships. Created by the family therapist Virginia Satir, it is designed to improve your existing relationships; you'll need to persuade your family, friends or work colleagues to do this exercise with you. It is called the Daily Temperature Reading because it takes the temperature of a particular relationship in the here and now. There is a belief that true love, great friendships and good working relationships just happen naturally. Often they do, but this exercise can help the process. It offers ways of confiding in other people, and confiding is an essential element in all kinds of relationships.

First, set aside half an hour when you will not get interrupted. Turn off your phones, computers, televisions. If there are two of you, sit facing each other. If you are a group, sit where you can all see each other. Take a minute or two to contemplate how you feel about yourself and your partner or the group. Like an agenda for a meeting, you have a list of five topics to get through. Try not to stray onto different subjects. The topics are: *i*) Appreciations; *ii*) New Information; *iii*) Questions; *iv*) Complaints with Recommendations for Change; and *v*) Wishes, Hopes and Dreams.

Appreciations

Take turns to share what you appreciate about each other. Be specific and precise. So instead of saying, for instance, 'I love being with you', be specific about what it is you love. For example, 'I love the way you ring me at midday to see how I am. It makes me feel cared for.' When you receive an appreciation, do not argue with it, or bat it back, or immediately say something like, 'Oh, and you too', because this will take away from its impact. Never put a 'but' on an appreciation, or try to sneak in a complaint by saying, for example, 'I would appreciate it if you would . . .' Reserve this section for sharing just what you appreciate about each other. You can decide between yourselves how many turns you wish to take to express appreciation.

New Information

This section is about sharing the events of your lives as well as being open about your moods, feelings and thoughts and about what is affecting them. It is important to keep one another up to date about what is happening to you. This section is for sharing objective information, such as, 'I have a dental appointment tomorrow', and subjective information such as, 'When I lost a tooth yesterday I felt so melancholy, it felt like the beginning of old age. Then I became more hopeful when I realized I still have time left.' The point is to say what is in the foreground for you, and keep it real, even if you have not worked out exactly what it is you are feeling and thinking. It is about not only keeping others informed of new facts but keeping them up-to-date on how you are working things out and what meanings you are making or trying to make. If there is time and if it seems appropriate, you can tell one another how you experienced hearing the information they have shared, or you can simply acknowledge it with a 'thank you' or a nod. If you have observations about what they have said, do not define the other person by making 'you'-statements. You could say, 'I have noticed you say you are sad when . . .' but not, 'You are always sad when . . .' Confine your statements to 'I'-statements, not 'you'-statements.

Questions

What assumptions are you making about your partner or the other people in the group? This is the moment to examine those assumptions. For example, you might say, 'The door slammed when you left the room yesterday. Were you angry or did the wind catch the door and slam it?' When I work with couples I often find that problems arise because they do not examine their own assumptions. Examining our assumptions and checking them out with our partner ensures that we have a relationship with the person instead of a fantasy of them, or avoid falling into the sort of 'I–I' relationship I spoke of earlier. This section is an opportunity to examine your assumptions and ask any type of question. These might be something as mundane as, 'What time are we leaving tomorrow?' or as pertinent as, 'I have experienced you as down and distant this week. Is anything going on?' Asking questions does not mean you will get answers, although you might. It is important to be patient with each other and to foster goodwill. Your question provides information for the other or others as well as being a question in its own right. There is no obligation to answer a question. If you wish, you can merely thank the other for their question, without answering it.

Complaints with Recommendations for Change

Complaints or worries should only be aired in conjunction with a suggestion for how that complaint or worry might be addressed. Without attacking, blaming, name-calling, playing the victim, interpreting or criticizing, describe the behaviour that causes you concern and then explain how it makes you *feel* (not think). Then say what you would like done differently. When you receive a complaint try simply to listen. Do not defend yourself. You do not have to alter your behaviour, although you may choose to. It is not differences that cause problems in relationships but how we deal with those differences. Because of our background and conditioning our response to hearing a complaint about ourselves can be defensive. When a response to someone's concern or complaint exacerbates the situation, the likelihood of a fully functioning relationship is decreased. It may help to remember when you receive a complaint that it is only nominally about you; it is really information about the person making the complaint. When we are able to work through qualms and complaints we can become closer through our successful navigation of the challenge they represent. When someone we love shares a concern, it is vital to develop the habit of listening with empathy and with a desire to understand. An example could be, 'When you come in from work and immediately start relating your day, my train of thought is interrupted, I forget what I was doing and I feel overwhelmed. What I would like would be for you to check in with what I'm doing and let me wrap that up, or mark my place and where I have got up to, and then I really want to hear about your day.' The other might respond with something like, 'I never realized, thank you for letting me know. Just put your hand up to say stop if I'm overwhelming you again.' Other complaints might be more tricky to hear, such as, 'I'm sick of being the person who puts the rubbish out in this house; I want you to do it for a change.' This complaint is expressed with a martyr-ish edge. It might have been better to phrase it as follows: 'As I put the bins out last night, it felt to me as though I am the only person who remembers to do this. Please could you do it next time?' The person on the receiving end may have been about to deliver the very same complaint because they feel that *they* are always left with this chore. Remember: the complaint is about the person making it. The best way to respond is, 'I hear that you feel that it is you who always takes the rubbish out, and you would like to change. Thank you for telling me.' It is best not to argue when you do this exercise. When you next do a Daily Temperature Reading, in the questions section you might say, 'It seems to me we both feel we are doing more than our fair share of chores. Perhaps we need to work out a system or get a cleaner. What do you think?' Remember, the idea is not to fight, and a good relationship is not about determining who is right and who is wrong. It's about finding a way forward together. A common intervention that psychotherapists make when working with couples is to say, 'You can choose between being right, or being together'. As I've said before, bear this in mind if you feel wrongly accused: the accusation is about how the other person feels and they will not feel better if they are made to feel wrong as well.

Wishes, Hopes and Dreams

Some people hold on to a belief that telling others of the things they really want will jinx the dream. In my experience the opposite is more often true. I advocate the sharing of wishes, hopes and dreams in order to get the support and encouragement we need to fulfil them. Before a race an athlete visualizes how he will jump every hurdle and cross the line at the end of the race. He may not win as a result of his visualizing exercise, but he gives himself a better chance of doing so – and so will you, as you share your hopes with others. Sharing our deepest hopes can make us feel vulnerable, so support your partner(s) in this endeavour, rather than challenging them. Sharing our vulnerabilities increases intimacy and deepens the connections between us.

The Daily Temperature Reading can be important to couples, families, work teams and others. To give it a chance, do it, say, every two days for a month as a couple, or weekly for two months as a group. Then evaluate what difference it has made in your lives.

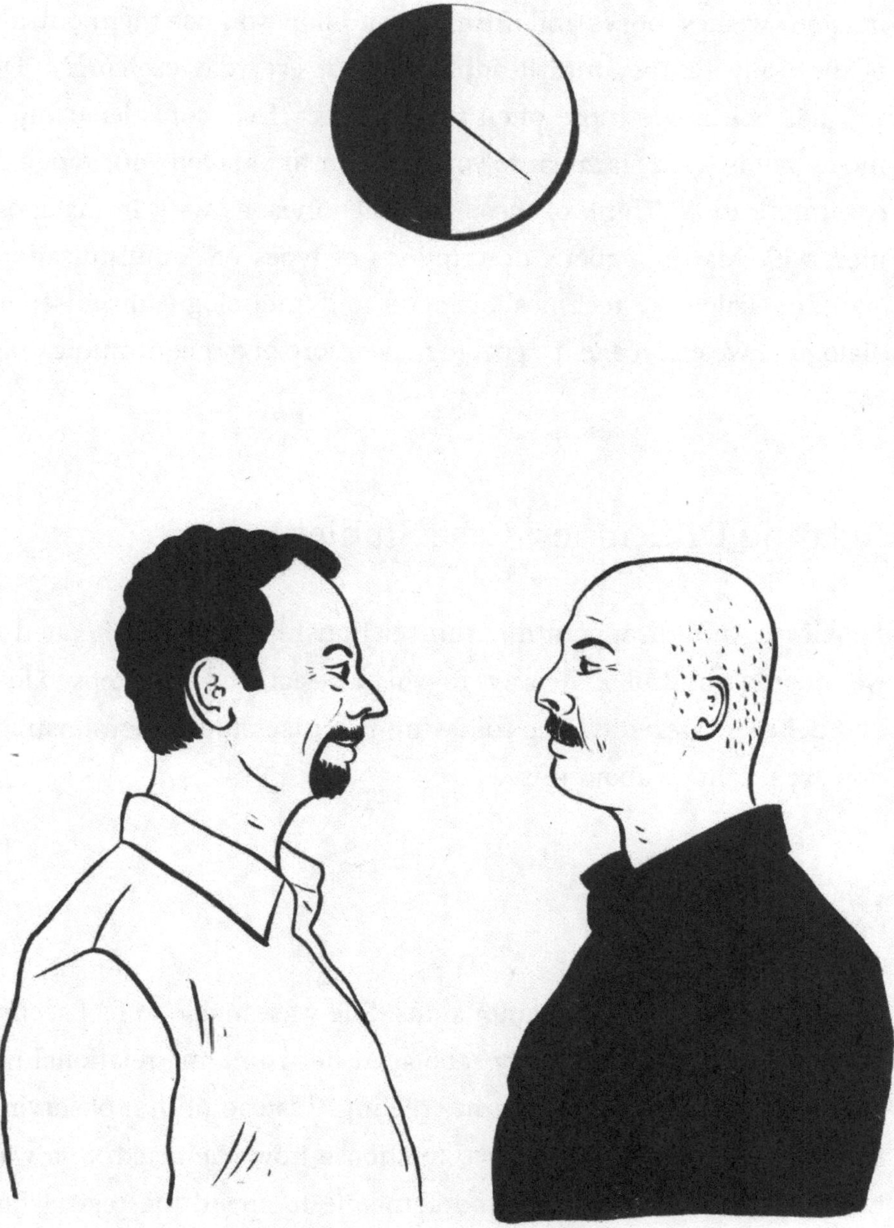

Think about these five modes of communication – appreciating; informing; questioning; complaining and recommending; and sharing your wishes, hopes and dreams – and how you use them outside of the Daily Temperature Reading, in your everyday exchanges. Do you use one mode more often than others? If so, consider using a mode that is not as familiar to you, in order to broaden your range of communication. Think of these five categories, as well, in juxtaposition with Martin Buber's descriptions of types of communication: 'genuine dialogue', 'technical dialogue' and 'monologue disguised as dialogue'. We can make it a goal to make more of our communicating count.

Relating Difficulties: Case Studies

Loneliness and disappointment in relationships can be mitigated if we become mindful of the ways in which we act, and take steps to feel and behave differently. The following two case studies demonstrate how we might go about this.

Zara

Zara was chaotic in her relationships. She was unable to feel secure with a partner and habitually sabotaged her romantic relationships at an early stage, by acting on her feelings instead of first observing them to give herself the chance to choose how she acted. She was twenty-eight and wanted to find someone to spend the rest of her life with. Using self-observation she noticed a certain pattern in her relationships and she noted down the pattern in her diary:

1. She would choose someone who was good-looking and/or charismatic.
2. She would go to bed with him at the earliest opportunity.
3. After sex, she would feel that she was 'in love' with him.
4. She would behave in a 'needy' way and ring him up too much.
5. The relationship died, usually after a couple of months.
6. She would be heartbroken.

This was the hole, the habit, the pattern – whatever you want to call it – that Zara was in.

She made a decision and set out a couple of guidelines for herself. When the next man came along, she would: *a)* not go to bed with him before they had established a relationship; and *b)* not act in a 'needy' way, *even when she felt needy.*

After a while Zara met a man at evening classes who seemed interested in becoming her friend. She did not assume they would become romantic, but they liked spending time together and met up for a drink once or twice a week. This went on for six months. Then they went on holiday together as friends, but came back as lovers. Zara felt the neediness rise up in her. She wanted to know what he was doing and where he was every second of the day: was he thinking about her? But instead of acting on this urge, she exorcised it, to some extent, merely by writing it all down in a private diary. This resolve not to 'smother' the man concerned appears to have been a good guideline, because their relationship continued to deepen, they married and now, decades later, they are still happily together.

So, although I am wary of rules, I have to admit that, in Zara's example, they did allow her to steer her life onto a happier course. Using self-observation you may discover chaotic patterns in your relationship and decide to implement a rule like Zara did, using it as a temporary splint until a more permanent, flexible middle way is found.

Sam

Rather than rules, Sam needed more flexibility in his life. He had rules such as never to talk about the weather, or to even ask the generic question 'How are you?' Sam deemed such ordinary, 'grooming' questions meaningless, and wrote off anyone who used them. His rules made him difficult to get on with and resulted in him living a lonely existence, with little contact with the outside world. He gained some comfort in thinking himself superior to the rest of the population, but feeling superior is no substitute for companionship and the positive difference friends make to a life. Sam became lonely and depressed. When the depression became unbearable he went to see his doctor, who referred him to a counsellor, Simon.

After he had learnt to trust Simon, which took a year of weekly sessions (neural pathways take time to alter), Sam was able to become aware of how he had established his own particular rule book, and how many of his rules were out of date. Supported by Simon, Sam experimented with change and allowed himself more contact with other people. He has not embarked upon a romantic relationship,

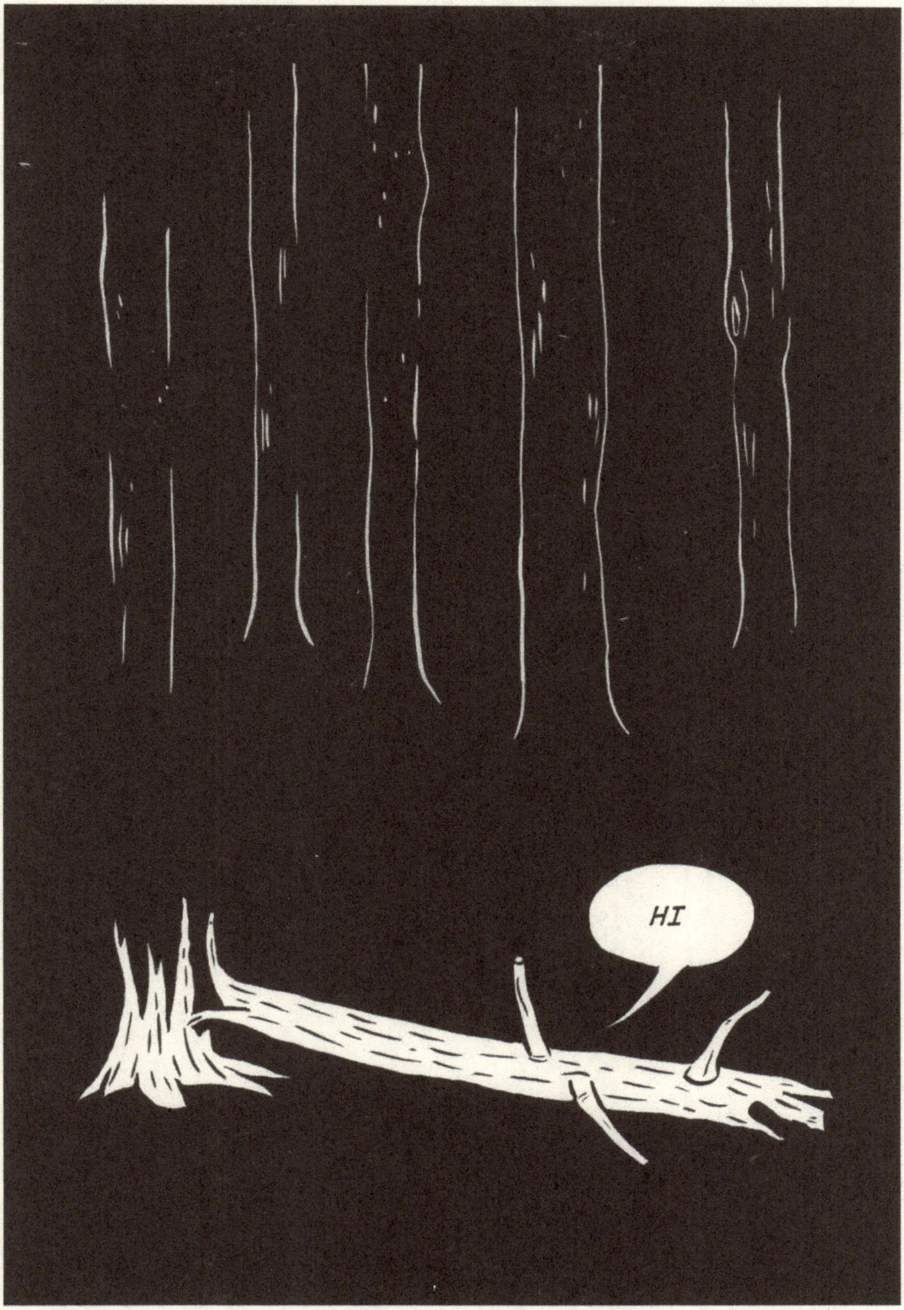
HI

nor become a party animal, but he has let a few other people into his life, is less lonely, less rigid and is no longer as depressed.

Philosophers ask themselves the question, 'If a tree falls in the forest but nobody hears it, has it, in fact, made a sound?' I wonder if this question is really asking, 'Would we exist if no one witnessed our existence?' Perhaps we have to ask that, because without another soul or souls to check in with, pass the time with, be affected by and affect, a part of us does seem to diminish. We do feel less human and we are more likely to go insane without the checks and challenges of other good-willed people around us. Solitary confinement is one of the most brutal, most stressful punishments we inflict on our fellow humans. If we are to stay sane, we must not inflict it upon ourselves.

3. Stress

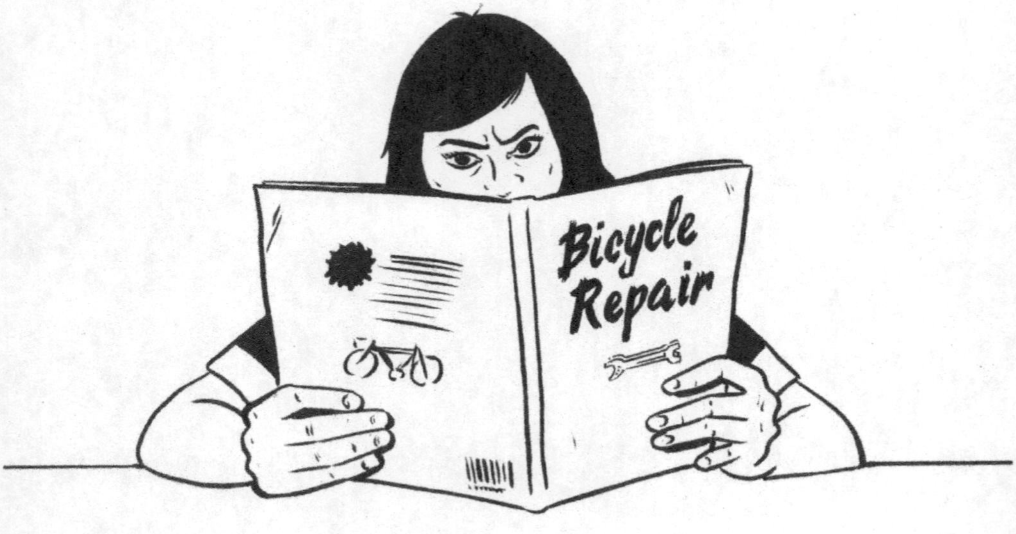
Bicycle
Repair

Learning

By improving our self-awareness and prioritizing beneficial relationships, we give ourselves a good chance of holding on to our sanity. Our brains never stop developing and we do have some choices about how they develop. The third cornerstone of sanity is concerned with how we keep our brains – and therefore ourselves – fit.

High levels of stress result in panic or in the brain dissociating. Dissociation is a disconnection amongst our thoughts, sensations, feelings and actions – experienced as a type of blanking out. Therefore high levels of stress are to be avoided. However, no stress at all means that the brain does not get any exercise. A brain is not unlike a muscle, in that the cliché 'use it or lose it' applies. Moderate levels of stress keep our minds in condition, and help us to stay sane. This 'good stress' promotes the neural growth hormones that support learning. Good stress, unlike the type that causes dissociation, can be experienced as pleasurable; it can motivate us or make us curious. More importantly, it triggers neural plasticity, which is why I get excited about it.

In psychotherapy, quite often, what the client and I are working towards is a position where the client is able to tolerate their feelings. We call this 'affect regulation', a process of inhibiting anxiety and fear to allow processing to continue in the face of strong emotion. To work at this level we cannot be too comfortable, because then new learning does not take place; but nor can we be too uncomfortable, for then we would be in the zone where dissociation or panic takes over. Good work takes place on the boundary of comfort. Some psychotherapists refer to this place as 'the growing edge' or 'a good-stress zone', or talk of 'expanding the comfort zone'. The good-stress zone is where our brains are able to adapt, reconfigure and grow. Think of the brain as a muscle and think of opportunities to flex it. The more we flex it, the better our brain functions.

The richer and more stimulating our environment, the more encouraged we feel to learn new skills and expand our knowledge. Such learning seems to have the side-benefit of boosting our immune system. There are some animal studies that show that an intellectually stimulating environment can compensate for the damaging effects of lead-poisoning. Two groups of rats were given water contaminated with lead. One group was put in a stimulating environment and the other was not. Professor Jay Schneider, who conducted the experiment, said that the magnitude of the protective effect of an educationally stimulating environment on the rats' ability to withstand the poison surprised him. I am sad to report the rats in the less stimulating environment did not fare so well. I am the same. When I go away on holiday to a new place I feel refreshed by having been stimulated by new sights, smells, environments and culture. This is an example of good stress. I like to imagine I can feel it doing me good, and the rat experiment suggests that it really might be.

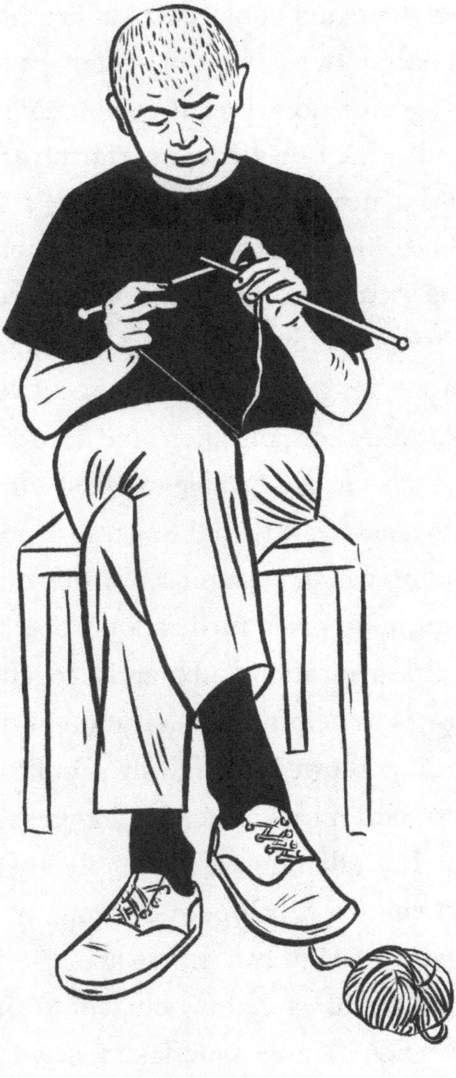

Physical Activity

To stay sane we need to increase the good stress that is generated by engaging not only in more intellectual pursuits but also in physical activity. The brain needs oxygen and the more oxygen it gets the better it functions. Two studies have demonstrated this clearly. In the first, two groups of sedentary elderly people were tested in four areas: memory, executive functioning, concentration, and the speed with which they could perform various physical tasks, from threading a needle to walking along a line. For the next four months, those in the first group walked for twenty minutes a day; those in the second group carried on as normal. Then they were tested again. Group 1 showed significant improvements in the higher mental processes of memory and executive functions that involve learning, planning, organization and multi-tasking. The implication is that exercise might be able to offset some of the mental declines that we often associate with the ageing process. The second study was carried out on patients diagnosed with a major depressive disorder. The first group was given medication alone, the second exercise alone and the third medication and exercise together. The results showed that exercise is as helpful as medication in combating depression, as all three groups showed statistically significant and identical improvement in standard measurements of depression.

It is often the case when we are considering embarking on a new activity (be it ballroom dancing, meditation or other new ventures) that we feel in two minds about it. However, if we *decide* to override that part of us that is reluctant to change (instead of merely *trying to* override it), and undertake a new regime anyway, we give ourselves the chance to experience the difference that new regime makes to us. If we are not feeling more stimulated, more interconnected, more alive, no harm will have been done and we can drop it. Starting a new habit means feeling the impulse to maintain your current way of being, but beginning the new regime anyway: it can feel like a wrench. We usually start to send ourselves messages – like 'this isn't really me' – clock such excuses and decide to persevere with establishing a new habit anyway.

The Nun Study

In his book *Aging With Grace*, David Snowden describes his long-term study of nuns. He undertook the study in order to examine longevity and incidences of dementia. He was also interested in links between the nuns' brain health and factors like intelligence and diet. His subjects provided an ideal opportunity to study the effect of education on long functioning life because the living circumstances of the nuns, in terms of exercise, diet, routine and financial circumstances, were similar, thus making education a measurable distinction between them.

In this study, Dr Snowden noticed that, while some nuns had mentally deteriorated so far that they could no longer live independently or feed themselves, others at the same age or older were still holding down full-time jobs. He found that the nuns who had university degrees had significantly longer, independent, functioning lives than those who had ended their education earlier. And the longer they continued to study, or embark upon and maintain new interests, the more lively their minds seemed to stay.

With another researcher, Jim Mortimer, Snowden also studied 'brain reserve'. They suggested that a brain that has been actively used in socializing and learning all through life builds more neural connections than a brain that has been less stimulated. So, in the former case, when part of the brain is damaged by Alzheimer's, the pathway is not necessarily permanently interrupted, but can find a new route around the tangle or plaque caused by the disease. Snowden and Mortimer also found that some nuns who displayed no signs of Alzheimer's when alive were found to have significant damage caused by it at autopsy, whereas the brains of those who clearly exhibited the condition in life had fewer signs of it when autopsied. Snowden and Mortimer have not yet come to any firm conclusions about the part continuing curiosity and learning plays in building up brain reserve, but circumstantial evidence suggests a connection.

Good stress keeps our brains plastic. A plastic brain can adapt, stay flexible, remain connected to community, and cope with the inevitable changes that life brings. Good stress motivates us by activating our curiosity, firing our enthusiasm and feeding our creativity.

The hormone dopamine is a key neurotransmitter in reward-reinforcement. We can stimulate its production in both healthy and unhealthy ways. The form of dopamine stimulation that I advocate is learning something new, and the thrill that comes with it – whether mastering a new musical instrument, succeeding with a new recipe, shooting a ball into a basket or learning to tell a successful joke. Dopamine production is also stimulated by addictive substances or activities, such as gambling. This is an abuse of dopamine and by using it this way we can overload our systems, causing health and emotional problems. Pleasure is good for us but feeding an addiction is not.

If we are, for instance, hard-working university researchers, we might consider that we are already doing enough learning. It is true that our neural pathways for research will be well developed; but learning how to dance the tango, cook a tagine or speak a new language will supply us with the good stress that builds more brain reserve. However, we need certain conditions for brain building. We must be doing something genuinely new, and we must pay close attention, be emotionally engaged and keep at it. New pathways will form if two or more of these conditions are met, but we will ideally meet all four at once.

Less challenging but also useful are the solo activities sometimes referred to as 'brain training' – such as crosswords, word search games and card games such as solitaire and patience – games that appear to be of limited value as transferable skills. For example, when we learn and practise Sudoku, we get better at Sudoku, but it has limited value that we can integrate into the rest of our life. In fact, as a Sudoku-and-other-numbers-games addict, let me offer a word of warning about such 'brain' games. I have noticed, as I play Bridge or Scrabble against a computer, or Suduko for an hour at a time, that my emotional side feels cut off. As a way of self-numbing I would say that number and letter games could compete with class-A drugs when it comes to shutting down our feelings. It feels to me as though the dopamine kick I get from it has a more addictive edge to it, than a learning edge.

If you too are a games addict, notice the difference in how you feel when instead you read a book. It may feel like it takes more effort, especially when you first start to develop this new habit. A novel, or a book on philosophy, is going to use both sides of the brain: not only will you have feelings about what you read, but your mind will also get more of a work-out because you will make connections between what you are learning and what you already recognize.

When I talk about the benefits of learning, sometimes people confide in me that what stops them embarking on learning something is a sense of shame that they do not know it already. Susan Jeffers wisely said 'Feel the Fear and Do it Anyway'. I say 'Feel the shame and learn something anyway'. No one likes to feel vulnerable[16] but unless we learn to tolerate some emotional vulnerability we will be endangering our growth, and if we do not grow we shrink – and if we do that we jeopardize our sanity.

Recently I was talking to a biologist about the benefits of maintaining the habit of learning. He asked me whether I was right- or left-handed. I said right. He told me that my chances of a full recovery after a stroke would be better if I was left-handed because left-handed people already have more neural connections than right-handed people. He added that if I started the habit of cleaning my teeth or working my computer mouse with my left hand I would begin to build 'brain reserve'. If I later suffered a stroke it would put me in a better position to recover from it.

Whatever new activity we begin to do – from left-handed teethbrushing, to learning a new language – we will make new neural connections, which can generate greater creativity and new ideas. A new idea has been likened to a shy woodland creature. To coax the shy woodland creature from the shadows into the clearing you must not scare it. Leave a little food for it and it will come out into the clearing where you can see it better. If you treat it well it will not go bounding back into the forest.[17]

Ideas rarely come from doing nothing. We stimulate our brains to come up with ideas when we learn new things or when we rehearse the things we are learning. I ran a five-day group for art students and art lecturers about the psychological processes of creativity. There was a general consensus that ideas came not from sitting around and waiting for inspiration to descend, but from working: trying things out, reading, learning and doing.

Learning Styles

There are many different ways of learning. Some of us absorb best when we read, while others prefer to learn visually from diagrams, videos and demonstrations. Auditory learners prefer to learn through listening, via lectures, talking things through and hearing what others have to say, gaining extra information from the tone and the nuances. There are also kinaesthetic learners, who learn through moving, doing and touching, preferring a hands-on approach through which they actively explore the physical world. So if we have always thought of ourselves as not being able to learn easily, it may be that we have not yet found the style of learning that best suits us; and, as the brain is plastic, we can, with practice, develop new styles of learning. The more we learn, the more we are able, by linking our areas of knowledge together, to come up with creative ideas. We would not know how physics and sky-diving go together unless we knew a little bit about both. Thus the more we know, the more we can create.[18]

I left school at fifteen and it took me a few years to come around to and enjoy learning. In my early twenties I had a repetitive administrative job. I knew that I felt under-stimulated. Boredom drove me to a College of Further Education recruitment evening. I signed up for Psychology and English A-levels and made new friends at these classes. I remember going round to a friend's house for the first time and being excited by her enthusiasm. She said, 'I'm not bored any more; I find myself thinking about the different motivations of characters in *Twelfth Night*.'

This is what learning does. It gives us more things to think about so we have less time to get bored, depressed and under-stimulated. It builds on our existing knowledge and expands it. It leads us to make more connections by linking together more neural pathways. It also connects our brains to other people's brains.

The next year I did Art and History. These became subjects that I have continued to build on with further reading and, in the case of Art and Psychology, further courses and a degree. Nothing but good has come from my taking a class. One year I did two evening classes, one in Film Appreciation and the other in Creative Writing. In the former I learnt that I disliked listening to people talking about film plots, while in the latter I did much better. In that class I met my husband. Learning new subjects not only builds new connections in our brains, but in our lives as well.

The Comfort-Zone Exercise

Get a large piece of plain paper and draw a circle in the middle. Inside the circle write examples of activities that you feel completely comfortable doing. Around the edge of the circle write down examples of

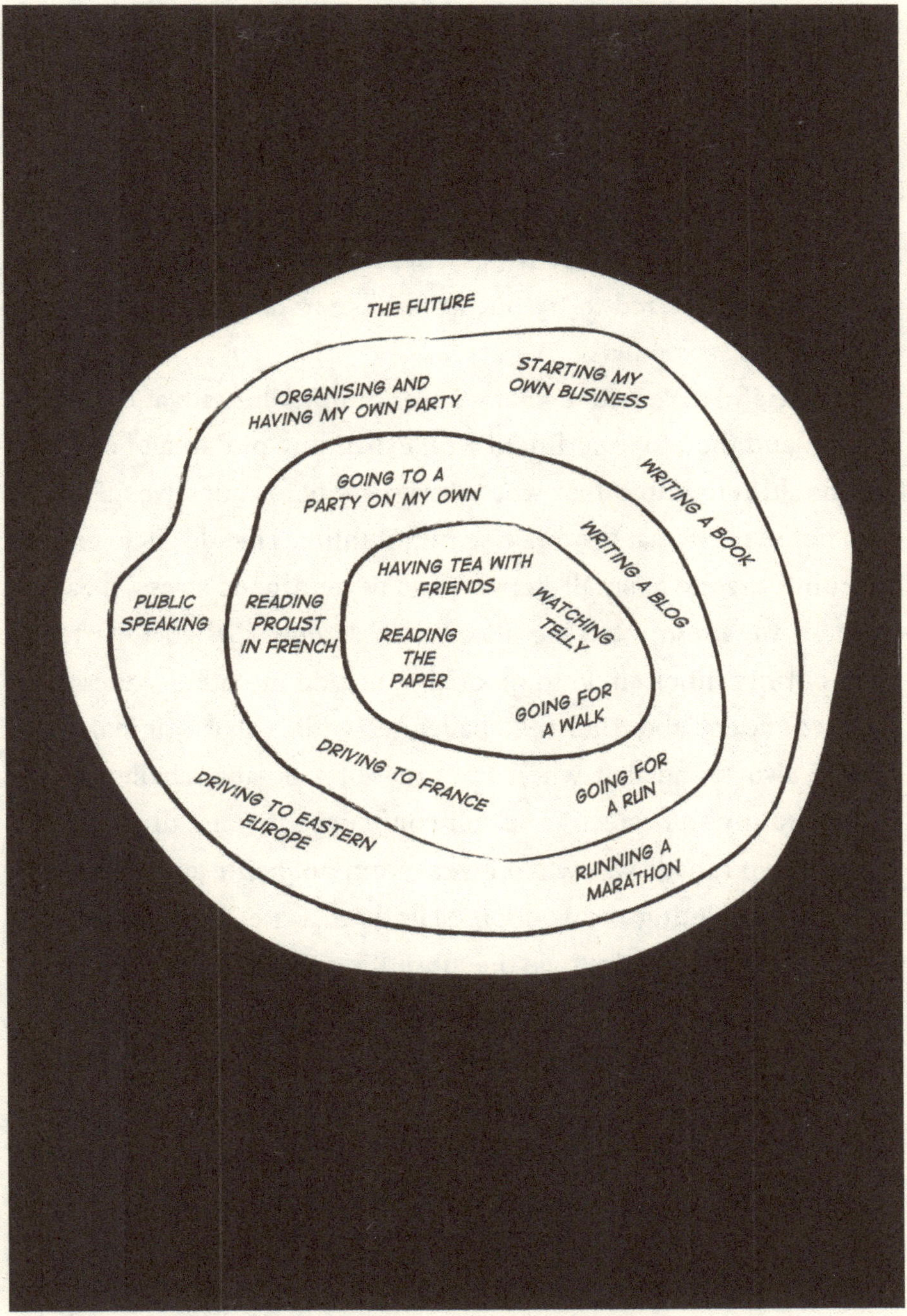

THE FUTURE
ORGANISING AND HAVING MY OWN PARTY
STARTING MY OWN BUSINESS
WRITING A BOOK
PUBLIC SPEAKING
DRIVING TO EASTERN EUROPE
RUNNING A MARATHON
GOING TO A PARTY ON MY OWN
WRITING A BLOG
READING PROUST IN FRENCH
DRIVING TO FRANCE
GOING FOR A RUN
HAVING TEA WITH FRIENDS
WATCHING TELLY
READING THE PAPER
GOING FOR A WALK

activities that you can do but that you have to push yourself a little bit to do – those activities that may make you nervous in some way, but not so much as to stop you doing them. Draw a larger circle around this circle of activities. In the next band write activities that you would like to do but find it difficult to get up the courage *to* do. Draw another circle around this ring of activities. After that write down those things you are far too scared to try but would like to do. You can create as many circles as you like.

It is useful to consider what we are comfortable with and what we are not, and then to experiment with expanding our area of comfort. We should remember that whatever we try is for ourselves alone. It does not matter what anyone else might think. The idea is to expand our comfort-zone in small steps. We go beyond 'good stress' into 'bad stress' if we attempt too big a leap across zones. When I started to push out my inner circle to gradually include the other zones I felt more confident about all the challenges within that original inner zone. I also found that when I set myself a do-able challenge and succeeded my self-esteem and self-confidence rose in all areas. The greatest leap I made was when I went from not being able to run 100 yards to completing the London Marathon. I am sure this is what gave me the confidence to go on submitting my book, *Couch Fiction*, after its first round of rejections. It was eventually published in May 2010. I have also experienced that if I do not keep on testing my limits, my comfort-zone shrinks back. Challenges that had seemed comfortable one year took courage to achieve the next. I do not want to get into that position again; so, onwards and outwards.

4. What's the Story?

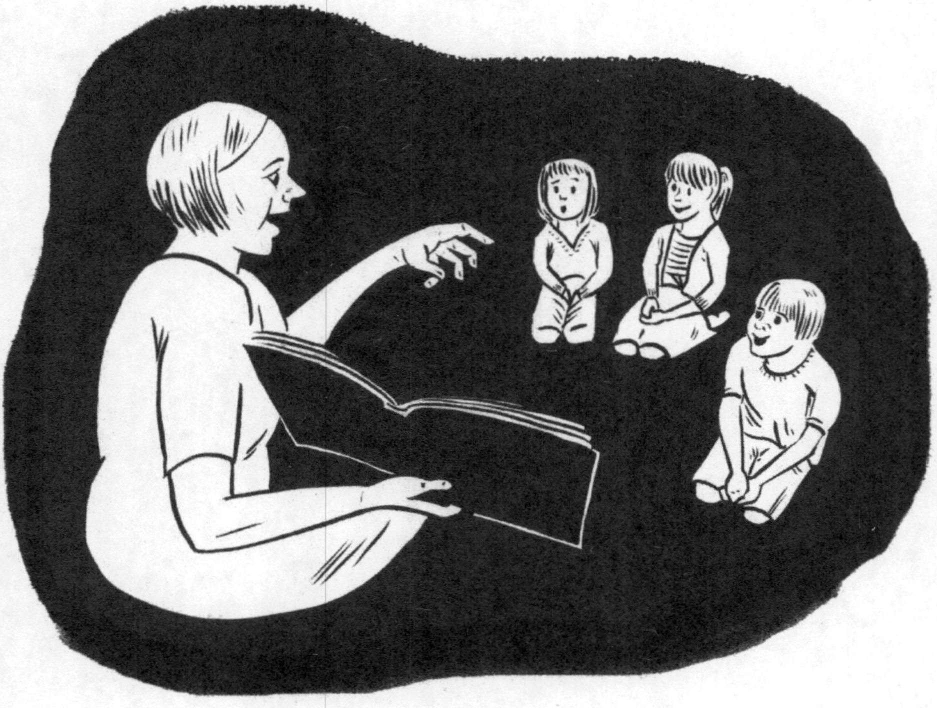

I have included this section on stories because a part of every successful therapy is about re-writing the narratives that define us, making new meanings and imagining different endings. In the same way, part of staying sane is knowing what our story is and rewriting it when we need to.

Our usual emotional, cognitive and physical response to the world – that is, our typical pattern for dealing with recurrent situations – will come from our own stories. Our way of being in the world will also come from stories that we read and that are told to us, from films, sitcoms and the news; they might be family legends, or parables and metaphors, or religious tracts and fairy stories. We make up stories, we read stories, we hear stories. Our lives interweave these stories and respond to them.

Our minds are formed by narratives. We evolved using stories and narratives that are co-constructed. As our earliest caregivers transcribed our sensations, feelings and actions into words for us, our narratives took shape. We used these narratives to integrate our experience into coherent meanings. Children and their parental figures narrate their experience together and, in doing so, they organize their memories and put them into a social context. This assists in linking feelings, actions and others to the self. These co-constructed narratives[19] are central to all human groups – from a family in the western world to the hunter-gatherers of the Kalahari Desert. The co-construction of story has negative and positive outcomes. The downside is that the parental figure can unduly influence the child with his or her own fears and anxieties, prejudices and restrictive patterns of being; but the upside is that co-forming narrative teaches ways of memorizing, as well as imparting positive values, group culture and individual identity. A child not only co-constructs the narrative of his or her life with his or her caregiver, but ideally listens to many other stories as well. We may think this is mainly just for entertainment and bonding, but the repeated telling of stories also helps to form structures in the child's mind that enable problem solving, meaning making, optimism and self-soothing. Wicked witches get their comeuppance, conflicts are resolved and we learn the concept of 'happily ever after'.

In the same way that stories are important in personality formation, they are also significant in the evolution of our species and the creation of culture. Before the invention of writing, stories, sagas and legends were handed down from generation to generation in the form of rituals and oral traditions that contained both education and the foundations of wisdom. Just as new learning forges new neural pathways to what we already know, so a new story adds to our existing stock. The appearance of certain themes across cultures and times – death and resurrection, for instance – testifies to their importance to the species as a whole. Such stories are used to pass down group identity, wisdom and experience for the next generation to build on, as well as giving them ways of coping, self-soothing and facing death.

Stories may unconsciously influence us to act in one way or another, but they also enable us to think about ourselves in an objective way.

When a client in therapy presents a problem, the therapist often asks them to imagine that problem belonging to a friend and, if that was the case, how they would counsel that friend. This use of storytelling helps us to gain some distance from ourselves and gives us perspective. We can also use stories to help us escape into our imaginations when there is no escape in reality. Children often create imaginary worlds where they can succeed and triumph. Though they may be limited in their choices in real life, they can use imagination and storytelling to soothe themselves during real-life experiences that might otherwise be intolerable. It is not only children who can do this. In his book *Man's Search for Meaning*, Victor Frankl explained that while he lived through suffering, atrocity and imprisonment at Auschwitz and other concentration camps he created a place of freedom in his mind and imagination. He ascribes his survival to this act of defiance and hope.

The great thing about a story is that it is flexible. We can change a story from one that does not help us to one that does. If the script we have lived by in the past does not work for us anymore we do not need to accept it as our script of the future. For example, the belief that we are unworthy of being loved and belonging is just that, a belief. This belief, this story we tell ourselves, can be edited. The effects of such editing can be more positively life changing than winning the lottery. Research has shown that after winning the lottery people take about three months to return to the mindset they had before the win. So, if they were generally optimistic and joyful, that's where they return to; and if they were self-loathing and misanthropic, they will be after their win as well. A lot of money does not change our emotional life. The way we talk to and about ourselves and the way in which we edit our own stories, can and does.

Creating a consistent self-narrative that makes sense and feels true to ourselves is a challenge at any stage in life. Our stories give shape to our inchoate, disparate, fleeting impressions of everyday life. They bring together the past and the future into the present to provide us with structures for working toward our goals. They give us a sense of identity and, most importantly, serve to integrate the feelings of our right brain with the language of our left.

Sophie was a fifty-year-old woman who came to see me. She interpreted her life story to mean that she was washed up and on the scrap heap, because 'it's a young person's world'. This worried me because people who interpret events in pessimistic ways are more likely to become depressed and ill, and live shorter lives than those who find positive meanings. Together we worked with her statement, not by arguing about whether it was true or untrue, but by examining how it made her feel and whether further meaning or meanings would not be more helpful. Sophie had just finished a fine-art degree and was finding it tough-going locating places to show her work. I told her a story (more of a myth – I do not even know if it's true) about a telephone-systems salesperson who made a very different kind of sense of rejection. Every time this salesperson was rejected by a prospective customer he was delighted, because it brought him one encounter nearer to his next sale. He calculated his hit-rate as one in fifty cold calls, so if he counted forty rejections he began to get excited, as he knew the sale would be coming soon. This made him more confident. He did very well and won the firm's salesman-of-the-year award. Sophie laughed at the story but it stayed with her and gave her the confidence to tell people that she really wanted to be selected for an artist's residency. When a residency did come her way, she told me, 'I did not have to approach anywhere near fifty people. It was more like seventeen. Holding the story in mind kept me enthusiastic when I talked about my work and what I had to offer.' By telling her story in a different way Sophie changed it, and that in turn changed the way she appeared to others.

We are primed to use stories. Part of our survival as a species depended upon listening to the stories of our tribal elders as they shared parables and passed down their experience and the wisdom of those who went before. As we get older it is our short-term memory that fades rather than our long-term memory. Perhaps we have evolved like this so that we are able to tell the younger generation about the stories and experiences that have formed us which may be important to subsequent generations if they are to thrive.

I worry, though, about what might happen to our minds if most of the stories we hear are about greed, war and atrocity. For this reason I recommend not watching too much television. Research exists that shows that people who watch television for more than four hours a day believe that they are far more likely to be involved in a violent incident in the forthcoming week than do those who watch television for less than two hours per day.[20] Not only does Hollywood supply a succession of movies in which the 'goodies' win by resorting to violence rather than dialogue, but even the news appears to be filtered for maximum emotional shock value, which means it has a bias towards bad news rather than good. Be careful which stories you expose yourself to. I am not saying it is not important to be informed about what is going on, but to be informed repeatedly about bad news will give us neither a balanced view of our world nor of the other people who inhabit it. In contrast to this torrent of bad news, I think it is important to seek out optimistic stories and foster the optimism within ourselves.

I am going to try to convince you that optimism is a good idea.

- Studies show that pessimism in early adulthood appears to be a risk factor for poor physical and mental health later on.[21]
- Optimism is shown to correlate with physical and mental good health.
- Optimistic people recover more quickly after operations and have higher survival rates after cancer. (They are more likely to follow their doctor's orders and so aid recovery.)
- Optimism puts you in a better mood and thereby decreases stress.
- Optimism is correlated with longevity while pessimism is associated with a reduced life span.[22]
- Optimists are more likely to trust others and therefore enjoy more satisfying relationships.
- Pessimists think they are cleverer than optimists but they really aren't.[23]

If I walk into a party with my head held high, with the optimistic attitude that everyone is pleased to see me or would like to meet me (and I them), I will catch someone's eye even if, hitherto, everyone in the room was a stranger to me. I will ask them about themselves and they may ask me about myself; we will probably find some common ground and I might learn something from them as a bonus. But more than that, I give myself the chance of forming what feels like a connection. It might last just a few minutes, or it may be the beginning of a long friendship, but in that connection I feel deeply nourished.

If, on the other hand, I walk into a party with my eyes on the ground, neither interested in meeting anyone nor thinking that anyone would be interested in meeting me, I will not catch anyone's eye and I will not enjoy the party. I will be thinking about ways to leave it. I will not be fully present at the party. Instead I will be present only with my prejudices; I will be projecting a fantasy, or an experience of the past, onto the present, and relating to that, instead of to what is going on around me.

The party is life. Sometimes, I confess, I enter the party in a state nearer the second scenario than the first and sometimes in spite of this somebody is still generous enough to make an effort with me and bring me round. Part of the story I tell myself is that if I am down, other people make me feel better.

What I have displayed here, even in my confessional paragraph above, is optimism. Whether optimism becomes established as a result of good things happening or, conversely, good things happen because they are visualized, hoped for, worked for and obtained, I do not know. But the meanings you find, and the stories you hear, will have an impact on how optimistic you are: it's how we evolved.

What happens if we never hear positive stories? How would it have affected your brain if you had never heard a 'happy ever after' story. If you do not know how to draw positive meaning from what happens in life, the neural pathways you need to appreciate good news will never fire up. Here is a story. A social worker who works with children was working with a family of three siblings aged six, eight and twelve. They had known only their own unsafe home, care homes and foster families all their lives. Their most recent placement was working out extraordinarily well. They had been placed in foster care with a couple, Brianna and Simon, who were empathetic towards the children and gave them some stability. They listened to what the children said, and were good at interpreting the children's feelings and able to provide them with support and loving care. My friend spent some time with them all and wrote her report recommending that the arrangement continue. The children were anxious about the meaning of her visit, so, contrary to usual procedures, she told them what she had written in her report. She said, 'You will not be split up. You are going to stay with Brianna and Simon. We are going to find local schools for you all and, as Brianna and Simon want to adopt you, we are going to begin that process.' The children were silent and seemed stunned, so my friend asked, 'What did I just say?' Each child said, 'We will be split up; we can't stay with Brianna and Simon; there aren't any schools for us and no one will adopt us.' My friend then repeated what she had said, and again the children could not hear it. She tried again and then the youngest child burst into tears. 'Why are you crying, Robbie?' she asked and Robbie replied, 'I think it is because I am so happy.' Eventually they all understood, but found it hard to take in.

The trouble is, if we do not have a mind that is *used* to hearing good news, we do not have the neural pathways to process such news. If we are in this situation we are probably unaware of it, because it is not as though we hear good news and do not trust it. Rather, it is as though we cannot hear good news as good news at all.

How easily do you absorb good news? If good stuff does happen to you, does it make you afraid in any way? Do you perversely comfort yourself by telling yourself it cannot last? If this is the case and if you were to begin to direct your mind to open itself to more optimistic ways of thinking you would probably experience a lot of head chatter telling you to stop. Note the head chatter, expect it and do not let it put you off. We need to point ourselves in the direction of listening for good news. Start a habit of looking for the positives in any situation, however dire. It will feel phoney at first. Often new behaviours feel false because they are unfamiliar; but an optimistic outlook is no more false than always assuming that nothing good will ever happen.

It is not easy simply to turn optimism on. It will take more than deciding that optimism sounds like a good idea. It will take practice and good people around us. You will need to keep up the practice of focused-attention exercises so you can pump up the neural pathways that can steer the mind. You may find that you have been telling yourself that practising optimism is a risk, as though, somehow, a positive attitude will invite disaster and so if you practise optimism it may increase your feelings of vulnerability. The trick is to increase your tolerance for vulnerable feelings, rather than avoid them altogether.

If we practise more optimism, disasters will still happen – but predicting disasters does not make them more tolerable, or ward them off.

At one time, when we went away for weekends, I would be quite low for the last thirty minutes or so of the journey home. I used to imagine that our house had been burgled. I pictured myself ringing the police, getting the broken window boarded up, ringing the insurance company. When I opened the front door, however, I would be delighted and relieved that it had not happened. When I began to practise self-observation, and noticed the fantasies I was having and the stories I was feeding myself, I decided to focus on other things when that particular fantasy visited me, and I was able to minimize the habit. When I got this pessimistic theme under control, I noticed that I not only enjoyed the last thirty minutes of the journey home more, but also the whole weekend. Only when I changed the story did I realize that my fantasy had been a cloud over the whole weekend. Sometimes we only realize that we have been living under a cloud when the cloud is lifted.

Optimism does not mean continual happiness, glazed eyes and a fixed grin. When I talk about the desirability of optimism I do not mean that we should delude ourselves about reality. But practising optimism does mean focusing more on the positive fall-out of an event than on the negative. It does not mean denying that you feel sad that, say, a relationship has not worked out, but rather acknowledging that you are now in a position to have a more successful relationship in the future. I am not advocating the kind of optimism that means you blow all your savings on a horse running at a hundred to one; I am talking about being optimistic enough to sow some seeds in the hope that some of them will germinate and grow into flowers.

The Jack Story

The deserts of America are lonely places; miles can go by without any other cars or a single house. In one of these wildernesses a driver heard his tyre blow. He was more annoyed than worried, knowing that he kept a spare tyre and a jack in his car boot. Then he remembered; he got the jack out last week and forgot to put it back. He had no jack. But things could be worse, because he passed a garage about three miles back. As he started walking, he talked to himself: 'There aren't any other garages around here. I'm at the garage man's mercy. He could really rip me off just for lending me a jack. He could charge me what he wanted. He could charge $50. There is nothing I could do about it. Goddamn, he could even charge $150. People are terrible to take advantage of others like that. Hell, what bastards people are.' He continued absentmindedly telling himself this story until he got to the garage. The attendant came out and said in a friendly way, 'How can I help you?' and the traveller said, 'You can take your damned jack and you can stuff it.'[24]

We can be unaware of the tales we regularly tell ourselves and even unaware of their effect on us. We act on fantasies as though they are realities. And when we visualize something it can happen, because – whether or not we are aware of our fantasies – that is what we expect to happen. We have all heard of people who would really like to have a life partner but tell themselves they cannot trust potential mates. Towards the potential partner they act as though he or she is not to be trusted, and keep testing them: *Would they stay with me if I was really nasty all the time?* They do not mean to do this; they do it because of the story they tell themselves about what others are. Self-fulfilling prophecies are just that: they come true.

Much of the story we tell ourselves goes back to the dynamics of our family of origin. We get fixed in a story like our fellow without a jack and his belief that man always takes advantage of his fellow man. Therefore we need to be self-aware. What stories are we telling ourselves about other people? What dynamic do our stories suck us into, and how do they determine the meanings we put on things and how we define them? We all like to think we keep an open mind and can change our opinions in the light of new evidence, but most of us seem to be geared to making up our minds very quickly. Then we process further evidence not with an open mind but with a filter, only acknowledging the evidence that backs up our original impression. It is too easy for us to fall into the trap of believing that being right is more important than being open to what might be.

If we practise detachment from our thoughts we learn to observe them as though we are taking a bird's eye view of our own thinking. When we do this, we might find that our thinking belongs to an older, and different, story to the one we are now living. For instance, we might be someone like Martin.

Martin always needs an enemy. In every story he tells, there is him and a 'baddie' of some sort. If you hear just one of his stories you might think, 'What a good thing Martin is crusading against such wickedness, be it a corrupt mayor, a political cause, non-paying customer or other scoundrel.' But then you begin to see that every tale features Martin, the crusading hero, against a 'baddie'. The plots of his tales are complex and involve the amassing of evidence on Martin's part. It is amassed through a filter, because once Martin has made up his mind about something, he looks for evidence that backs up his position, and no longer sees anything else. Polarized against the 'baddies' are the 'goodies': if you get into Martin's good books you can do no wrong – his judgement of you will always be positive. When you first get to know him, you may not notice anything amiss, but after a while you may recognize the same patterns reccurring. It seems like the dynamic is already set in Martin's head, and the people around him are simply fulfilling the pre-existing roles he has available. Thus he replays the dynamics of his childhood over and over again. We tend to do the same.

This is why it is important to understand our past. Contemplation, psychotherapy or an exercise like the genogram (which I will describe in more detail later on) can help us do this. Our dynamic is also wrapped up in the stories we tell, the tales we hear and our background fantasies. All this contributes to the meanings we make that shape our behaviour.

A dynamic such as Martin's is usually formed by his childhood experience. Perhaps one or both of his parents had the same dynamic and therefore the same filter through which they viewed the world. Or perhaps Martin's experience was of huge injustice; for example, not being believed when he was telling the truth, or being punished when he was innocent. These grievances fester in the unconscious as: 'I was right; they were wrong.' Indeed 'they' were *so* wrong that Martin needs to keep finding 'them' and *proving* them wrong. He needs to feel himself in the right and be seen to be right, over and over again. So he searches out the enemies and wrongdoers he needs to regulate his own emotions and thus feel okay. He needs an enemy to be 'wrong' so he can feel 'right'. If he sticks to his dynamic unquestioningly he will not develop or learn and the ghosts and stories of his past will prevent him having true contact with people in the present. He will compromise all his relationships.

There are many dynamics that are passed down by previous generations or established by childhood adaptations to an environment that the individual no longer inhabits. An example is our attitude to money: we may be striving for money at the expense of our relationships, or believe we have less or more than we actually do. Money is often a metaphor for how secure we feel in our relationships. For example: if we cannot face up to our fear of losing love, we displace that fear by reiterating reasons to be mean with our money.

Then there are our attitudes to place. If we are always moving, never satisfied with this town or that house, this country or that continent, and come up with brilliant reasons as to why we need to move again, the solution is probably to be found in our own psyche, rather than in the geography of a particular place or the ways of its inhabitants.

There are any number of examples I could come up with to illustrate stuck patterns of thinking, reacting and doing, to show how we use reason to prevent us from discovering more about our feelings. We need to look at the repetitions in the stories we tell ourselves about other people – at the *process* of the stories rather than merely their surface content. Then we can begin to experiment with changing the filter through which we look at the world, start to edit the story and thus regain flexibility where we have been getting stuck.

In my personal therapy I uncovered many such stories and was able to trace the origins of some of them. When exploring my patterns for acting in groups, I used an exercise called the genogram. A genogram is an elaborate family tree, which traces not only blood lines, but lines of behaving, relating, character traits and attitudes. I have explained how to create a genogram in the exercise section at the back of this book. Looking at my genogram I saw that both of my parents come from large families. Then there was something I had not noticed before, which became obvious once it was on paper in front of me: both of my parents had a sibling to whom they were apparently less close than to their other siblings. Both of my parents also idolized one of their own parents.

Then I looked at the way I myself behaved in group situations. In psychotherapy training you usually belong to many groups: your main training group, plus different groups for different modules of the training. I noticed that I always idealized one member of each group and felt annoyed by or dismissive of another. It came as a revelation to me that this pattern was repeated in all my groups, and it dawned on me as I worked with my genogram that I had a pattern for behaving in these group situations that might be embedded in the past rather than be a response to the given situation in the present.

Once I discovered this I had more choice about how to act. Rather than letting that behaviour continue automatically, I resolved to observe the impulses I had to admire one person and demonize another. If I found myself demonizing a person I practised focusing on what was positive about them. By doing this I changed my negative filter for a positive one. Sometimes it is necessary to over-steer in the opposite direction for a while, in order to find your true trajectory.

The next group I engaged with was an interview panel for a new job. I had applied for my first job as a therapist, at a centre for recovering drug and alcohol addicts, where I would have to run therapy groups. The interviewer asked me what my group style was. I told them how I had traditionally behaved in group situations and I expected it to cost me the job. However, I did get it. I told them I was surprised, considering I had revealed my habit of favouritizing and demonizing in groups. The supervisor told me that it was because I was *aware* of this impulse that she had faith that I would not act on it, and that is why they considered me a safe group leader. After that trust was shown towards me,[25] I did not act on my old impulse, even though I still felt its pull. I was able to do that because

I had learnt to stop and observe my instincts, rather than unthinkingly going along with them. In this way I changed the story of how I act in groups.

As I have said previously, sometimes a new behaviour feels false or unreal but is merely unfamiliar. In my experience what 'feels' true might not actually be the truth, or good for us; it might merely be familiar. And, conversely, what feels 'false' might not be; it might just be new. I can sometimes still feel a compelling impulse to demonize and idolize members of a group, and if I give into it, it feels temporarily satisfying. It takes willpower and practice to be aware that I feel the impulse; it feels more comfortable to ignore it. But, gradually, resisting those impulses becomes my nature too. I can free myself from an old dynamic. I can let neural pathways laid down in my childhood relationships grow over, and I can forge new paths over uncharted territory, paths that serve me, the people around me, and possibly the world, more advantageously. Although we are always in danger of reverting to old unsatisfactory patterns, especially in times of stress, new behaviour can become automatic too, and loses its 'phoney' feel.

Each of us comes from a mother and a father, or from a sperm bank, and each of us was brought up by our parents or by people standing in for them. Many of us have siblings, uncles, aunts and cousins. All of these people have an impact on who we are, as do their ancestors. Those ancestors, too, had problems and triumphs, and any learning or habits these experiences gave them they tended to pass down. Red hair or skin tone are easily spotted as inherited characteristics, and it's not difficult to spot, for instance, an inherited aesthetic taste. Using the genogram we can see how we form and

GRANDAD

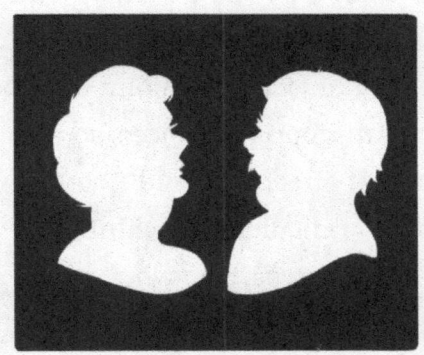

PETER 54

ME

keep (or do not keep) relationships, how we act in groups, how we make decisions and use thought and emotions, and generally find our place in the world. In the genogram these inherited characteristics are as obvious as hair-colour or sense of taste. The point of the exercise is to free you up to make more appropriate choices, so that it is YOU who is making the choices that affect you, and not your great-grandparents. You may feel it is ridiculous to think that your ancestors are influencing you now, but part of who we are derives from previous generations, in ways that can be either productive or unproductive. You can find exact instructions for the genogram exercise at the end of the book.

Through the millennia, stories, songs and rituals have been passed down by the elders to the young of our tribes. Some of the stories and their meanings get lost. I wonder what else is lost with them? In an age of 24/7 news we tend to be all-consumed with the stories of the here and now; the ever unfolding crises and negative things happening in the world. Do our elders still want to tell their stories? Do we still know how to listen if they do? And if we do not, what are we hearing instead?

I am going to finish with a couple of stories that illustrate, first, how change can come about through dialogue and, second, how wisdom is passed from one generation to another.

Die Meistersinger: *The Master Singers*

Die Meistersinger von Nürnburg is an opera by Wagner. It is a story about a singing competition. The Meistersinger ('master singers') is a guild-like institution that runs the competition according to strict, pedantic, unbending rules that provide structure and discipline but stifle creativity and joy. Enter Walther the romantic genius, whose chaos injects brilliance, originality, passion, artistic integrity, erotic feeling and, unfortunately, a riot into the proceedings. Here we have the two elements of life we must steer between: rigidity, represented by the Meistersinger, and chaos, represented by Walther.

The hero of the opera is Hans Sachs, a cobbler, who persuades the Meistersinger that rules are only useful if they are flexible and applied when real need arises. Sachs listens to both sides, appreciates their opposing points of view and engages them in dialogue. He is a learned and thoughtful man who understands the need to steer a course between chaos and rigidity. We see him pondering man's illusions and the madness of human existence and wondering how to apply philosophy to the problem of getting the Meistersinger to appreciate Walther's merits and Walther to see the necessity of some rules to preserve the history and story of their country. Thanks to his thoughtful, reflective and flexible thinking and his wisdom, all ends well. Only one of the Meistersinger, Beckmesser, remains unconvinced and unchanging. Beckmesser is tripped up by his own self-interest. He tries to cheat and ends up isolated and unhappy. Sachs, unlike Beckmesser, understands that there is no shortcut to flexibility; it demands integrity, hard work and close attention. Our job is like Sachs's. We too, have to negotiate that line between rigidity and chaos.

My Wooden Spoon

I sometimes look at a busy street and think: in a hundred years, we will all be dead. On this same street a hundred years ago, perhaps another woman thought the same thing. Perhaps, however, like me, she consoled herself with the thought that love is generative and lives on in the next generation, passed on in the habits of love we inculcate in our pupils, children and friends. I have my late aunt's paintings around me, my late mother's ring on my finger and her words inside me still urging me to tell my daughter to 'be careful' every time she leaves the house. My grandfather's gruff sarcasm lives on in my father and in me, so he is not really dead. When my daughter lays out a sewing pattern, my fondness for needlework lives on in her.

This deeply moving process, that connects human to human in a cascade of memory passing through generations, can be symbolized by particular objects that are passed down along with the knowledge of our ancestors. I am the proud owner of a wooden spoon that is worn into an un-spoon-like stump. In the pre-electric whisk days of the 1960s, my aunt taught me to cream the butter and sugar for a cake mixture; we always used the same spoon. Even then the spoon was worn out. My aunt had, in her turn, used it as a child. I use a whisk now; but the sight of that spoon in the drawer brings tears to my eyes if it catches me unawares on an hormonal day. My aunt will be forgotten eventually; my daughter may not talk about her to her children; but I am sure that my daughter will teach her own children how to make cakes. Along with cake recipes she will pass down the love I received first from my aunt. Oh yes, my aunt will live on, even if her name gets mentioned less and less and her spoon is thrown away.

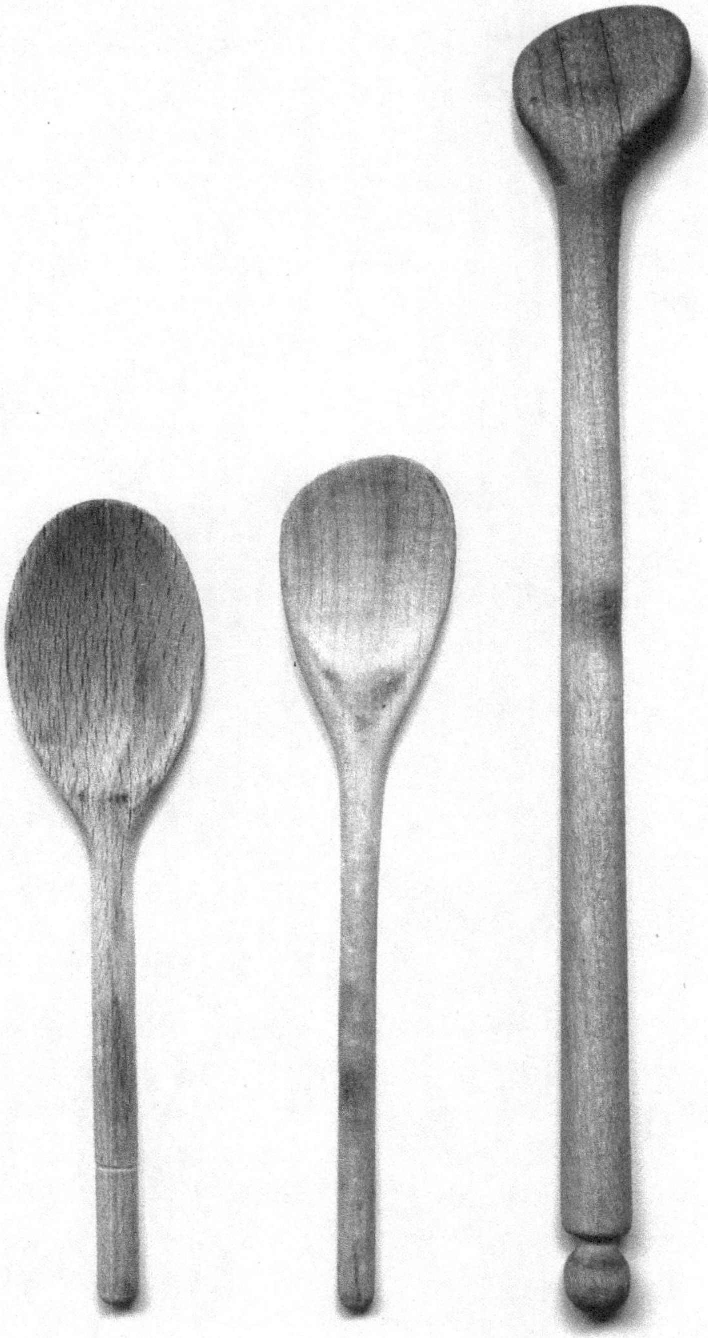

Conclusion

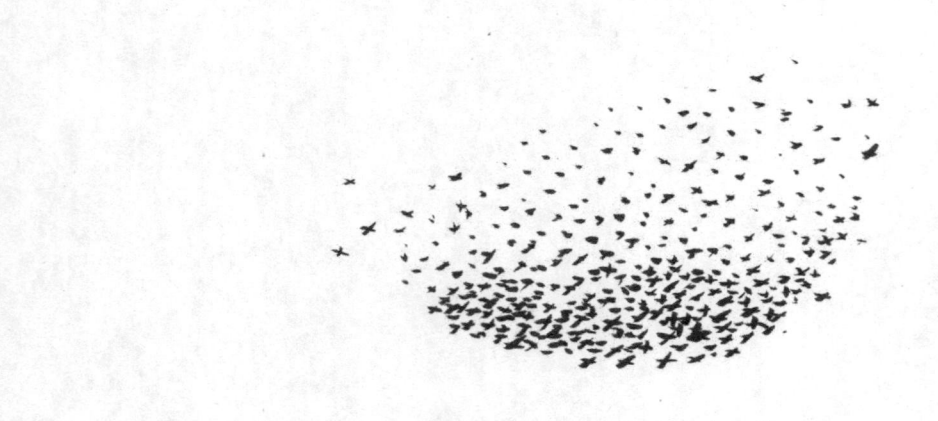

So how do we stay sane? We can develop our faculties of self-observation so that we can have the capacity to observe even our strongest emotions, rather than being defined by them, allowing ourselves to take in the bigger picture. Self-observation helps us to avoid too much self-justification and getting stuck in patterns of behaviour that no longer work for us. We can prioritize nurturing relationships and allow ourselves to be open. We can relate – not as who we *think* we should be, but who we actually *are*, thus giving ourselves the chance to connect and form bonds with others. We can seek out 'good stress' to keep our minds and bodies fit for purpose, and we can be watchful of the stories we hear and the belief systems we live our lives by. We can edit our story at any time, to right ourselves if we veer off course either into chaos or rigidity.

Is it that easy? No, it isn't. One of the things that can give us the illusion of sanity is certainty; yet certainty is a trap. On the other hand, we can swing too far in the opposite direction and become so unsure that we never set off on any path. Extremes appear not to be the best way forward for sanity. I say make a mark, put a foot onto the path, see (and feel and think) how it lands; and then you can make a good guess about where to put the next foot. And if you start to go off in the wrong direction, it is never too late to change course.

I hope reading about how to stay sane has been helpful. To get more out of this book, work through the exercises in the next section.

Exercises

I hope that this book will be useful to you, even if all you do is read it. However, in order to make connections, reading on its own is rarely enough. To really take on board the lessons in this book it is necessary to work experientially. It is one thing to know about something and another to embody it. In order to embody the habits of self-observation it is necessary to practise them; merely knowing about them is not enough. The point of a set of instructions that comes with a model-aeroplane kit is not to supply you with reading material, but to guide you in the practical steps you need to apply in order to build the kit. This exercise chapter is similar to such instructions. The exercises are not simply for reading, they are for doing. Either tackle these exercises on your own, with another person or in a group. Do not tackle too many exercises at once. Personally, one per day would be enough for me: this gives me time to allow insights to come up from the unconscious, and for any self-adjustment to take place.

1. The One-Minute Exercise

For sixty seconds focus all your attention on your breathing. Breathe normally and return your attention to your breath whenever it wanders, without trying to change how you are already breathing. Attempt this without thinking in words.

It takes years of practice before we can maintain this sort of alert, clear attention for even a single minute. This is not an exercise at which you can fail. It is about your experience of the practice. This simple breathing exercise provides a foundation for subsequent exercises, but do not wait until you can achieve it before trying other exercises. Simply return to it often.

When one minute is up, notice how the exercise was for you. How did directing your focus feel? Did you notice a change in mood? How did doing the exercise affect you and how long do its effects last?

2. The Thirty-Minute Exercise[26]

- Commit to doing this exercise and allotting the full thirty minutes to it.
- Get yourself a notebook and something to write with.
- Turn off the phone, computer, radio and television. Resolve not to pick up a book or a newspaper, and choose a time when you will not be disturbed.
- Get yourself a clock or stopwatch and set it for 30 minutes.
- Sit with your back supported. You can put your feet up but do not lie down, as you may go to sleep, which is not the purpose of this exercise.
- Focus your attention on your breathing and empty your mind of other thoughts.
- Thoughts will come into your head but do not stay with any

one thought. Label it and write it on your pad with one or two words, then let it go. When the next thought comes into your mind, do the same thing. If the urge to stop the exercise comes into your mind, treat that like any other thought, jot it down and focus your attention back on your breathing.
- Do this for thirty minutes.

Now look at all the thoughts you have written down, sort them into one of the following categories and then total the thoughts in each category. The numbers at the end of each category are my own results for this exercise:

- Sensory-awareness thoughts: e.g. sounds, sights smells sensations – 4
- Planning thoughts: to-do lists of wants or needs – 3
- Anxiety-provoking thoughts: worries or self-deprecating thoughts – 2
- Playing back of memories – 0
- Fantasies about non-existent situations, relationships or events – 0
- Envious, angry, rebellious, critical thoughts: wanting to stop the exercise or critical thoughts about others – 5
- Take-over: any thoughts you were unable to clear and that took over the exercise? – 0

You can add more categories to suit the types of thoughts you have.

The aim of the exercise is first to see what happens for you; for you to notice how you experience the exercise. You are probably pretty good at noticing the words you use as you talk to yourself, but it is interesting to listen to those thoughts that do not have words.

Secondly, this thirty-minute sample of your thoughts might be an indication of the percentage of your daily thoughts in the various different areas; so, for example, if you spend 80 per cent of your thinking life in fantasy and 20 per cent feeling critical, you can look at that and think: 'I have a choice. I may want to experiment. Perhaps it would be more satisfying to allot more of my thinking time to noticing what I can see or smell or if I focused instead on what I appreciate?' The point of the exercise is to become more self-aware. You cannot change anything unless you know what it is you are changing. The only way you can get this exercise wrong is to not do it, or abandon it early. But even then you can start again.

This is an extract of the summary I made and the conclusions I came to when I had finished the exercise:

> I do not know which category to put my fleeting thought about appreciating marmalade in; maybe it should have gone in memory rather than sensory awareness. Anyway, don't suppose that matters. I notice I've written 'too fat' down; can't remember having that thought, but I'm guessing I was thinking about myself – that definitely goes in 'Anxiety-provoking'. I had quite a lot of resistance to doing the exercise – five protests, I notice on the pad. The other thing I noticed is that all the protests happened in the first ten minutes and that the first half seemed to go slowly; then I surrendered to the exercise and the second half almost went too fast, and I was sorry when it was over. After I had finished resisting

it, it felt as if I was keeping myself company and that was a good feeling. I wonder if that was because I was then open to what popped into my head? I'm not sure what that resistance is about but it felt very familiar. Next time I feel that resistance I will be curious as to what it is about; whether it is a matter of long-term gain or short-term gain. In this instance I feel satisfied that I listened to it but put it on one side. Had I acted on it, it could be seen to be self-sabotaging. I do find it incredible how a simple exercise like this really does feel like I paid myself some positive attention and gained from it. I'm not sure whether the meanings I have extracted are anything more than post-rationalization, but appreciating that can be satisfying too.

This exercise gives us information about ourselves that we may not otherwise have appreciated. When we do the exercise once a week and compare the results, we can monitor changes in our thinking patterns. It also lets us get a feel for which thoughts foster our creativity and curiosity and may lead to growth, and those that, by contrast, lead us down the dead-end of post-rationalization.

3. A Self-Observation Exercise to Do Whilst Working

Try this: When you are next doing chores around the house – cooking, cleaning, washing, etc. – focus with complete awareness on what you are doing, mentally recording each feeling, thought, sensation or memory as it enters your head. For example, 'Now I am washing a cup; I feel the warm water and soapy suds; now I'm putting the cup on the draining board and noticing the sound of one against the other; now I am thinking about the war in Afghanistan; now I am pulling the plug', and so on. You might want to have a shower with complete awareness, or wash the kitchen floor, or eat a meal. This is a simple way to develop self-observation and concentrate on living in the moment.

4. The Focused-Attention Exercise

For this exercise I like to take between forty-five minutes and an hour, but you may want to start with five minutes of focusing, and build up in increments. It may help to have someone read this exercise to you while you are doing it, or you can record yourself reading it aloud, and play it back.

Think of this as a work-out for your brain, so do not go to sleep. Sit on a chair with your back straight, your feet on the ground and your eyes open. First, and without changing it, notice how you are breathing . . . When your mind wanders, and it will, bring it back to your breathing . . . Notice how your abdomen expands as you breathe in . . .

Looking down at the ground in front of you, notice what your eyes alight upon; become aware of the colours, textures and shapes you can see . . . Spend a minute or two looking and noticing without judging what you see . . . Return your attention to your breathing . . . Imagine the shape the air makes inside your body . . . Notice the in-breath . . . Notice the out-breath . . .

Notice all the sounds you hear ... Notice the sounds outside the room ... Notice the sounds in the room ... Spend a couple of minutes alternating your attention between all the different sources of sound you can hear ... Now return your attention to your breathing ... Notice the sensation of your out-breath as the air leaves your nostrils ... Notice the different sensation of the air coming into your nostrils on your in-breath ... Be aware of any taste in your mouth and smells in the room ... on your in-breath, pay attention to smell ... and on your out-breath pay attention to taste ... Where on your tongue is the sensation of taste happening? ... At what point in your cycle of breath is your sense of smell heightened? ...

Come back to your breathing again ... Imagine the clean air travelling through your body to your feet ... Be aware of what the soles of your feet feel like ... What does the skin on your feet feel right now? ... Where is most pressure felt on the feet? ... Then pay attention to what the skin feels on your right hand ... What, if anything, is it touching? ... Now turn your attention to your left hand ... Think about the external temperature your hands can sense ... Return to your breath ... If your eyes are not closed close them now, as you notice how you are breathing ...

Turn your attention to your digestive system ... Move your awareness slowly through your mouth ... oesophagus ... stomach ... intestines ... bowel ... bladder ... rectum ... Come back to your breathing, notice your in-breath ... then your out-breath ... Notice the turn at the top of the breath ... How long do you take after breathing in before the out-breath starts? ... Be aware of that pause ... Be aware of the pause at the bottom of the breath ... Now take your awareness to your heart ... notice your pulse ... stay there for a while, focusing on your heartbeat ... Return to noticing your breathing and pause there for a minute ...

Focus on the chatter in your head; spend a while observing the thoughts you are having ... Come back to your breathing ... Now imagine yourself being able to breathe underwater, like a fish ... Imagine yourself deep in the ocean, looking up to the surface of the water ... That surface is your mood ... Is it stormy? ... Smooth? ... Now you are a bird flying high above the water ... With the power of your thought you can make the water rough or smooth ... Return your attention to your breathing ...

Now turn your inner focus to the person who is closest to you at the moment ... How do you relate to that person? ... How do you feel when you think of them? ... Broaden the net to those you have spoken to today ... Do you feel connected or disconnected to them? ... How do you feel connected or disconnected to your closest family and friends? ... To your community? ... Your country? ... Your world? ...

Come back to your breathing once more, be aware of the rise and fall of your breath. Remember what you have just done; you have explored your five most immediate senses: sight, sound, touch, taste and smell. You have explored inner, physical sensations and you have noticed your thoughts and your feelings. You have visualized your feelings as the surface of the ocean while you have observed them; you have felt your sense of connectedness with others, and now you return to your breathing once more ...

As you notice your breathing, notice yourself noticing your breathing ... Notice that you can focus your attention purposefully to any of these areas ... You are not at the mercy of your thoughts, you can direct them ... You can deliberately notice something ... or you can deliberately or absentmindedly notice your attention wandering ...

Write or draw what it was like for you to do this exercise. What is in the foreground for you now, as you remember doing it?

5. The 1 2 3 4 Breathing Exercise[27]

Sit supported or lie down. Become aware of your breath. As you breathe, give each stage of your breathing a number:

1, Inhale
2, Top of in-breath
3, Exhale
4, Bottom of out-breath

Get used to counting with the breath. If you spend too little time at the top or at the bottom of the breath to apply numbers 2 and 4, slow yourself down until you are counting and breathing easily.

Now, as you count and breathe, bring in the observing part of your mind. Notice the subtle differences of emotion you experience with each stage of the breath. First of all, compare 1 and 3, then compare 2 and 4. Notice which is the most comfortable stage of the breath cycle for you and which is the least comfortable. Spend as much time as you need to do this.

When we have become aware of the nuances of our emotion on each number, we are going to exchange the numbers for a mantra. So you get the whole phrase in, you might need to lengthen the breath; if you are breathing slowly and have plenty of time, do not feel the need to speed up. Replace the numbers with the following phrases:

1, *I take from the world*
2, *I make it my own*
3, *I give back to the world*
4, *I come back to myself*

You can think about whether the phrases correlate with the moments of the breath cycle when you felt most and least comfortable, and whether there is any new information for you there. You can also use these mantras to meditate upon any interaction about which you feel self-righteous or otherwise emotionally charged. For example:

1, *(breathing in) I noticed someone taking my parking space (I take from the world)*
2, *(top of the breath) I imagined they did it on purpose to spite me (I make it my own)*
3, *(breathing out) I shouted at them not to park there (I give back to the world)*
4, *(bottom of breath) I felt self-righteous (I come back to myself)*

Then you could use the mantra to think about what you will do differently afterwards:

1, *(breathing in) I will notice someone taking my parking space (I take from the world)*

2, *(top of the breath) I will not take this personally (I make it my own)*
3, *(breathing out) I tell them I have paid for the space and public parking is around the corner; I make a bigger sign for the space (I give back to the world)*
4, *(bottom of breath) I feel satisfied (I come back to myself)*

A more positive example could be:

1, *(breathing in) I was taught by my aunt to bake (I take from the world)*
2, *(top of the breath) I made up my own recipes (I make it my own)*
3, *(breathing out) I pass my learning on (I give back to the world)*
4, *(bottom of breath) It feels good (I come back to myself)*

When discovering these exercises you may alight on a favourite. The 1234 Breathing Exercise is mine. I do it at least once a week and usually more often. I love how, for me, it mirrors the experience of being alive, of taking in or reaching out and then returning to the self. It also mirrors how we each put our own particular spin ('I make it my own') on what we perceive.

6. The Crowded-Place Exercise (Feeling, Thinking, Acting)

The Crowded Place Exercise helps us discover which 'being zone' is our most comfortable. To use ourselves optimally we need to be operational in three 'being zones': thinking; feeling; and taking action. Normally we are more comfortable in one or two of these zones. The Crowded Place Exercise may help us become aware of which zone we go to first, and remind us to use all three zones in order to maximize our inner resources.

To start with, do this exercise quickly, without rereading each part. You will need something to write with and your notepad (or write the answers on this book). Your answers do not need to be long. You are looking for first impressions here, not deliberations. (I have used the pronoun 'I' throughout the exercise – the 'I' is you and not me!)

i.

- I am imagining I am in a crowded place. I am feeling ....
- In this crowded place, I have my family and friends near me and I feel ....
- The crowd surges forward and somehow I become separated from my group. I feel ....
- I am surrounded by hundreds of people but I am on my own. I feel ....
- The crowd disperses and I am on my own. I feel ....

ii.

- I am in a crowded place. I think ....
- I have my family and friends near me. I think ....
- The crowd surges forward and somehow I become separated from my group. I think ....
- I am surrounded by hundreds of people but I am on my own. I think ....
- The crowd disperses and I am on my own. I think ....

iii.

- I am in a crowded place. What I do next is ....
- I have my family and friends near me. What I do next is ....
- The crowd surges forward and somehow I become separated from my group. What I do next is ....
- I am surrounded by hundreds of people but I am on my own. What I do next is ....
- The crowd disperses and I am on my own. What I do next is ....

Now answer these questions:

- Thinking back over this visualization, did you see yourself as a child, one of the adults, or the person most in charge of the group?
- Do you think it is important that you stick to the role you imagined for yourself?
- How much difference was there between the feeling, thinking or doing answers? (If the answers were the same go back and do it again!)
- Which came easiest to you, the feeling, thinking or doing answers?
- How flexible or rigid are you about what responses you have? Do you see that you have a choice? Or is there no choice in how you respond?
- Do you believe that your thinking influences your feeling and doing. Or does your feeling influence your thinking and doing? Or for you, is it doing that seems to come first followed by either feeling or thinking?
- Which would you say was your most dominant zone of being: feeling, thinking or doing? And your least practised zone of being?
- If you think about some of the other choices that affect how you act, think or feel, and imagine yourself doing them, how does that feel?
- If you think of the days ahead, what choices do you have in how you think, feel and act? Patterns of behaving are habitual, but what is it like just to play in imagination about changing some of those patterns?

- What would the pattern look like with one or two very minor changes?
- What would major changes look like?
- How many of your answers reflected pessimism?
- How many of your answers reflected optimism?

iv.
- Feel your response to doing this exercise.
- Think about your response to doing this exercise.
- *Did* you do this exercise? Do you often miss out the 'doing' in your life? Is it a pattern?

This exercise may help us to become aware of which 'being zone' we go to first and remind us to use all three zones – thinking, feeling and taking action – in order to maximize our inner resources.

I also use this exercise when working with couples or groups, to discover which zone each person is most comfortable in. When this is understood and communicated, people can better understand each other and improve their relationships. For example, I asked one couple I was working with to describe to me a typical argument between them. They told me they were expected at a friend's house for the weekend. Their host had said, 'Start out after breakfast and I'll see you when I see you.' The man assumed this meant everyone in the car by half past eight, ready to hit the road. The woman had assumed it meant she could give the kids some cereal in front of their cartoons while she leisurely packed, listening to her favourite Saturday-morning radio show. By nine o'clock, seeing the rest of the family still in their pyjamas, he started to raise his voice and she responded in kind.

The man was a 'do-er' and the woman was a 'feel-er', but they did not understand this, and found each other's approach to this everyday situation incomprehensible. Doing the Crowded Place Exercise with each other, and learning that they each had a particular 'being zone' that was more developed than the other zones, helped them better understand each other and predict each other's responses to situations. This allowed them to be more specific in what they each needed and to come to a compromise – not because one of them was right and the other wrong, but because they had come to respect that they were different and that each needed to consider the other accordingly.

7. The Genogram Exercise

This exercise can take anything from a couple of hours to a week, depending on how much time you give it. It is best not to rush it, so attempt it when you have the time to do it justice. The genogram is probably one of the most comprehensive tools to aid self-awareness that exists, giving you nearly as much insight into yourself as you might get from a good therapist. But it comes with a warning. Look after yourself while you do it. Listen to your instinct. If you feel overwhelmed by the information you are uncovering, take that feeling seriously and take a break or stop. You can always come back to it later, or when you have more support.

i.
In the centre of a massive piece of paper draw a horizontal line. At each end of it put a very short vertical line – to a small square for your father on one end and, on the other end, to a circle for your mother.

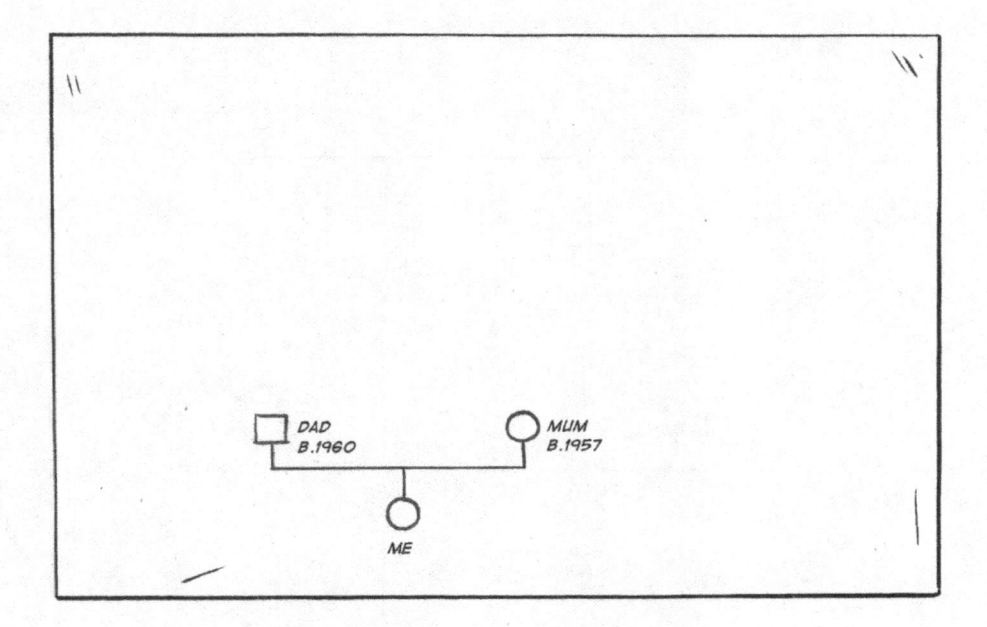

[Diagram: a rectangular frame containing a family tree with a square labeled "DAD B.1960" connected by a horizontal line to a circle labeled "MUM B.1957", with a vertical line descending to a circle labeled "ME"]

If you were brought up by a gay couple, that would be two circles for two women or two squares for two men. Put their names next to their symbol and their birth date. If either one of them has died put an X through the circle or square and put in their date of death. If there has been a divorce or a separation mark the date of that with a double dash through the horizontal (marriage) line.

ii.

Next, put yourself and your siblings on the map, squares for males, circles for females. Put a star in your own circle or square, because you are starring in this exercise. Put in any miscarriages as a little dot.

iii.

Now put in your grandparents. Put in your aunts and uncles, in the right birth order. I'm not saying this is an easy thing to do, but keep

276 How to Stay Sane

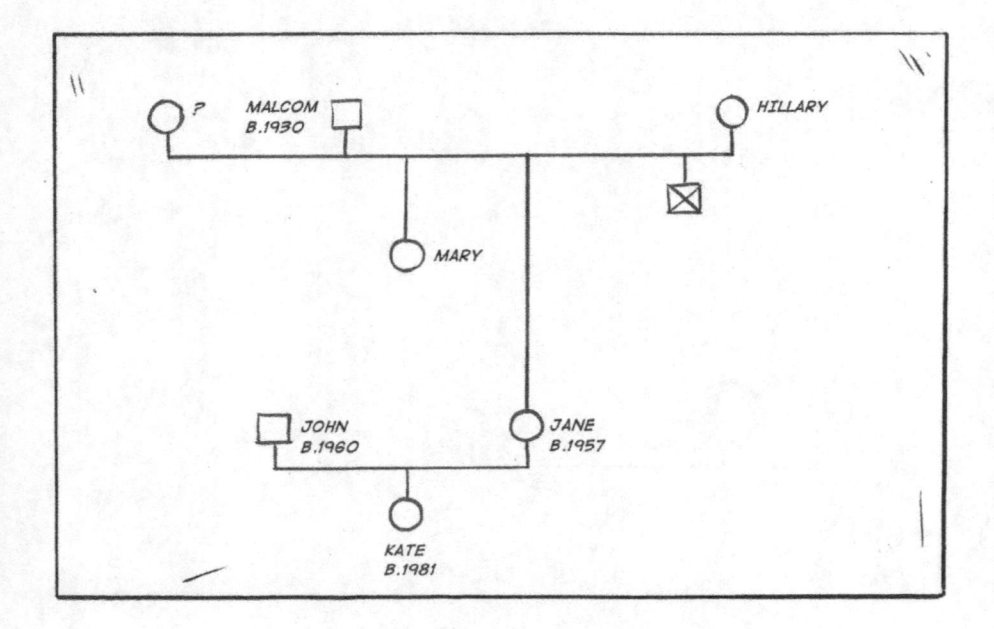

[Genogram diagram showing: Malcom (b.1930) with "?" partner and Hillary; Mary as child of Malcom; a deceased child of Malcom and Hillary; John (b.1960) married to Jane (b.1957); Kate (b.1981) as their child.]

at it. It's at this stage I usually start again, on an even bigger piece of paper. Now you'll have a map of your closest relatives, parents, siblings, grandparents, aunts and uncles.[28] Now add your relatives by marriage and any additional blood relatives – your children, your nephews, cousins, nieces; include them all. Pick five adjectives to describe each person – get other members of your family to help you, but avoid sentimental nostalgia and be realistic.

iv.
If an individual has had more than one marriage or live-in partnership, show this by extending the marriage lines. Put in any non-relatives who lived with your family, such as a lodger or anyone who was especially important to you or your family – maybe with a line of a different colour.

Exercises 277

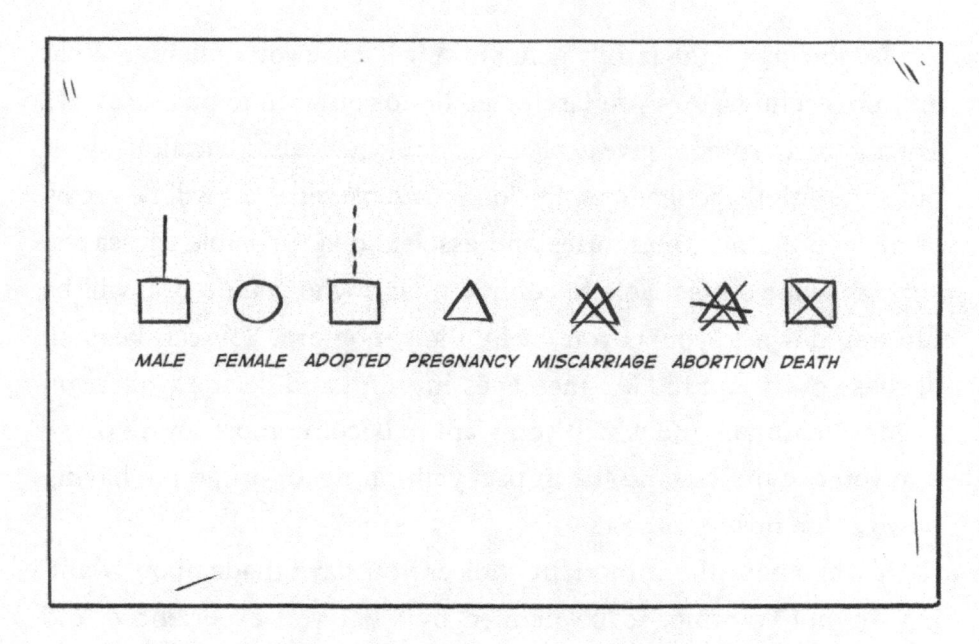

[Symbols diagram: MALE (square), FEMALE (circle), ADOPTED (square with dashed line), PREGNANCY (triangle), MISCARRIAGE (X'd shape), ABORTION (X'd shape with cross), DEATH (square with X)]

Here are all the symbols you need on the maps. As you can see, you use different lines between two people to show if a relationship was close or conflicted, violent, loving, and so on.

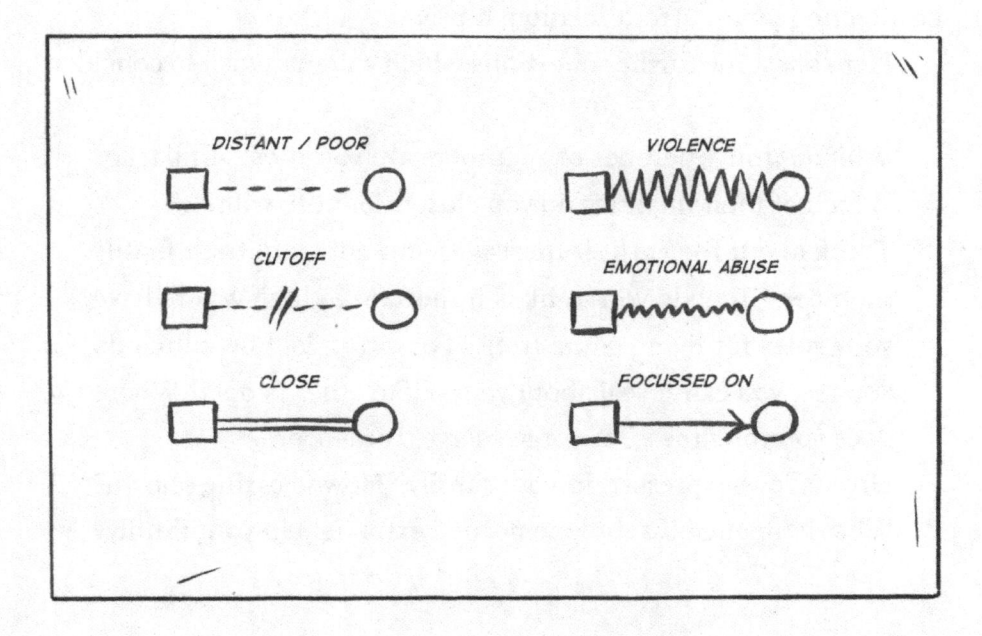

[Relationship symbols diagram:
DISTANT / POOR — dashed line
VIOLENCE — zigzag line
CUTOFF — dashed line with //
EMOTIONAL ABUSE — wavy line
CLOSE — double line
FOCUSSED ON — arrow]

As you create the family genogram, what are you noticing? What are your feelings? Are you fascinated or do you want to push it away? Try not to interpret or give explanations for the feelings straight away, but stay with those feelings. By doing this exercise you will be recovering impressions, memories and associations. Invisible messages, such as who you feel able to confide in and who you do not, will be filtering down to you as you create the genogram. You can keep all of these overt and hidden messages in mind and decide which you need to maintain and which you want to become more aware of, so that you can understand the impact your family or origin are having on your life now.

Think about the important choices you have made about wanting, or not wanting, to be defined by what you experienced and noticed in your family. Make a list of these things. Have these choices changed since you first made them? Which ones still operate in your life? Looking at these past relationships, can you trace how they may be affecting your current relationships?

Here are some further questions which you may wish to consider:

- Which family member or members are you most similar to? Which of their qualities do you closely identify with?
- Think about the earliest messages you got from each family member. What do you think is important in life? Where have your rules for living come from? For example, how much do you feel you can reveal about yourself to other people? Where does your openness, or your reserve, come from?
- How is love expressed in your family? How is caring shown? What happened if someone needed extra help in your family?

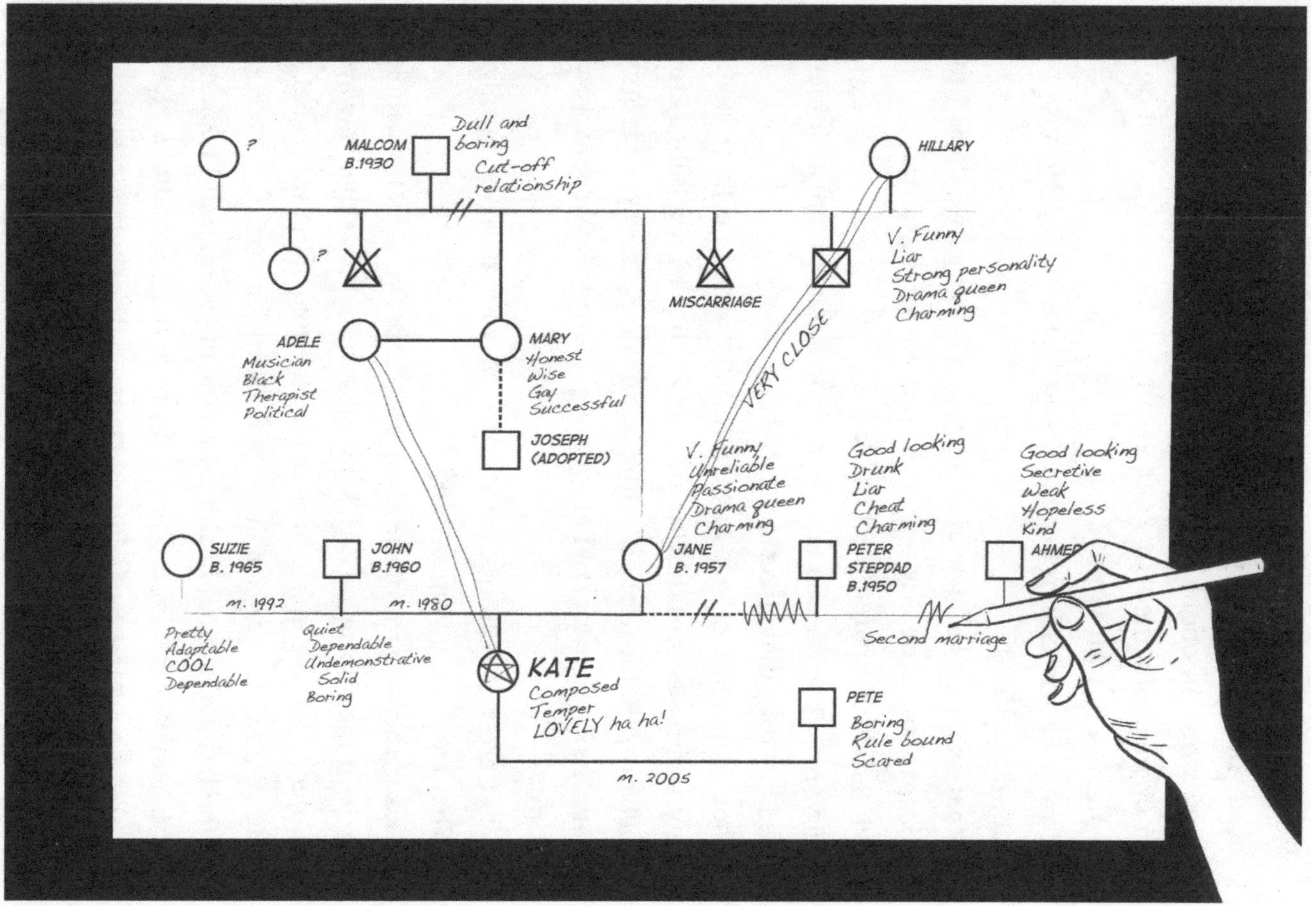
?
MALCOM
B.1930
Dull and
boring
Cut-off
relationship
HILLARY
?
MISCARRIAGE
V. Funny
Liar
Strong personality
Drama queen
Charming
ADELE
Musician
Black
Therapist
Political
MARY
Honest
Wise
Gay
Successful
JOSEPH
(ADOPTED)
VERY CLOSE
V. Funny
Unreliable
Passionate
Drama queen
Charming
Good looking
Drunk
Liar
Cheat
Charming
Good looking
Secretive
Weak
Hopeless
Kind
SUZIE
B. 1965
JOHN
B.1960
JANE
B. 1957
PETER
STEPDAD
B.1950
m. 1992
m. 1980
Second marriage
Pretty
Adaptable
COOL
Dependable
Quiet
Dependable
Undemonstrative
Solid
Boring
KATE
Composed
Temper
LOVELY ha ha!
PETE
Boring
Rule bound
Scared
m. 2005

Who did they go to, and how did they get support? When you need support how do you get it?
- How were emotions expressed in your family? How were emotions contained in your family? How were emotions repressed in your family?
- How were the children treated and brought up? How were they disciplined?
- What is your fantasy of a happy family? How does this compare to the reality represented in the genogram?
- What did your parents get right?
- How have the various family members related to each other, and how has that affected your life?
- Look for family crises. Is there a pattern? Have there been any complete breakdowns of contact between siblings, for instance? Bankruptcies? Other disasters? Can you identify patterns of blaming? What are the patterns for chaos in your family?
- What are the patterns for divorce in your parents' family? What are they in your family?
- Look at the patterns of the relationships between all the people on your map. Who got on? Who was estranged? Is there always someone who seems to have to play the role of the scapegoat – the outcast? Is there a culture of favouritism, too?
- Who has had mental-health problems in your family? Looking at the mental-health problems through the generations, does it seem to come from family traits or from outside events? What evidence is there of the effect of traumatic experiences being passed down generations?

- Look at your own relationship between you and your mother. Look at her relationship with her own mother. Do the same for your father and his father. Look at their relationships with both their parents.
- What is the pattern of the relationship to authority in your family? What were your grandparents' individual relationships with authority like? Your parents? Yours? How have their relationships with authority impacted upon yours? Repeat this question with regard to the opposite sex, ethnic minorities, poor people, rich people, foreigners, etc.
- How did the patterns you have noticed help to shape your character, your identity?
- What are the beliefs about the 'right way' of doing things in your family? What is the right way to make small talk or embark on a romantic relationship, for instance? What are the shared values, spoken and unspoken?
- Do you feel in debit or credit, as far as affection and attention go? Do you feel understood by or unknown to your family of origin?
- How were the expectations you have of relationships formed?
- Are there any jobs or occupations that each generation seems to take up? What feelings do you have about the passing on of hobbies or professions?
- How do the people on the genogram talk about the other people on the genogram? Have you noticed that before? How has it influenced how *you* talk about other people?
- What was it like to be with your siblings when your parents were not present? Who played what role? Were you

dismissed or valued? Who held the limelight? Who disappeared into the shadows? How has being a member of all these different-size groups affected you today? Do you feel there is safety in numbers? Or do you feel cowed by large groups? Are you fine being with one other person while feeling threatened in a three? If it is hard for you to be in a group today, can you trace where this came from by looking at your family genogram?

- What are the stories that the older generation frequently told the younger generation? Are you passing them on in your turn? Are there similar rhythms to the stories you tell each other? Do you tell no stories at all?
- How did your parents use television? Has this been passed down? Think about how food has been eaten in your family. Sitting around a table as a group? In front of the television? Or are family meals never taken?
- What has been your ancestors' attitude towards religion? How has this affected you?
- How open or how secretive has your family been? With each other? With people beyond the family? What is your own attitude towards secrets?
- What is the emotional legacy you have inherited? Which ways of believing, behaving, thinking and feeling have you inherited from your ancestors?
- What has been your conditioning as to the right and wrong ways of doing things?
- Was thinking more highly regarded than feeling or doing in your family? Or was being able to emote or to act given more approval? What is the legacy of this for you?

- What stands out as the most important (positive and negative) things you have learnt from being in your family?
- What are the male and female attitudes to work in your family? To money? To sex?
- What part does immigration or emigration play in your family? Or staying put? How does this affect you today?
- How are you tackling this exercise? How do you imagine your ancestors' attitude towards it would have been?

These questions are not exhaustive. If other questions and lines of enquiry have come up for you, pursue them. These are just examples of questions you can answer more fully with the help of your genogram. Draw and write on it. You may want to create several with different themes.

From the genogram you may be able to remember stories and family legends that are not toxic, but that nurture and nourish. Every family is a mixed bag and it's important not to throw away the good as we pick out the less helpful myths we have overtly and covertly been told.

I compare this exercise to clearing out a cupboard, one I may not have looked into for a long time. Each object may have an emotional charge, but I need the space for new things; so, rather than keep everything or chucking away the lot, I need to be with each object, decide how I feel about it and either keep it or let it go.

This is a small sample of the exercises you can do to develop and maintain self-awareness. Some people might do them with a therapist or in a therapy group, but you can also do them on your own or with friends. Doing these exercises, like the job of staying sane, is an endeavour that is never finished. I have done the genogram many times and always find something new. I practise the 1234 Breathing Exercise and the Grounding Exercise as part of my daily routine. I go through phases of keeping a diary and I like to keep the expansion of my comfort zone in mind. I would not claim I feel completely sane at all times but I feel this practice helps me in my efforts to achieve this.

Notes

Introduction

1. I first read of this idea in Dan Siegel's book *Mindsight*.
2. Adapted from an idea by Louis Cozolino's *The Neuroscience of Psychotherapy*, (Norton, 2012) p.26

1. Self-Observation

3. This exercise is an adaptation from a similar exercise in Janette Rainwater's book *You're in Charge: A Guide to Becoming Your Own Therapist*, (De Vorss & Company, 2000).
4. There is further information about these experiments here: http://nobelprize.org/educational/medicine/split-brain/background.html.
5. This idea is expanded upon in Alice Miller's book *The Untouched Key: Tracing Childhood Trauma in Creativity and Destructiveness* (Virago, 1990).
6. Simon Baron-Cohen explained the possible behavioural consequences of lack of empathy in his book *Zero Degrees of Empathy: a New Theory of Human Cruelty* (Allen Lane, 2011).

7   T-cells are a particularly important part of our immune systems and they can be measured to assess our health and ability to fight diseases.
8   http://www.huffingtonpost.com/ocean-robbins/having-gratitude-_b_1073105.html?ref=fb&src=sp&comm_ref=false
9   Julia Cameron, in her book *The Artist's Way* (Pan Books, 2011), refers to this method as 'Morning Pages'.
10 http://lapleineconscience.com/wp-content/uploads/2011/11/Holzel-etal-PPS-2011.pdf

2. Relating to Others

11 Neuroplasticity is the brain and nervous system's capacity to change structurally and functionally as a result of input from the environment. Plasticity occurs by forming new neural pathways which allow new ways of thinking, reacting, feeling and relating to become familiar as the new pathways become established.
12 Carl Rogers founded a school of humanistic counselling based on empathy rather than interpretation.
13 Spoken by a trauma consultant in the opening credits of the Channel 4 series, *24 Hours in A&E*.
14 I got this from Kate Fox's book, *Watching the English* (Hodder, 2005).
15 Kate Fox, *Watching the English*.

3. Stress

16 For more on the power of vulnerability, see this 'Ted Talk' by Brene Brown http://www.ted.com/talks/brene_brown_on_vulnerability.html.
17 This idea is from Robert M. Pirsig's *Zen and the Art of Motorcycle Maintenance* (Vintage, 1999).
18 To learn more about the different learning styles try Googling Howard Gardner; e.g: http://www.infed.org/thinkers/gardner.htm.

4. What's the Story?

19 I first read about co-constructed narratives in Louis Cozolino's *The Neuroscience of Psychotherapy*.
20 http://en.wikipedia.org/wiki/Cultivation_theory.
21 Maruta, Colligan, Malinchor & Offord, 2002; Peterson, Seligman & Vaillant, 1988. Quoted in *The Healthy Aging Brain*, Cozolino (Norton, 2008).
22 Cozolino, *The Healthy Aging Brain*.
23 I made that one up but I believe it.
24 I got this tale from *You're in Charge: A Guide to Becoming Your Own Therapist* by Janette Rainwater.
25 Someone else's faith in you when you have doubts in your ability can carry you through to success, if you allow their optimism to override your pessimism.

5. Exercises

26 This exercise is slightly adapted from one in *You're in Charge: A Guide to Becoming Your Own Therapist* by Janette Rainwater.

27 This exercise was inspired by a workshop I attended at a UKAPI conference in 2003 run by Jochen Lude.

28 If you Google 'genogram' you will be able to find software to help you make the genogram. I have not used it myself but perhaps it is useful.

Homework

A large number of books, articles and conversations contributed towards the ideas in this book. The following were particularly useful and are highly recommended not only for their inspiration and the information they contain but as good reads in themselves.

SIMON BARON-COHEN, *Zero Degrees of Empathy*
Presenting a new way of understanding what it is that leads individuals to treat others inhumanely, this book challenges us to reconsider the concept of evil.

LOUIS COZOLINO, *The Healthy Aging Brain: Sustaining Attachment, Attaining Wisdom*; *The Neuroscience of Human Relationships: Attachment and the Developing Social Brain*; *The Neuroscience of Psychotherapy: Healing the Social Brain*
Louis Cozolino is a master at synthesizing neuroscientific information to make it accessible to non-scientists. He illustrates the deep connection between our neurobiology and our social lives as well as demonstrating the practical applications of his knowledge.

NORMAN DOIDGE, *The Brain that Changes Itself*
An explanation of neuroplasticity and how our brains can repair themselves through the power of focusing and exercises.

MARIA GILBERT AND VANJA ORLANS, *Integrative Therapy*
Explains, in depth, the workings of psychotherapy: its concepts, techniques, strategies and processes.

ALICE MILLER, *The Untouched Key: Tracing Childhood Trauma in Creativity and Destructiveness*
I regret that this book is currently out of print, but if you can get hold of a copy it will explain how childhood trauma can lead to either creativity or destructiveness, and the factors that make the difference.

PHILIPPA PERRY, *Couch Fiction*
This introduction to psychotherapy shows, in graphic-novel format, how therapy works and what to expect from it.

JANETTE RAINWATER, *You're in Charge: A Guide to Becoming Your Own Therapist*
This practical self-help book offers ideas and exercises that enable the reader to act as their own therapist.

DANIEL SIEGEL, *Mindsight*
Contemplative practice can be used for sustaining good mental health and to alleviate a range of psychological and interpersonal problems. This book explains how, and offers case studies.

DAVID SNOWDON, *Aging with Grace*
This book shows us that old age does not have to mean an inevitable slide into illness and disability; rather, it can be a time of promise and productivity, of intellectual vigour and freedom from disease.

Acknowledgements

I'd like to thank Alain de Botton for his faith in me that I could write a self-help book and for continuing that faith when I was short of it myself. I am grateful to various readers for their encouragement and feedback: Julianne Appel-Opper, Dorothy Charles, Lynn Keane, Nicola Blunden, Daisy Goodwin, Stuart Paterson, Galit Ferguson, Jane Phillimore and Morgwn Rimel.

I'd like to thank the Pan Macmillan team, Liz Gough, Tania Adams and Will Atkins for their editing skills. Thank you to Marcia Mihotich for her illustrations and for being a pleasure to work with. I am grateful to Gillian Holding for a useful anecdote. I am very much indebted to Stella Tillyard for all her reading of various stages of the manuscript and her belief, encouragement, friendship and practical help. Any errors in this work are all mine. I am deeply grateful to my loving husband Grayson and daughter Flo who help to keep me sane, every day.

How to Change the World
John-Paul Flintoff

By the same author:

Comp: A Survivor's Tale

Sew Your Own: Man Finds Happiness and Meaning of Life – Making Clothes

Contents

I. Introduction 297

II. How to Start to Make a Change
   1. Overcoming Defeatism 303
   2. What Drives Us? 315
   3. Some Thoughts on Strategy 331
   4. Bearing Witness 347
   5. What You Will Need 353
   6. Taking a First Step 359

III. What Needs Changing, and How
   1. Add Beauty – and Fun 371
   2. How Does Money Fit In? 377
   3. Make It Appealing 387
   4. Love Helps 397
   5. Aim for a Peace Prize 403

IV. Conclusion 417

Homework 425
Appendix: 198 Ways to Act 431

'Imperfection is an end. Perfection is only an aim'
– Ivor Cutler

I. Introduction

If you had the chance, would you change the world? Of course you would. There are plenty of things that you would change right now, if you were given a magic wand.

After all, the world is desperately in need of improvement. So much so that sometimes we lie awake at night, turning over for hours on end as we worry about it. During the day, we huff and curse at the many smaller things that seem wrong. And in sunnier moments we allow ourselves to dream, conjuring parallel worlds that seem entirely delightful.

But whatever our disposition, we often conclude that to change the world would be hard work, if not impossible. And so we don't even try.

That's a shame, because actively creating change brings benefits for ourselves as individuals, too: we discover deeper reserves of empathy and opportunities to be creative, and we can cultivate a habit of fearlessness. Better still, it turns out that changing the world produces a deep, lasting sense of satisfaction – not only when we've 'finished', as if that were possible, but at each step along the way.

If you have read even this far, you are already interested in changing the world. You may also be confident that you can do something. But not everybody will share that confidence. In which case, it's as well to remember that the ideas set down in this book are validated by ancient wisdom and the latest in scientific research. And they're not merely theoretical, but grounded in historical fact: they've been shown to work. By the time you have finished reading, you should be better equipped to make change, and also more determined to do so.

To back up the analysis, the book is full of anecdotes, from across history and around the world. Some of these stories are of great historical significance, but I have also included stories from my own life, or from the lives of people I know, precisely in order to show that changing the world is not only the business of 'great souls' like Gandhi, Mother Teresa or Nelson Mandela.

I make no apology for using these personal stories. On the contrary, it would be shameful to argue that everybody is capable of making change if I didn't mention some of my own experiences. They are not intended to seem outstanding: they just happen to be mine. Feminist theory teaches that 'the personal is the political', and if that's the case then the evidence to prove it will almost by definition appear rather unremarkable. But it's evidence all the same, and shows that the small, everyday actions of 'ordinary' individuals have the potential to be world-changing.

The point of this book is not only to offer a few intellectual propositions for you to absorb. We learn best by doing, and a book like this is useful only if you put it into practice. As you are reading, think how it might apply to your own situation.

And then try it.

II. How to Start to Make a Change

1. Overcoming Defeatism

How can I, one individual in a world of billions, hope to change anything? There are many reasons why this kind of defeatist question comes so easily to us. They include the way we have been brought up, a lifetime of putting up with things that frustrate or dismay us, and painful memories of failed attempts to Do Something.

But the fact remains that we are all making a difference all the time. The real problem is that if we're only affecting things unconsciously then we are probably not producing the effect we would wish for.

Some people may find it hard to believe they are making a difference all the time. In which case, it may help to abandon the global perspective for a moment and zoom in to our daily human interactions – in which we spend every moment either deciding what must happen next or going along with somebody else's ideas. Either way, our actions are all purposeful, and all produce effects. Our day-to-day lives are hardly the stuff of history, you might argue. Certainly not compared with Julius Caesar invading Britain, Genghis Khan sacking Baghdad and Christopher Columbus discovering America. That's how many people understand history. 'The history of the world is but the biography of great men,' wrote Thomas Carlyle. But the 'great man' theory of history has been on its way out for years. Nowadays, we recognize that those men couldn't have done what they did on their own. And we identify historical significance in hitherto overlooked episodes.

The Russian novelist Leo Tolstoy was one of the first to observe that history should more accurately be considered to consist of the combined effect of the many small things that ordinary individuals do every day: 'An infinitely large number of infinitesimally small actions'.

As Tolstoy saw it, we are making history from the moment we get up in the morning till we go to bed at night. And it's not only the things we *do* that make history, it's also the things we don't do. That's obvious when you think about, say, voting in an election or not. But taken to its logical conclusion it also goes to show that we are making a difference even *after* going to bed: because we are sleeping instead of, say, working all night on some earthshaking political manifesto, or patrolling the streets to feed the homeless.

And that's fine, by the way: we all need to sleep. But Tolstoy's insight requires us to recognize that we are *all* responsible for the way things are. 'We are each absolutely essential, each totally irreplaceable,' says the Native American activist Leonard Peltier. 'Each of us is the swing vote in the bitter election battle now being waged between our best and our worst possibilities.'

And yet the old idea ingrained in us throughout school, that history is about the actions of dominant individuals, is hard to shake off. Indeed, it seems that, even in democracies, it is positively encouraged.

On the twentieth anniversary of the Berlin Wall coming down, 'world leaders' flew in to Germany to deliver speeches to the listening masses.

It was striking that they came to take credit for this particular historical event, because world leaders had had very little to do with the Wall's collapse. In reality, the barrier between East and West Berlin was pulled down because many ordinary Berliners did something very small. Having witnessed 'people power' effecting significant change in several neighbouring countries, and following massive protests elsewhere in East Germany, they merely turned up at the border to see what was going on. Soldiers at the control post, overwhelmed and likewise conscious of what had recently happened in neighbouring countries, opened the way for them to cross freely from one side of the city to the other. Soon after, the wall having ceased to be an effective barrier, it was pulled down. The fact that 'world leaders' took the credit does not diminish the achievement, but does suggest that, when changing the world, we can't necessarily expect recognition for it.

When we talk about the ways the world frustrates us, we often reach for terms like 'the system' or 'the status quo', and, shrugging, complain that we are powerless. We might do this if a great wall were built through the middle of our city, preventing us from seeing friends and relatives, but also in the face of much lesser hardships. Let's imagine for a moment that we want to hold a street party, but find ourselves obstructed by petty civic regulations that were drawn up for entirely other purposes: we give up. With terms as abstract as 'the system' and 'the status quo', it can be hard to see our own complicity in the problem. The truth is that we have a choice. We could try to change the regulations that obstruct us, or even disregard them. The choice is entirely ours.

The Berlin Wall: when enough people came, the soldiers had to let them through.

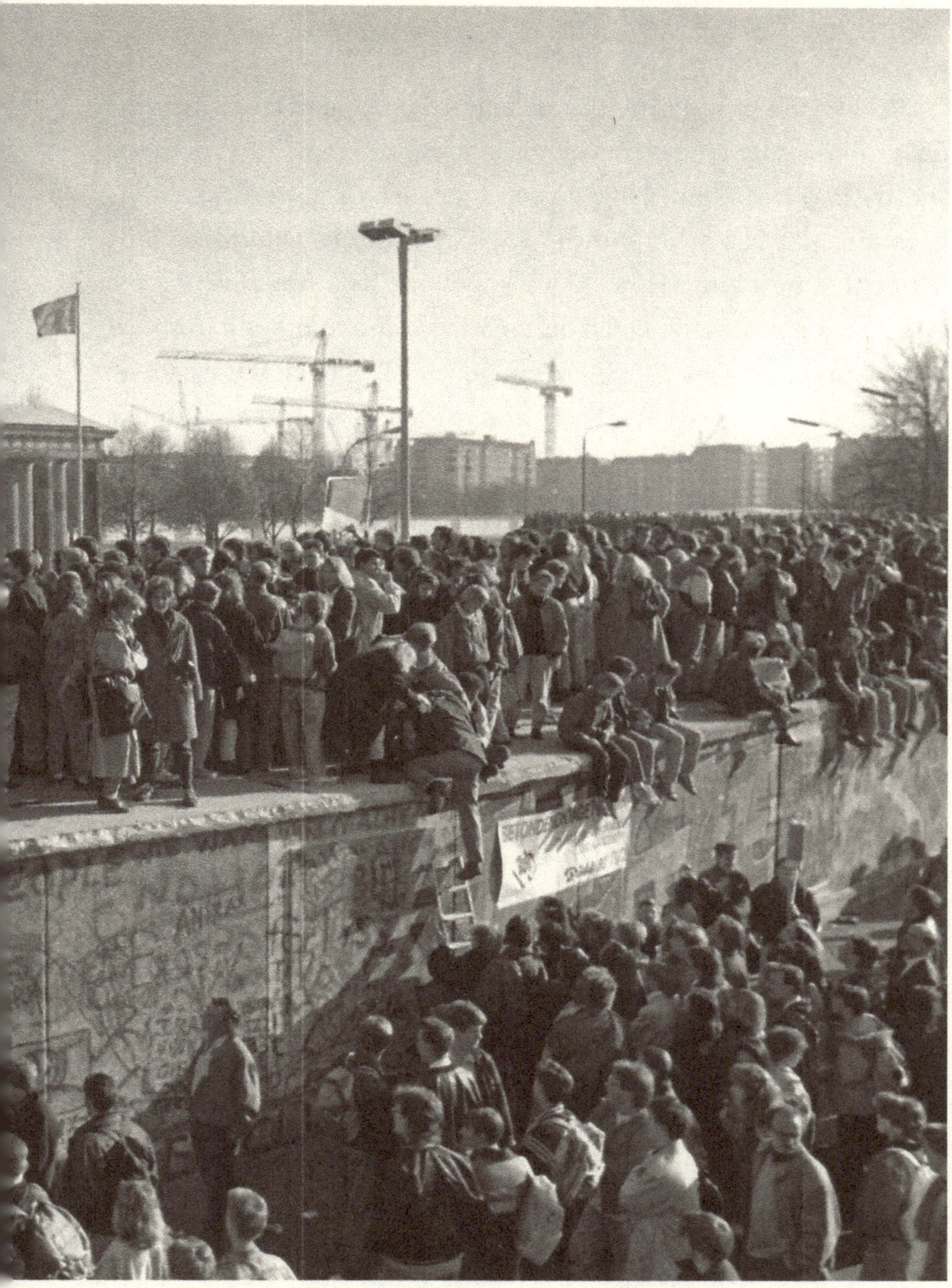

To put this into terms that a child could understand: imagine for a moment that the status quo is a powerful king. Shut your eyes and try to picture him. How do you know he's a powerful king? Is it because he has a big crown? A golden throne? No, those only tell us that he's king. How do we know that he's *powerful*? It's the other people nearby, lying flat on their faces and trembling. It's *their* behaviour that makes the king seem powerful, not his. If they got up off their faces, turned their backs and started to tell jokes, or smoke cigarettes, or have a snooze, the same imaginary king, with the same big crown and golden throne, would no longer seem very powerful at all. Now imagine the powerful king is an actor on stage, and that those prostrate before him are also actors. An actor lying flat on his face before a seemingly powerful king knows that there is an alternative: at any moment, he could get up and do something else, with tremendous effect. In real life we also have the ability to step outside of our normal role and do something else, but we often forget it – if we ever knew.

This is partly because conventional wisdom, and the kind of kings-and-queens-and-presidents history taught to children from a young age, hold that power is vested at the top. Like the Wizard of Oz, parents and teachers encourage children to believe that they, and other 'authority' figures, are all-powerful. As we grow into adults, we are encouraged to believe that employers and governments are all-powerful too. And for as long as we believe it, they truly are.

It may seem bizarre to dress up this everyday business as turning our backs on a powerful king, but many people around the world do indeed feel powerless in the face of bullies – whether they are rulers or employers or indeed friends or family – and it can be liberating to remember that, whatever the consequences, obedience is entirely our own choice.

Tolstoy was baffled that people did not recognize this. He couldn't understand why ordinary Russian peasants, having joined the Tsar's army, were prepared to kill other Russian peasants, perhaps even their fathers and brothers – just because the Tsar told them to. Troubled by this and other questions of social justice, Tolstoy gave up the fashionable life and retired to his farm. While he was there, he was contacted by a young, politically active Indian man then living in South Africa. Tolstoy wrote back, and subsequently published his 'A Letter to A Hindu'.

Describing the subjugation of India by the British East India Company, Tolstoy wrote: 'A commercial company enslaved a nation comprising two hundred millions. Tell this to a man free from superstition and he will fail to grasp what these words mean. What does it mean that thirty thousand people, not athletes, but rather weak and ordinary people, have enslaved two hundred millions of vigorous, clever, capable, freedom-loving people? Do not the figures make it clear that . . . the Indians have enslaved themselves?'

The young Hindu Tolstoy wrote to was Mohandas K. Gandhi, who had a privileged background like him. But Gandhi had felt for himself the humiliating effect of injustice when he was thrown off a train in South Africa for having dark skin. From that moment on, he devoted himself to fighting oppression. Moving back to his native India, then under the control of Great Britain, he started a non-violent campaign for freedom.

Gandhi emphasized the importance of a change of will as a prerequisite for a change in patterns of obedience and cooperation. There was a need for (1) a psychological change away from passive submission to self-respect and courage, (2) recognition by the subject that his assistance makes the regime possible and (3) the building of a determination to withdraw cooperation and obedience. Gandhi felt that these changes could be consciously influenced, and deliberately set out to bring them about:

> My speeches are intended to create 'disaffection' as such, that people might consider it a shame to assist or cooperate with a government that has forfeited all title to respect or support.
>
> The moment the slave resolves that he will no longer be a slave, his fetters fall. He frees himself and shows the way to others. Freedom and slavery are mental states. Therefore the first thing to say to yourself: 'I shall no longer accept the role of a slave. I shall not obey orders as such but shall disobey them when they are in conflict with my conscience.'

Naturally, the British were outraged. Still today, some people find it hard to accept the legitimacy of civil disobedience. The law must be respected, they might say. But to take that position is to argue that, once Hitler's regime came to power, it was the duty of all Germans to obey it completely. Few today believe that. On the contrary, most believe that under certain conditions, disobedience and defiance are absolutely justified.

The daily reality is that obedience is never universally practised by the whole population. Many people sometimes disobey the law, or break lesser regulations, and some people do so frequently. Some do it for selfish reasons and some do it for nobler ones. Dramatic instances of mass disobedience are only more visible evidences of this general and everyday truth.

If you have picked up this book because you already have an idea for changing the world, involving, say, the manufacture of a cheap and comfortable shoe, you may be a little alarmed by the turn things have taken: Gandhi's talk of mental slavery, and my own reference to Hitler. What has this to do with you? Well, it's true that we do not need to believe we are slaves, or live in a dictatorship, in order to take part in changing the world. We need only to believe that something is seriously wrong (the cost, and discomfort, of shoes currently available?) and to resolve that we are not willing to put up with it any longer.

All the same, I mention Nazi Germany for a purpose. I want to argue that even if you think your efforts may not be decisive, it's imperative that you try.

Sceptics often say that ordinary people's non-violent political efforts could not have defeated the Nazis. Are they right? Hypotheticals can never be proven, one way or the other. Rather than get bogged down in debate about whether non-violence 'might have' beaten the Nazis, Gene Sharp encourages us instead to consider how the Nazis actually *were* opposed non-violently, both within Germany and in occupied countries.

An academic who has held tenure at Oxford and Harvard, Sharp published his first work in 1960, with a foreword by Albert Einstein. In the first volume of his magnum opus, *The Politics of Non-violent Action*, Sharp demands that we remove our blinkers and recognize that political power is our own power – and that it does not reside only in the ballot box. In that book and elsewhere, Sharp provides a stunningly comprehensive account of non-violent resistance to the Nazis, often overlooked by military historians.

There are too many instances to list here, but the following paragraphs hint at the variety of approaches.

When prisoners started to escape from a Polish prison, a young woman telegrapher risked her life by simply failing to send a message calling for reinforcements.

In Norway, citizens looked right through German soldiers, as if they didn't exist, and refused to sit next to them on public transport. If this sounds mild, it seriously rattled the Germans: it became an offence to stand, on trams, if there was a seat available. Who could have imagined that Nazi morale was so fragile?

In Denmark, the king wore a yellow star in sympathy with Jews who were forced to wear them. When Danish officials were instructed to round up Jews for deportation, they let the information get out, allowing plenty of time for people to go into hiding. Many Danes simply disregarded the Nazi-imposed curfew, staying out at night as long as they liked.

In Holland, some 25,000 Jews successfully went into hiding, many of them with help from non-Jews.

In Germany, a group of non-Jewish citizens protested publicly after their Jewish husbands and wives were taken away. The protest took place at the height of the war, and in the centre of Berlin. Incredibly, the protesters got what they wanted: their spouses were returned home and remained safe for the rest of the war.

Twice, German field marshals walked out on Hitler during meetings.

Doctors who disliked the regime exempted young men from military service. (They came to be known as 'Guten Tag' doctors, because that was how they greeted patients, instead of saying 'Heil Hitler'.)

German musicians undermined the prohibition on playing American jazz by making up German names for the tunes they liked.

The best-known opposition to Hitler was organized by the White Rose Group, which produced anti-Nazi propaganda distributed by post to households across the country, chosen at random from the phone book. The leaflets started to appear in 1942, when the war was still going well for Germany. 'We will not be silent!' one read. 'We are your bad conscience!' The leaflets were found all over the country. Nobody suspected that the White Rose consisted of a tiny group of friends in Munich. Their last leaflet was smuggled out of Germany and millions of copies were dropped over Germany from Allied planes. News even reached the concentration camps. 'When we heard what was happening in Munich,' one inmate later recalled, 'we embraced each other and applauded. There were, after all, still human beings in Germany.'

Some of these actions are almost laughably small: playing American jazz! But as we shall see, even the smallest act of subversion has the potential to inspire others.

If it hadn't been for these minor setbacks, Hitler's regime might have been even worse than it actually was. To put it another way: if more people had dared to resist, the Nazis' worst outrages might have been prevented.

To say this is not merely to pass judgement on people living long ago. It's to challenge ourselves, right now. Because it's easy to imagine that we'd have acted boldly if we'd been in Germany at the time.

But the honest question to ask is whether there is anything we should be doing *today*, about something that is going on right now. To ask ourselves if there have been times when we knew we should have done something, but didn't, and to remember how awful that felt. And then resolve to do everything we can to avoid feeling that way again.

2. What Drives Us?

Some people may be lucky. They will know exactly what they want to change. But for many it's uncertain. There are so many problems, and so many ways to deal with them. Surprisingly often, we find ourselves impaled on a paradox: we desperately want to do something, but have no idea what it may be.

To look for inspiration to the great breakthroughs of the past does not always help, because one of the most common effects of success is to be taken for granted: what once seemed impossible looks ordinary after it's been accomplished. For the same reason, the role taken by particular individuals has a tendency, with hindsight, to seem inevitable, or pre-ordained. We find it hard, for instance, to imagine Gandhi leading a life of inoffensive middle-class respectability. But he might have done. He didn't, because he found that other things mattered more to him than the conventional legal career for which he had trained.

We too, if we hope to change the world, must try to understand what drives us. In particular, we need to understand whether to follow our interests, or a sense of duty.

Historically, many people tried to follow the teachings of religious authorities, perhaps in the hope of a better afterlife. Immanuel Kant promoted the idea of duty for its own sake, regardless of reward in heaven or punishment in hell. He suggested that we act morally only when we have put aside all motives stemming from our desires or inclinations. But this can lead to rigid fanaticism, as the philosopher Peter Singer points out in his book *How Are We To Live?*

> Before his trial, the Nazi Adolf Eichmann suddenly declared with great emphasis that he had lived his whole life according to Kant's moral precepts and especially the Kantian definition of duty . . . on occasions he felt sympathy for the Jews he was sending to the gas chambers but because he believed one should do one's duty unaffected by sympathy he steadfastly stuck to his duty. Another Nazi, Heinrich Himmler, told SS troops assigned to kill Jews that they were called upon to fulfil a 'repulsive duty' and that he would not like it if they did such a thing gladly.

The eighteenth-century philosopher David Hume opposed Kant's view. He believed that every reason for doing anything has to connect with some desire or emotion if it is to influence our behaviour. If Hume is right, the only way to answer the question, 'What should I do?' is by first asking, 'What do I *want* to do?'

But there's a danger here, too: we might want to pursue narrowly selfish interests. This is fine, up to a point, but there comes a time in most people's lives when that no longer seems adequate — often when we become truly conscious of our own mortality.

For centuries, people used the awareness of death deliberately to focus the mind on living well while we can. A story found in many variants across medieval Europe told of three proud, handsome and rich young courtiers riding in the forest, where they encountered three rotting corpses. The corpses said to the men: 'As you are now, so once were we. As we are now, so shall you be.' One can readily imagine how such an incident might get the young men thinking, because something similar happens in real life. People who recover from near death say the experience is character-building, and gives a clearer perspective on what is really important. The Buddha had a similar insight. After growing up in a palace, protected from the problems of the world, he went out one day and saw an old person, a man grievously ill, and a dead body. He asked his chariot driver whom these things happened to and was stunned by the answer: 'To everyone, my lord.' Buddhists acknowledge the great value of these dreadful sights by calling them Heavenly Messengers – because they spur us to seek awakening.

According to the philosopher Stephen Batchelor, in his study of Buddhism and existentialism, *Alone with Others*, we all 'know' that we must die, and that the things we leave will eventually fade or crumble away. But most of us habitually behave as though the opposite were true – as if we were immortal. And we refuse to accept our cosmic insignificance because to focus on it can be terrifying: our entire world is just one planet circling round one star in a galaxy that contains about 300,000 million stars and is itself one of several million galaxies. The sun will eventually grow cold, and life on earth will come to an end, but the universe will continue, utterly indifferent.

Authentic existence means accepting our inevitable death, and cosmic insignificance – and deciding to live purposefully all the same.

Jean-Paul Sartre conveyed our situation in a paradox: 'Man is condemned to be free', while Albert Camus likened our lives to the hard existence of Sisyphus, obliged by the Greek gods to push a

'As you are now, so once were we. As we are now, so shall you be.'
A vivid sense of our own mortality does tend to concentrate the mind.

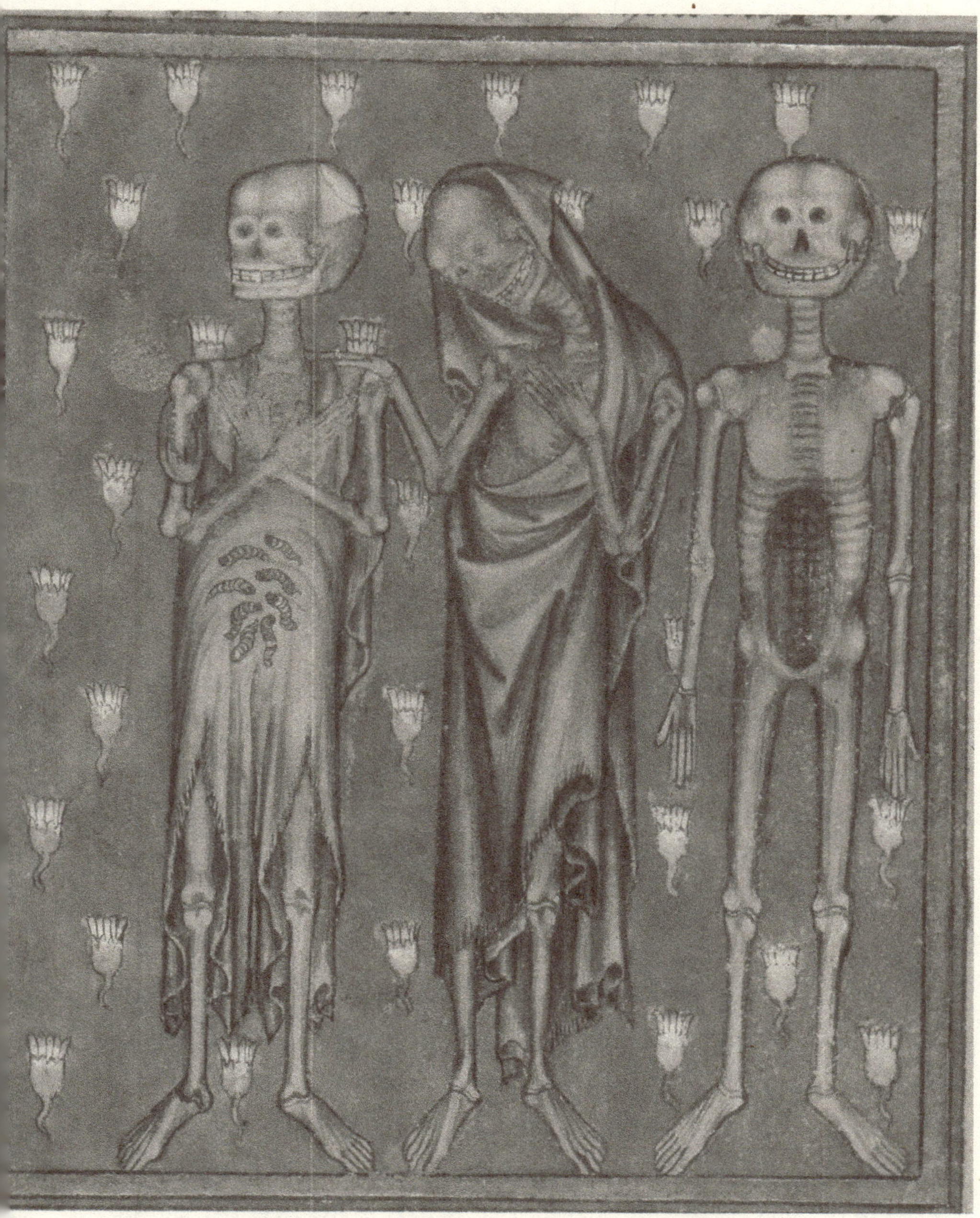

heavy rock uphill then watch it roll back down, again and again for all eternity.

Today, as Singer has pointed out, the assertion that life is meaningless is no longer regarded as a shocking discovery. It's repeated every day by bored adolescents. But that doesn't mean we can't do something meaningful within it, on our own terms. Even Sisyphus, Camus believed, can find satisfaction if he really tries: 'There is no fate that cannot be surmounted'.

But it can only be surmounted if we confront it directly. If we do that, we find the courage to move through to empowerment and growth. That's confirmed by the psychiatrist Chris Johnstone. In his work with alcoholics and addicts, he makes the obvious but necessary point that if we forbid ourselves to talk negatively about something, 'We block the awareness of grievances that need an airing as a prelude to dealing with them'. Johnstone describes our grievance as a 'call to adventure' that sends us out into the world to make things better, just as the 'heavenly messengers' set the Buddha on his path to enlightenment. Many children's stories start with something similar – a catastrophic turn of events, or a shocking revelation, that pushes the unwilling hero into the world to right wrongs before returning home triumphant.

There is something counter-intuitive about welcoming the thing that makes us unhappy. But if you don't truly accept that there's a problem, you might lack the determination necessary to fix it. This is particularly obvious when people who are worried about, say, climate change ask experts whether we are going to 'make it'. If the expert says yes, people lapse back into business as usual. If the expert says no, everybody falls into despair. Neither attitude will make change happen.

Studies have shown that inducing fear about the way things are, without simultaneously giving people a sense of purpose, can actually suppress their immune system – it will make them unwell. The psychiatrist Viktor Frankl based his life's great work on this insight, which he saw for himself as a prisoner in Nazi concentration camps. The prisoner who had lost faith in his future was doomed. In his book *Man's Search for Meaning,* Frankl quotes Nietzsche: 'He who has a "why" to live for can bear almost any "how".' If we find a reason, we can overcome anything.

> Man is not fully conditioned and determined but rather determines himself whether he gives in to conditions or stands up to them. Man does not simply exist but always decides what his existence will be, what he will do in the next moment. By the same token, every human being has the freedom to change at any instant . . . One of the main features of human existence is the capacity to rise above [our] conditions, to grow beyond them.

The search for meaning must always come before the pursuit of happiness, Frankl insists, as we must have a reason to be happy. Once the reason is found, one becomes happy automatically. But when Frankl talked about meaning, he didn't only mean some grand, ultimate purpose, of the sort that might appear on our gravestone. He meant the potential meaning inherent and dormant in every situation we ever encounter. 'The perception of meaning boils down to becoming aware of what can be done about a given situation.'

In recent years, his suggestion has been confirmed by the 'positive psychology' movement led by Martin Seligman. Using scientific methods, Seligman and his colleagues compared the experiences of groups of people enjoying different types of pleasure. One group was sent out to experience sheer hedonism – say, having a foot massage or eating chocolate. Another group was asked to do things that they felt were 'meaningful'. The satisfaction enjoyed by this second group was shown to be both deeper and longer lasting. Several individuals reported that the 'afterglow' didn't only improve their day but also the way they felt about themselves generally.

Changing the world, in other words, feels good – better than pursuing narrowly selfish interests, better even than having your feet massaged while you eat chocolate.

The particular 'meaningful' actions taken are not ultimately important in this context. Others, doing the same things but without stopping to think *why*, would not have shared the sense of satisfaction. To give a simple example: your neighbour is unwell and you take their dog for a walk; you might do so because you genuinely *want* to help them at this difficult time, or you might do it resentfully. The first will make you feel good, the second won't.

This explains how it can be that, if changing the world consists only of everyday actions, some people are actively doing it and others are not. There's a distinction to be made between people who are changing the world merely by existing and others who seek *deliberately* to make a difference: only the person who actively seeks to make change truly understands that there is a choice to be made about how we lead our lives, and can observe clearly the effect they are having. To change the world is to have a sense of purpose, and

Is this a fun way of helping your neighbour, or a chore?

that's something we can all cultivate. Just ask yourself, every so often: 'Why am I doing this?'

Questions like this help us to find what Chris Johnstone (echoing Hume) calls 'the want behind the should'. We won't be motivated to change the world if doing so threatens to be a dreary obligation – but if we can find ways to do it that overlap with the things we most enjoy in life, we're more likely to stick at it.

When we are immersed in activities we love, we are living by our intrinsic values. These are not the general values that everybody pays lip service to but a collection of ideals that are important to us individually – values that get us out of bed in the morning, or make us turn off the TV if something upsets us. Many people will share some of our values, but taken as a whole they are uniquely ours.

One way to grasp your own values is to ask yourself: what do I think of as a good life, in the fullest sense of that term? What kind of life do I truly admire, and what kind of life do I hope to be able to look back on? To be more specific, write a list of things to accomplish by the time you die. What steps are needed to make them happen?

You might also try writing ten different answers to the question 'Who Am I?' Find the reason you are excited by each answer, and see if you can find a pattern. Then put the answers in order, from favourite to least favourite. Everybody will do this differently, but it's likely that most people's answers will include relationships (I'm a father, a son, a husband, a brother, a friend, a neighbour, and so on), ways in which they have made a living, and outside interests. It takes work to determine what we find exciting in each case, but it's worthwhile because it teaches us something about ourselves that we might never previously have considered.

A similar exercise involves making a note of events or relationships that have made you feel truly alive in the recent or distant past, and then (just as important) trying to analyse why. Answer the question honestly – don't assume that a 'worthy' answer is required. For instance, if you happened to feel truly alive playing golf, write that down. Then ask yourself: was it because you like being outdoors, or because you are competitive at sport, or because you like the opportunity to chat with people, or some other reason? Once you have identified the reason, ask yourself why you enjoy *that*. Write down the answer, and keep breaking down the pleasure you derive from the activity until you get to the 'ultimate' reason why you enjoy it. Then ask what other things you could do that would lead to the same kind of ultimate satisfaction. The exercise might go something like this:

What do I enjoy? Playing golf
Why? Because I like seeing my friends
Why? Because I enjoy open, unhurried opportunities to chat with friends
Why? Because I am a sociable person, and like to find out what makes people tick

From this you could conclude that you might find satisfaction volunteering to talk to people, perhaps as a trained counsellor. It might involve a bit of work, but trying to change the world for the better in that area could make you just as happy as a round of golf.

Another thing we might do is look back at times when we have made a difference, no matter how small, and try to remember what that felt like.

Standing in front of a tank: to focus too much on this kind of monumental struggle can be misleading.

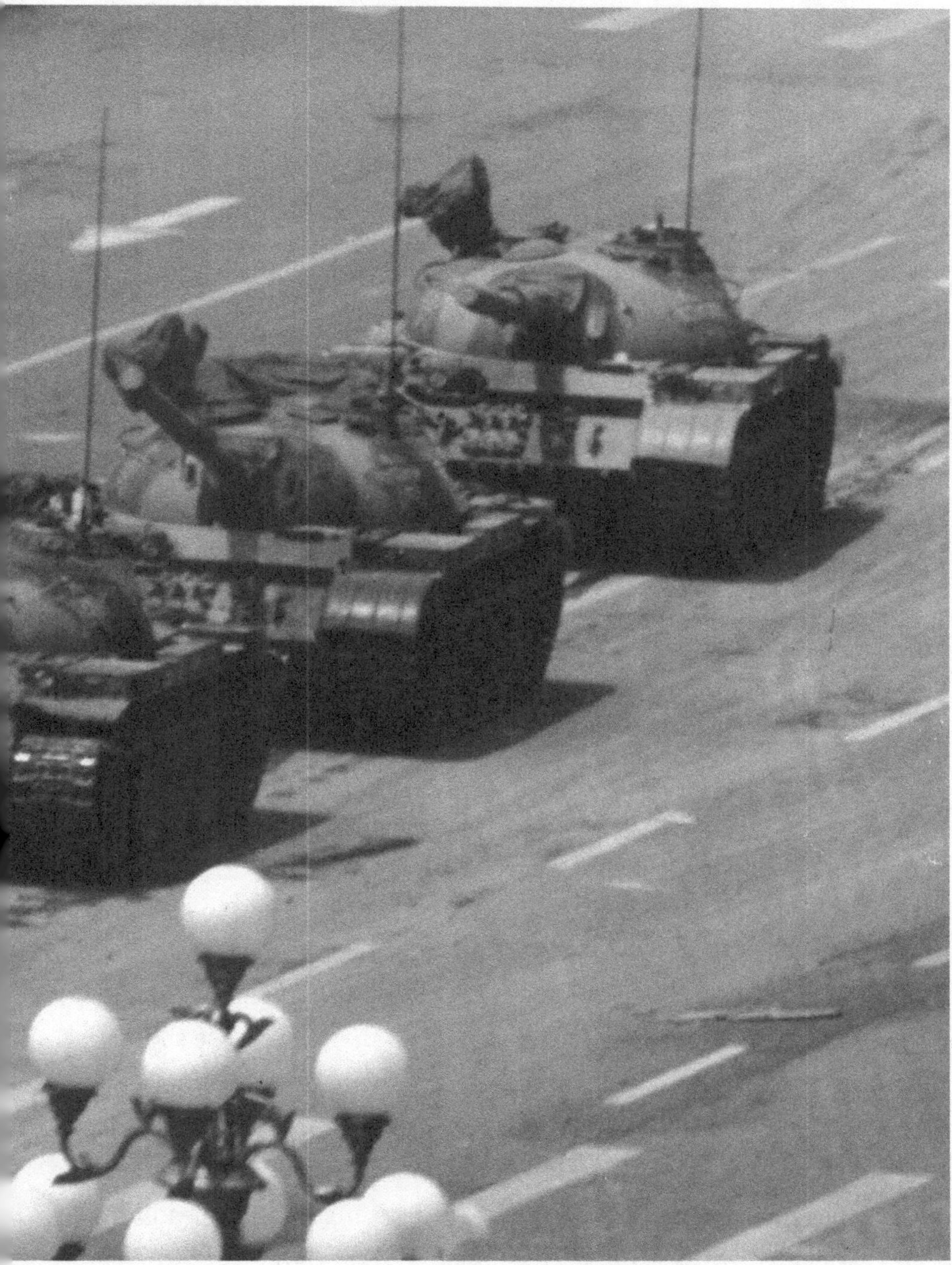

It's imperative to actually do the exercises. Reading them and skipping on won't help at all. Only by doing the exercises can you hope to find a better sense of the things that give your life meaning.

This helps to determine how we should act, because the question we are looking at is not 'What is the meaning of life?', but 'How can I make my life meaningful?' And the answer to that requires action.

To focus too much on monumental struggles – such as that of the lone Chinese student who, in Tiananmen Square in 1989, went with his shopping bags to block a column of tanks – can be misleading. Ethics appear in our lives in much more ordinary, everyday ways. The Victorian artist and writer John Ruskin once asked why we give medals to people who, in a moment and without much thought, save somebody's life, but we give no medal to people who devote years to bringing up a child.

Even the mundane can acquire grandeur if it's held in a wider perspective. A researcher once asked men working with stone what they were doing. One said his job was to square off the stones and move them. Another said he was working to provide for his wife and children. A third, while conscious that he was doing both those things, said he was building a magnificent cathedral, for people to worship in long after he'd gone. Each of them was doing great work, but only one recognized how great it was. We can even impose a kind of grandeur on everyday parenting, of the sort Ruskin described, if we see it as the work of a 'good ancestor', striving to pass on the best of our distant forebears to people as yet unborn.

The novelist and philosopher Iris Murdoch insisted that leading a good life involves not only occasionally making grand gestures, whether standing in front of tanks or giving blood (a less dramatic way to save lives). 'The exercise of our freedom is a small piecemeal business which goes on all the time, and not a grandiose leaping about unimpeded at important moments.' It's about the way we conduct ourselves from one moment to the next.

It's also, crucially, about how we observe the world around us. Murdoch believed we should cultivate a kind of 'mindfulness'. By making a habit of focusing our attention on everyday things that are valuable or virtuous, we hone our ability to act well at decisive moments. 'Anything that alters consciousness in the direction of unselfishness will do,' she wrote.

And that's because, if we are really interested in changing the world, we have to put other people first. Every attitude we assume, every word we utter, and every act we undertake establishes us in relation to others. We may be alone in the realms of our private thoughts, perceptions and feelings, but the world we want to change consists of other people.

And this gives us an important clue as to where we might find the meaning we are looking for: in helping others. Because if we are not doing that, we are still pursuing narrowly selfish interests.

3. Some Thoughts on Strategy

Having understood what drives us, we should be in a better position to choose between the many issues that deserve our attention. One way to do this might be to write a list, putting the issues into an order of priorities. Perhaps like this:

- War
- Poverty
- Environmental degradation
- Famine
- Political corruption . . .

And so on. But each person's list will be different, sometimes radically so. The issues that worry somebody in one part of the world may not bother another person elsewhere (even if they 'should'). For example, it is hard to imagine making famine our mission if we have no experience of it, and do not even know where a famine is to be found. As the last chapter explored, if we're not interested in something, we won't be inspired to do much about it. For this reason it's imperative to release yourself from the idea that the list I have just given is somehow more worthwhile than the one that you would draw up yourself. It's true, however, that a third person might insist that my list is more worthwhile if you were to write this:

- Do more baking with the children
- Play more American jazz
- Bit of stonemasonry

But if you were to consider your list from a wider perspective it might be seen to have a grandeur of its own:

- Do more baking with the children = *passing the best of our ancestors to people yet unborn*
- Play more American jazz = *undermine Hitler*
- Bit of stonemasonry = *building a magnificent cathedral for people to worship in long after we've gone*

In other words, if your chosen mission does not immediately appear very ambitious, that may only be because you are admirably modest and haven't yet found the words to express its cosmic significance. If that bothers you, keep asking, 'Why am I doing this?' But fundamentally it's not important, so long as you are pursuing something meaningful to you, and it involves, at some level, helping others.

All the same, it may help to provide a systematic analysis of the kinds of issues facing us. One way to do this is to divide them into four types:

i. Problems that affect everybody, but for which nobody (or hardly anybody) can imagine a remedy that they, as individuals, can administer. These might include living in a state of war, or under a ruthless dictatorship, or in a lawless environment where violent crime or corruption is widespread.

ii. Problems that appear to affect only some people, and not the population as a whole. For example: the many situations, throughout history, where rights were withheld from certain racial or religious groups, or from women or children; or extremes of poverty that make it almost impossible to live a happy life.

iii. Problems that pose a threat to everybody, but are recognized only by a small minority. This might include issues like climate change, destruction of natural systems, population growth, or resource shortages.

iv. Not problems but opportunities. If the streets around us are ugly, that may bother us a great deal. We may have imagined elegant and efficient ways to run public infrastructure. Or alternative electoral systems. We may have come up with an invention that has the potential to transform people's lives, created beautiful art, or written something insightful.

If the fourth type is on your mind, you are entitled to pursue it without worrying that you should first put an end to war, topple dictators, save the planet, feed the hungry, and cure the sick. The world would be immeasurably poorer, after all, if everybody devoted themselves solely to remedying those great ills, and nobody was available to, for instance, tend gardens any more.

To identify your own greatest concerns, you might try to draw up a shortlist – a top five, perhaps. It may help to ask yourself what you would do if you knew you were certain to succeed – if failure was, magically, impossible. By asking the question that way, we get rid of the nagging internal voice that says we couldn't possibly manage such a thing, and who the hell do we think we are, anyway? So today my own list would read:

i. Organize a Christmas party for my street.

ii. Find someone to fund a prize for the designer who works out how to extract fibre from nettles cheaply, for use in high-quality sustainable clothing.

iii. Encourage the cooperative movement to launch a parallel currency, creating liquidity for its members at a time when banks are not helping.

iv. Talk to local cafe about providing space for local artists (including children) on its walls.

v. Set up a webpage enabling local people to upload news.

At all times, strive to be specific. Surprisingly often, people worry about, for instance, 'poverty' or 'animal rights', but have no clear idea what it is about these topics that they want to fix. Nobody can get rid of poverty altogether, because (as Ruskin pointed out) rich and poor are relative terms, like north and south. So what is it about poverty that bothers us? To get to the heart of the matter, we must keep asking ourselves why something is a problem. At first, this seems silly: how can anybody not understand that poverty is a problem? But unless we are specific about what the problem is, we can't hope to find a specific solution.

It's impossible to overstate the importance of this point: if you don't know what you want to fix, it can't be done.

After going through the process carefully, we may discover that our generalized concern about 'poverty' boils down to, say, finding ways for everybody in the world to be clothed and fed. From here, we might decide whether it is clothing or feeding that interests us most. And when we have pinned down exactly what the problem is, we can move on to thinking of ways to help fix it.

Having decided which cause to take up, we must consider the different approaches we might take. Should we stand for election and work to change the law? Join a campaign group? Or 'just' carry out good works quietly by ourselves?

It depends on what it is you are trying to change: each of these approaches is valid, and can produce results, but each also has its downsides. In formal politics, we may achieve a great deal at a stroke, but it could take years before we do this, and we will frequently be required to compromise on the way. We may, for instance, go into politics with one particular mission in mind, and find that our entire career is given over to other things, including policies we don't particularly believe in.

If we act alone, on the other hand, we avoid compromising, but may never feel satisfied that we have achieved enough.

Sometimes, it's perfectly obvious which route needs to be taken. The lawyer and environmentalist Polly Higgins concluded that the best way to stop extensive destruction of ecosystems was to create a new international crime of 'ecocide'.

While it remains legal to engage in destructive practices, she concluded, businesses will continue to do so, if only on the flimsy basis that, if they didn't, somebody else would. And as long as damaging businesses remains legal, they will continue to attract funding and research that would otherwise go towards safer but more expensive projects.

An international law like the one prohibiting genocide would be enforceable against individuals, not companies, and people would be deemed culpable even if they were 'only following orders'. Thus, a law against ecocide would turn subordinates into whistle-blowers: every individual around the world automatically becomes a steward of the environment.

Higgins was inspired by reading about the abolition of the slave trade in Britain in the early 1800s. Campaigners decided it was no use seeking piecemeal improvements in conditions for slaves. They wanted to abolish slavery altogether. In the UK, at the time, 300 companies were engaged in facilitating the slave trade. They fought hard against abolition, arguing that it would lead to a loss of jobs, and that the public wanted slavery to remain in place. They promised better conditions for slaves – fresh hay for bedding was one idea – and said it was best to let the market regulate itself. But slavery was banned, and subsidies for the trade were withdrawn, to be moved to support more benign businesses instead. Within a year, British slave companies were profitably trading in other commodities, including tea and china. 'Corporations and the economy, when faced with the risk of collapse, can reinvent their wheels overnight,' says Higgins, who continues to campaign for change.

To introduce a new law is no small matter. That's not to say it can't happen, but only to warn that a great deal of work must be done first, and by a lot of people, if representatives of nearly 200 countries at the UN are to accept the need for a new law, and enact it.

I talked about this recently with somebody who has devoted herself for decades to formal politics – as a lifelong member of a mainstream party, and a former candidate for the British parliament. I was struck by her determined insistence that the only way to get things changed is to stand for parliament or to vote for people who will enact the 'right' laws. Slavery was abolished, she said, by parliament. Homosexuality was legalized by parliament. Education flourishes because parliament decided that all children must attend school.

I agreed that parliaments made laws in the way she described, but said that the parliamentarians would not have voted for these things if there was not already a strong mandate in the country at large – indeed, they'd have had no right to do so.

The mere enacting of legislation doesn't necessarily make a great deal of difference. Even before the slave trade was abolished, it was entirely possible for people to decide to give up owning slaves, and many who gave the matter some thought did exactly that. What's more, despite the trade having been abolished, slavery continues illegally today. Similarly, while homosexuality has been decriminalized in many countries, this does not mean that gay people are freed

Hope is not a passive thought; it is a call to action.

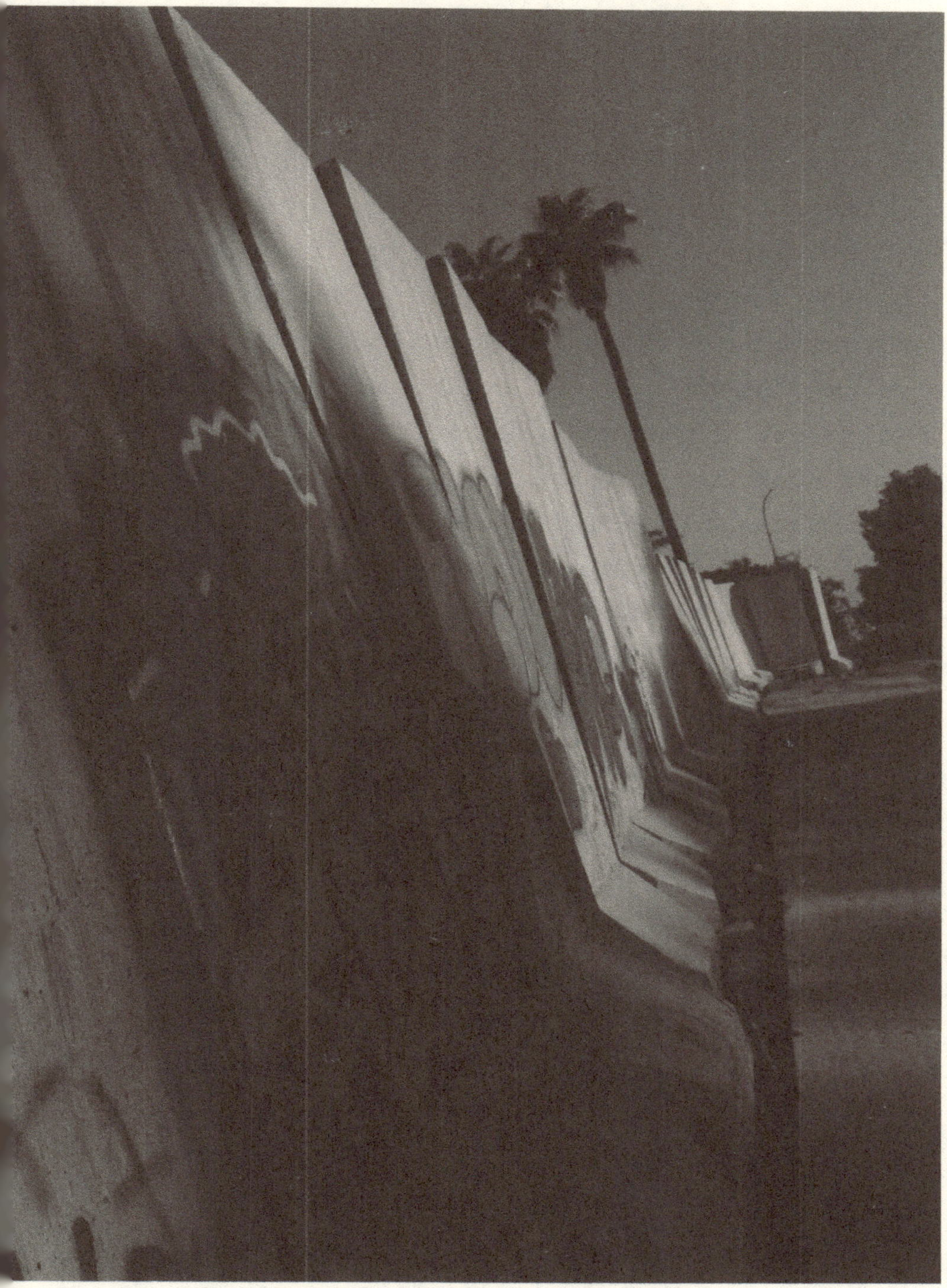

from ordinary, everyday prejudice. And though parliament obliges parents to send their children to school, astonishingly large numbers of children leave school unable to read.

The tenth-century Danish King of England, Canute, was once told by his advisers that he was so powerful he could stop the waves if he wanted to do so. To prove them wrong, he went to the beach and commanded the waves to stop. It would be well if people remembered that parliament's power is no greater than Canute's: merely banning or legalizing something does not *necessarily* make a great difference. The thing that makes a difference is people deciding to comply – and as we've seen, they can change their behaviour without the intervention of parliament.

If you want people to feel that they have the capacity to change things, it's extremely important to draw attention to the ways they can do that *themselves*. If, instead, you insist that they must wait for somebody else to do it on their behalf, you make them feel powerless, and rob them of responsibility, which is necessary and wholesome. Unless we feel that we can do something ourselves, we have no hope, says the writer and activist Rebecca Solnit. 'Hope is not like a lottery ticket you can sit on the sofa and clutch, feeling lucky. Hope is an axe you break down doors with. Hope calls for action.'

Another friend frequently complained about the greed of bankers. I asked him which bank he uses. It was one of the global giants, implicated historically in all kinds of shady behaviour. He would like banks, he said, along with railways and other utilities, to be taken into national ownership. I pointed out that he could have the kind of banking he wants right now if he switched to an account run by a bank that is owned by ordinary people like him, as a cooperative with strict ethical-investment policies. Why wait – perhaps for ever – for parliament to make obligatory what he could have at once? He said he was too lazy to change, and anyway wanted parliament to make ethical banking a matter of policy, so that it would be available to everyone.

I was puzzled that a man who gives up hours to knock on strangers' doors on behalf of a political party could describe himself as 'too lazy', but I assured him it doesn't take long to move bank accounts, and that the facility is *already* available to everyone who cares to take advantage of it. If people don't want it, that's fine. What right does he have to try to impose on others something he can't even be bothered to take advantage of himself?

The best that can be said for parliament is that it enacts legislation as a projection, by no means perfect, of the will of the majority. People who are not happy about the status quo, like my friend, often assume that they need only to get parliament to enact a new law and then their own vision will be imposed on everybody else. But in order to make that happen, it may sometimes feel like we have to wage war on government itself.

People who have tried to make change in the past have often done so spontaneously, and intuitively. How much more effective might they have been, Gene Sharp wondered, if they'd had a better idea of what had been done before? And so he set about compiling a list of methods of non-violent action, which stalled for years at precisely 198. (The term 'non-violent action' is inelegant, and may strike some people as countercultural. But nobody seems to have been able to devise a better way to describe the many everyday methods of creating change that happen not to involve violence.)

The techniques Sharp lists include examples that go back as far as recorded history, and come from all over the world. Number 67, 'flight of workers', can be said to have been used by Moses and the Israelites as a way to register dissatisfaction with the conduct of Pharoah. Number 90, 'revenue refusal', was used in Ancient China by unwilling taxpayers, who buried their possessions and took to the hills when the tax collector was known to be on his way. Number 57, 'Lysistratic non-action', may have been used by women in Ancient Greece to end war by refusing sexual relations with bellicose men, but Sharp has found evidence of the technique being used in recent history by both women of the Iroquois nation and in Southern Rhodesia, as it was then called. It was used in Kenya more recently, by women who included the wife of the president.

Some of the techniques appear almost boringly familiar, such as technique number 2, 'letters of opposition or support'. But they can still be effective, and in certain contexts, even that step requires courage. In her book *Wild Swans,* Jung Chang describes the enormous hardship her family suffered during China's Cultural Revolution, due in large part to her father's decision, as a loyal, high-ranking official, to write a letter of comradely concern to Chairman Mao. And even in supposedly free-thinking countries, it can be dangerous to put in writing opinions that go against the general consensus. You may not be incarcerated, but you may lose your job.

Other techniques require physical bravery, such as technique number 171, 'non-violent interjection', as practised by that anonymous

Chinese man before the tanks at Tiananmen Square. Or technique 66, 'total personal non-cooperation'. During World War II a conscientious objector in the US named Corbett Bishop declined to eat, dress himself or even stand up. His limp body had to be carried in and out of court and a variety of prison cells. He was forcibly fed by tube. Eventually, after considerable newspaper publicity, he was allowed home without agreeing to anything.

Many of the techniques compiled by Sharp usually require the participation of more than one person. Technique 193, 'overloading of administrative systems', was used in the US during the Vietnam War. The law relating to the draft required individuals to give notice within ten days of 'any change in address or status'. The large numbers of people opposed to the war decided to take this so seriously that officials were overwhelmed. People wrote in to state that they had moved to a different room in the same house. Others wrote that they were thinking of travelling, then wrote again to say they had changed their minds. The same technique has been used more recently to crash official computer systems.

Sharp's list of 198 methods of non-violent action is included in the appendix to this book, and rewards further study. As we scrutinize it, we observe a broad distinction between the various techniques.

The first group is gathered by Sharp under the general heading of 'protest', but if that puts you off, think of it as 'raising awareness'.

The second group of techniques is described by Sharp as non-cooperation. You may prefer to think of this as simply ceasing to have dealings with systems or people you dislike – for instance, not buying items made by companies that exploit their workers, or refusing to fly in order to reduce CO_2 emissions.

The third group can be classified as active interventions to disrupt the status quo, perhaps by building alternatives to what is currently available. Again, these innovations need not be especially 'alternative' in the pejorative sense. Nor do they need to pose a threat to the status quo. One fantastically successful example was the Scout movement, founded by the soldier Robert Baden-Powell because he was dismayed by the poor state of recruits sent to fight for Britain in the Boer War. He decided to do something about it, and took a group of young men to camp for a few days on a small island. Despite that modest beginning – and his narrowly pro-British, militaristic motivation – the Scout Movement spread around the world and became utterly mainstream.

As with warfare, it's necessary to have a strategy before you choose your tactics. But the techniques need not always be negative, in the sense of involving withdrawal or hostility. Japanese unions, working for employers who used just-in-time delivery, invented the 'go-faster' strike to support their demand for better pay. I came across a similar example from the UK. A library was threatened with closure owing to budget cuts. Local residents joined forces to withdraw every single book from that library, leaving every shelf bare. (In a witty flourish, they arranged it so that the very last book to be taken out would be Mary Norton's novel, *The Borrowers*.) Which is to say: they opposed the planned closure by showing that they really did use the library.

The tactic is so elegant that it appears obvious, and even unremarkable. But in light of it we can see the ineptness of others who, out of desperation in a similar situation, might have chosen different tactics – throwing paint over the local mayor, for instance, or embarking on a hunger strike.

How do we decide which techniques are required in our own case? We might start by brainstorming, either by ourselves or with help from friends. It doesn't actually matter whether they share our aspiration, only that they are willing, briefly, to pretend they do and to come up with some ideas. They may enjoy the exercise more if they *don't* share your view, as this allows them to think freely. A psychological experiment carried out decades ago found that businessmen taking a creativity test scored very poorly indeed until they were asked to take the test again, 'as if they were hippies', whereupon the same dull individuals put down ideas that were startlingly imaginative. In the same way, if people who don't share your particular concern allow themselves to pretend briefly that they do, they may provide better ideas than a group that is genuinely like-minded.

Whether brainstorming alone or with others, the key thing is to put ideas down on paper. It doesn't matter whether they are earnest or frivolous, practical or impractical. Just put down whatever comes to mind, without censoring, explaining or defending anything. Don't criticize or even praise other people's ideas either, till the process is complete.

When you have collected a large number of ideas – at least twenty – read through them carefully. Remove any that do not seem helpful. After that, take a fresh look and select the ones that seem most helpful. After just five minutes of brainstorming, you may discover ideas that verge on genius.

4. Bearing Witness

Of course not everyone will identify a particular mission of their own. The good news is that this need not stop us having a powerful effect, because we can change the world both by passing on news about things that need fixing, and by helping promote other people's attempts to fix those things.

It's possible that these two types of message appeal to slightly different personality types – pessimists may gravitate towards pointing out problems, while optimists are likely to enjoy talking about and coming up with solutions. But both types of information are important. You may know already, but to find out which appeals to you more – and perhaps more importantly, what *kinds* of problems and solutions you are interested in – pay close attention to the sort of stories you tell people. Do you talk about climate change worsening? Shops closing? People's bad manners? Or are you more likely to enthuse about exciting new inventions and tell people about opportunities to see inspiring events? If this doesn't work, read several newspapers over a single weekend, and write a summary. Which kinds of stories grabbed you? Did you focus more on problems, or solutions? It doesn't matter if writing doesn't come easily. Bearing witness has always been an important part of changing the world.

For Jung Chang, who worshipped Mao as a child in China, the process of enlightenment was gradual. Crucially, she was able to question ideas with others – if only close relatives. In *Wild Swans* she discusses the effect of her younger brother Jin-ming's more sceptical view of the regime:

> Jin-ming often made sceptical comments . . . which kept us laughing. This was unusual in those days, when humour was dangerous. Mao, hypocritically calling for 'rebellion', wanted no genuine inquiry or scepticism. To be able to think in a sceptical way was my first step towards enlightenment. Jin-ming helped to destroy my rigid habits of thinking.

The importance of these voices – educated, questioning and critical – cannot be underestimated. Jung Chang's mind, and those of countless Chinese citizens around her, were changed not by laws or initiatives or rebellions, but by the commentary that they heard all around them.

When Mao's efficient deputy Zhou Enlai died, Mao's wife and her political faction known as the Gang of Four ordered that mourning for Zhou be played down. But many people ignored the order, and showed grief in order to express disapproval of the Gang. Soon afterwards other, small acts of protest were seen across China: at the endless mass meetings, speakers read their prepared scripts in flat, expressionless voices, and their audiences wandered around chatting, knitted or even went to sleep. As acts of subversion, these seem unremarkable but the cumulative effect was decisive – after Mao died, his wife and the Gang of Four were quickly and easily arrested.

If we decide to take a more direct approach to spreading awareness and enlightenment, we should proceed with caution. Remember that there is only one way to get anybody to do anything: by making them *want* to do it. And that applies even to changing their minds.

Don't begin by discussing things on which you differ, advised Dale Carnegie in his bestselling self-improvement manual *How To Win Friends and Influence People*. Begin by emphasizing areas of agreement. The idea is to keep the other person saying yes, yes, and at all costs to stop them saying no, because once they've said no, they may feel that to change their mind would be to lose face. You are more likely to get them to say yes if you have attempted to understand their interests. Try sincerely to see things from the other person's point of view, Carnegie adds. Don't just pretend, because if it's not sincere, it's useless.

This is how salesmen work. It's also how the Ancient Greek philosopher Socrates worked. He asked people questions to which the answer was likely to be affirmative, and kept doing it until they had moved, often without realizing it, into accepting a position they would have rejected only moments before. To give an example from my own experience: the man who owned the flat I used to share with friends wanted to increase our rent at the end of the year. We could not afford to pay the increase. I called him to say we would have to leave, with regret, but asked if he had been happy with us as tenants. Yes, he said. I said that I expected he might have to pay a fee to an agency to find new tenants. Yes, he said glumly. I asked if he would lose money if the flat were empty for a short period. Yes, he said, he would. I pointed out that the increased income he hoped for by raising the rent would be lost if the flat stayed empty for as little as two weeks. Did he think that was a possibility? It was, he said. I added that even after paying the agent's fee, he might end up with tenants he didn't get on with. Might it not, on reflection, be better all round if he kept the rent at the level we could afford? He agreed to do so, and we stayed another year.

This kind of open conversation will not always work out the way we want it to but it's infinitely better than strident confrontation, which can be irritating and cause distress. It could even be worse than that: lecturing people about, for example, environmental collapse without at the same time giving them a sense of agency could make them depressed and even ill because, as Frankl saw, people need a sense of purpose if they are to cope with adversity. Research suggests that this partly explains high sickness levels among the long-term unemployed.

To paraphrase the late philosopher Raymond Williams, the key thing is not to make despair convincing but to make hope possible.

This is what Trenna Cormack has tried to do. Instead of being a prophet of doom, she became a prophet of hope. A few years ago, at a party, a young woman (Cormack) came up to me and asked if I might be interested in looking at a book she had written and published herself. Out of mere politeness, I said I would. And when I did so, I was very impressed. Cormack had been in the paying audience at an event some time earlier called 'Be the Change' – a phrase borrowed from Gandhi, who conjured us to 'Be the change you want to see in the world'. The topics covered by the speakers at the event included many that are often presented in dismal terms, including environmental crisis and social injustice, but Cormack was startled to find the discourse was generally upbeat. 'I found myself in a hall full of people who cared passionately about creating a better world,' she said. Over three days, they heard from many speakers engaged in a variety of inspiring activities. 'I thought to myself, "This is brilliant! There should be a book about this."'

And then the question was turned to the audience: 'This isn't just about sages on stages. What are you going to do to *be* the change you wish to see? What's yours to do?' Cormack gulped and realized that the book she had imagined was to be her own work. She made arrangements, interviewed dozens of people who inspired her, wrote them up, published the book herself, and went out to promote it herself too.

She did not set out to highlight any particular cause of her own, but through her efforts she helped others' causes to be better known.

A Canadian art dealer named Fred Mulder did much the same to spread awareness of people actively working to overturn intractable problems. Mulder used to give money to good causes but without feeling entirely satisfied. Then he got together with a handful of others and set up The Funding Network as a forum for philanthropists (even modest philanthropists, with only small heaps of cash to disburse) to learn together about social-change projects and help fund them as a group. Representatives of interesting and worthy causes are invited to 'pitch' to TFN audiences of would-be funders at regular networking events. In less than a decade, thousands of sponsors have raised millions of pounds for hundreds of good causes, and spin-off networks have been established internationally.

But it's not necessary to go to the same lengths as Cormack and Mulder. Even just the odd word here and there can be helpful. A friend of mine had, on a few rare occasions, spoken to me of the help he had found at Alcoholics Anonymous, an organization of which I then knew little; but those few words enabled me, when the dire need arose, to recommend AA to another close friend, who was thereby utterly transformed.

5. What You Will Need

By now you should have discovered what sort of cause you want to help with, and your place within it. So we are almost ready to start our adventure, but one last thing remains necessary. We must consider the resources we may need, and the allies.

Physical resources may be important, but what I have in mind at this point are personal qualities: skills, experience, mental and emotional capacities. Things that you might list on a job application – but also some that you probably wouldn't.

To get a better grasp of my own skills, I recently drew up a list of my work experience, including some things I had done only as a pastime, holiday job, or tiresome duty. I resolved from now on to stop thinking of myself only as a writer. I am also an artist, a baker, a career coach, a carpenter, a cleaner, a cook, a copywriter, a decorator, a dog walker, an English-language teacher, a film-maker, a gardener, a map-maker, a bike messenger, a minicab driver, a poet, a police-checked child minder, a qualified first-aider, a printer, a publisher, a rubbish collector, a Scout patrol leader, a second-hand bookseller, a tailor, a typist, a waiter, a washer-up and possibly much else. I have to say that drawing up this list gave quite a boost to my self-esteem.

We can all draw up a list of work experience, skills and hobbies, but we rarely look for potential in our limits and our shortcomings.

We might be surprised to find something valuable there. This sounds like another paradox, but it's not.

Take Richard Reynolds. He lives in a tower block in a part of London with few green spaces. A few years ago he started to clean up the municipal planter on the vast roundabout near his home, removing all the cigarette ends people had discarded. Then he began to put in some plants. Over time, he learned which plants did well, and which didn't. Sometimes vandals destroyed plants. At other times local officials interfered, telling him he had no right to do what he was doing. But other local people were inspired, and joined him. Gradually they moved on to other spaces, including a large traffic island, which they planted with rows of lavender. Over time, word got out about Reynolds' work, and he heard from others doing similar things elsewhere. They set up a movement of 'guerilla gardeners', which has since gone mainstream. Not long ago I walked past one of London's big department stores and saw Reynolds' face on materials in its window display. The store was selling 'guerilla gardening kits'. The seeds he had planted were flourishing, in more ways than one.

The point to remember is that Reynolds' success stems from a very peculiar blessing: he has no garden of his own.

To see the potential even in our shortcomings, failures, and what we lack requires us to take a fresh look at our entire lives. If we are to recognize their value, it's not our resources that must change: it's the way we see them. This means seizing any opportunity to transfigure them, rather than overlooking, or shunning them. It's about being creative, and looking on the bright side – not coming up with reasons to be cheerful that are far-fetched and implausible but finding genuine value and potential. In all likelihood, we will find strengths even – perhaps especially – in areas that we don't much like to think about.

It is often argued that the strongest among us are those who have been through the greatest difficulties. (As Nietzsche put it, what doesn't kill us makes us stronger.) The charity Peace Direct offers financial support and advice to community-based peacemakers all around the world. Many of the individuals carrying out the work are former child soldiers, who have done shameful things. Ordinarily, that background would be viewed as a shortcoming, but in the circumstances it makes these individuals well-qualified to help others seek peace.

In other words, what we need is often exactly what we already have.

A less sensational way to look at this might be to consider whether, say, the work that you find boring may after all be the means by which you can achieve wonderful things. In the ancient Buddhist 'Song of Zazen', Hakuin Zenji wrote: 'How sad that people ignore the near and search afar, like someone in the midst of water crying out with thirst'. This nearly describes something that happened during the Cold War. Russia and the US were racing to get into space, and an American named Paul Fisher took it on himself to spend a vast fortune developing a pen that would write in outer space. NASA duly bought his pens and distributed them to astronauts. The Russians, meanwhile, made do with an alternative so modest that NASA somehow overlooked it – a pencil.

Having considered our resources, we should then take a similarly forensic approach to assessing our allies, because as we have seen, it's unlikely that we will achieve a great deal working entirely alone.

Chris Johnstone, in his work with addicts and alcoholics, encourages them to draw maps of their support network. We might usefully do the same. To begin, write your name in the middle of a piece of paper, and around it write the names of the people who give you the greatest support. Then draw an arrow from each one towards your own name, varying the thickness of the arrow to indicate the amount of support they give (a thick arrow means a lot of support). Now map the support you give to other people by drawing arrows in the opposite direction. Add more names, if necessary.

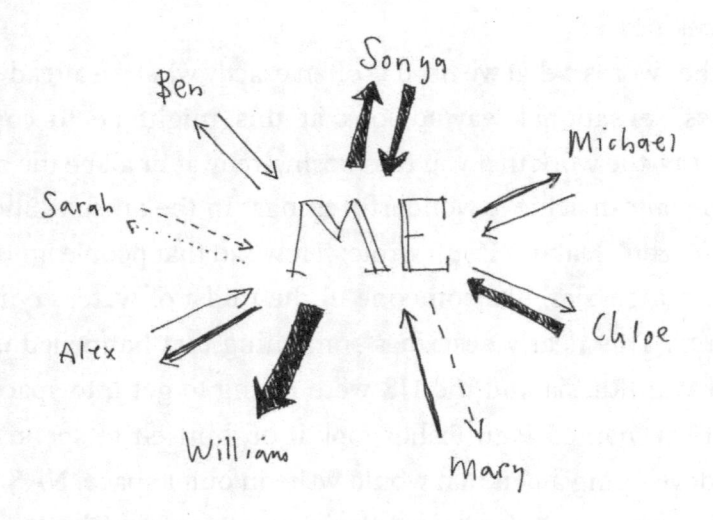

After drawing such a map, you might consider whether there are changes you would like to make – relationships to strengthen, or others to back away from. In the example I've provided, you see that I am giving lots of support to William, but getting nothing back, while Chloe is giving me a great deal of support, and getting little in return. Johnstone suggests that the most promising relationships may not be the ones where the support is strongest but where it is mutual. 'They are valuable resources in your life,' he says. 'Treasure them. Mutual-support arrangements are stronger than one-way flows.'

Now that you have mapped your network, go and tell people what you plan to do and ask for help explicitly, says Johnstone, because when you do this, you liberate helpers to do more than merely nod supportively when you come to them. They start coming to you with ideas. They may even make your project their own.

Instinctively, we find it difficult to ask for help like this. We think it might be an imposition. But there's plenty of evidence that people like being asked: it's flattering. The only reason people might not like being asked is if they can't see a way to say no. So when you ask for help in your mission, make it clear that you don't mind if your people tell you they prefer not to help, for whatever reason – either now or at any time in the future.

If they know they are free to excuse themselves, they will almost never feel the need to exercise that freedom – and together you can do great things.

6. Taking a First Step

Having considered what drives us, and examined carefully the things that need doing, the techniques we might use, and the resources and allies we need, we should be ready to start. But when we think about issues that are huge in scale, we can be overwhelmed. From our first school physics lessons we've grown up with the idea that to move a massive object requires huge force. This is true, but newer insights from physics show that this force can just as easily be derived from a number of smaller movements.

Chaos theory teaches that seemingly insignificant initial circumstances can effect global, even universal events. As the theory has it: a butterfly flaps its wings in one country and helps to cause a tornado in another. The same idea applies in our lives. In her workshops, the environmental activist Joanna Macy uses the following exercise to dramatize something like the 'butterfly effect' in human terms.

She explains the exercise in her book, co-authored with Molly Young Brown, *Coming Back To Life*. It works best with a large group of people, in a large open space. Macy gives instructions: select two other people in the group, without indicating who they may be, and move so as to keep an equal distance between yourself and those two people at all times (not necessarily at the midpoint between them).

People immediately begin to circulate, and each movement triggers many others in an active, interdependent fashion.

> Participants find they are by necessity maintaining wide-angle vision and constant alacrity of response. The process is purposeful, suspenseful, laced with laughter. It speeds up for a while, then may abate, accelerate, and again slow down toward equilibrium, but it rarely comes to stasis.

This continues for four or five minutes, then as activity lessens Macy invites people to pause and reflect on what they experienced. Often participants mention a temporary eclipse of self-consciousness, as perceptions focused not on their own actions so much as on other people's. They've become aware that they are part of something bigger than themselves.

Sometimes, Macy (who joins in the exercise herself) waits for a while before deliberately upsetting the system's balance. Interestingly, people rarely notice who started such a chain of events, but afterwards remember the sudden flurry of activity – and how small, intentional change by just one person can create wide effects.

So: somebody has to go first, or that intentional change won't happen. But why should it be us? One reason we hold back from doing what needs to be done is that nobody *else* seems bothered about it. This comes down to something fundamental about human beings: we're social animals and we learn the right way to behave by observing others.

And yet every single breakthrough occurred because somebody decided to do something new. That first person's actions 'gave permission' to others – if only to do what they already wanted to do.

Not long ago, my colleague at the School of Life, Dr Nick Southgate, told me about a video on the internet, apparently recorded on somebody's phone, featuring a crowd of people in a field at a music festival in Canada (www.youtube.com/watch?v=GA8z7f7a2Pk). In the film, a solitary figure dances in an open space, without the slightest hint of self-consciousness, and continues to do so for some time. A few people walk past but studiously ignore him. Eventually another man joins in. This second man puts energy into his movements but appears self-conscious, occasionally looking back into the crowd with a grin, for reassurance. The first man welcomes him, but carries on as before. Then a third man arrives, seemingly a friend of the second one, and makes moves that are obviously intended, more than anything else, to be amusing.

Then three more young men arrive together, and three more dash behind them. People near the camera whoop approval. Six more arrive. And then comes the tipping point: everybody rushes to join in, suddenly desperate not to be left out.

What held them back? Maybe they were too busy filming the dancing man on their cameras: it's sometimes easier to be a spectator. There are certainly an awful lot of versions of the event available to watch on the internet. One is particularly instructive: for five minutes, the person holding the camera and his neighbours make horrible remarks about the dancer. But as more people join in, their tone changes. 'Wow, it's a revolution, man!' says a male voice. 'One man can change the world!' says a woman. And after six and a half minutes of filming, she says, 'I wanna go down [and join in]!'

What Dr Southgate told me about the dancing man is instructive for anybody hoping to make change:

> This is an interesting example of what it means to go first. If this one guy doesn't start dancing, the dance will not happen. He does this at lots of festivals. It's his thing. Most times, he dances and no one else dances (or only a few, and it dies out). He knows he has to get up and dance alone for a long time before anything happens. And sometimes he will fail, but if he gets up and does it again, eventually the time and the place and the people will be right and his dance will be seen and his call will be heard.

You might not have thought it was so hard to get people who had chosen to attend a music festival to dance. But the point to emphasize is this: don't worry about other people. If you put enough energy into your own efforts, soon enough they may find it impossible not to join you. Or as Gandhi famously put it: 'Be the change you want to see in the world'.

What the dancing man showed was that we *can* change the ethos of the group around us. Chris Johnstone, in his work with addicts, found that if they were to overcome a climate of cynicism and putdowns, it helped to stop thinking about what other people 'should' do and concentrate instead on what they themselves *will* do. His insight applies to us all, and the social environments we find ourselves in, whether at work or at home or in public life. The key is to recognize the way we ourselves participate in each context. By simply refusing to undermine anyone around you, and instead giving positive encouragement to others, you change the culture you live in. And as Johnstone says, 'styles of interaction are contagious'.

It may help to give a more obviously historic example. In the southern states of America, as recently as the 1950s, black people were second-class citizens. Among many other indignities, they could not attend the same schools as white Americans, use the same public toilets, drink from the same water fountains, or sit and eat in shops frequented by white people. Many believed that to complain about this petty humiliation would only result in trouble.

But one day in 1955, four African-American passengers on a bus in Montgomery, Alabama, were asked, as usual, to give up their seats to newly boarded white passengers, and stand. Three complied, but Rosa Parks, a seamstress, refused. At a stroke, she threw off what Gandhi called mental slavery, and substantially inspired the civil-rights movement that followed. But it's important to understand that, just by going first and providing inspiration, she did not become the 'leader'. Going first does not necessarily mean taking charge of everything that follows.

A few days after her arrest, a group called the Women's Political Council called for a one-day bus boycott:

> This has to be stopped. Negroes have rights too, for if Negroes did not ride the buses they could not operate. Three fourths of the riders are Negroes, yet we are arrested, or have to stand over empty seats. If we do not do something to stop these arrests, they will continue. The next time, it may be you, or your daughter, or mother.

Virtually everybody complied, and it was decided to continue with the protest. The original ambition was only to modify slightly the system of segregation, so that black people would not be obliged to stand if there were empty seats available. But the success of the one-day boycott increased people's confidence, and led to calls for wider reforms.

In the months that followed, black people stopped using the buses altogether. They took taxis, walked, or shared cars – a sizeable car pool was organized, largely through church groups.

The protest led to reprisals. The use of taxi journeys at reduced fares was prohibited. Negro drivers, including one prominent protester, Martin Luther King, were arrested for minor, often imaginary driving offences. A hundred prominent protesters were arrested and charged with violating an anti-boycott law. Insurance policies on cars in the car pool were cancelled.

Then victory came. The US supreme court, acting on a suit filed by the protesters, declared segregation on buses to be illegal, not only in Nashville but across the US. But protesters decided to continue to avoid the buses until the ruling came into force, and segregation actually ended. Raising the stakes, the Ku Klux Klan rode through the Negro district. But this didn't have the usual effect. Instead of finding the inhabitants terrified, locked away in houses with the lights off, the Klan found people were sitting on doorsteps to watch. Some even waved.

On the first day the buses were officially integrated, there were no problems. But then white extremists began a reign of terror, with beatings and shootings. Churches and homes were bombed. The Klan paraded again and burned crosses. But the protesters

I shall not be moved: Rosa Parks started the bus boycott, and wider civil rights campaigns, by refusing to give up her seat to a white passenger.

kept their discipline. Many in the white community were repelled by the violence that was supposedly being enacted on their behalf, including the local newspaper, church ministers and a local business association. The terrorism abruptly ceased. Segregation on buses, in Montgomery and everywhere else, had ended, and pretty well everybody accepted a state of affairs that would have seemed unthinkable less than a year before.

Soon after, as a result of the wider struggle, black people were granted equality in other areas too.

But that may seem to suggest a kind of historical inevitability. Civil rights for black people were not inevitable. Rosa Parks is a celebrated symbol of the struggle, but she didn't pull it off on her own. A vast number of other people, perhaps inspired by her example, took personal responsibility and refused to submit any longer.

It would be a mistake to presume that these individuals were exceptional, or indeed that they acted without fear. They felt the fear and did it anyway. Diane Nash was only twenty-one years old, in 1959, when she coordinated sit-ins at lunch counters in Nashville reserved for white people. Like others involved, Nash had been trained beforehand in how to conduct herself, at a workshop on non-violence. But she was surrounded by an angry, shouting mob and for a period of fifteen minutes she wobbled: 'I gave myself a short period to make a decision. Either I would resign as chairperson because I could not be effective, or I would overcome the fear and get my mind back on my work,' she recalls, in Catherine Ingram's *In The Footsteps of Gandhi*.

In the event, Nash managed to calm herself, and stayed. In the years since, she has been upset by the way historians and the media focus on a few prominent leaders, such as Parks, or Martin Luther King:

> Martin was not the leader. He was the spokesman, a very competent, eloquent spokesman. He was a great man. But if people think of him as superhuman or a saint, then when something needs to be changed they are tempted to say, 'I wish we had a leader like Martin Luther King today.' People need to know that it was just people like themselves who thought up the strategies and managed the movement. Charismatic leadership has not freed us and it never will, because freedom is, by definition, people realizing that they are their own leaders.

III. What Needs Changing, and How

1. Add Beauty – and Fun

Bringing about positive change often takes the form of reducing suffering. But many of us, while recognizing war, poverty and environmental collapse as grave problems, just don't feel inclined, or qualified, to fix them.

We may feel that there's something a bit dutiful, grey and depressing about attempting to save the world from famine, or eliminating disease. (Quite apart from it being hard work.) We recognize that the task might appeal to *someone*, but it doesn't appeal to us. In fact, the prospect of getting involved in something like that may make us glum, or leave us bored. And recognizing that is important, because feeling bored is a sure sign that we have not found the kind of meaningful activity that makes life not just endurable but actually enjoyable.

But there are two ways to change the world: to decrease suffering or increase pleasure.

And we may instinctively prefer the latter. Like many others, we may be drawn to the aesthetic side of life. If this sounds rarefied, that's not intended. It's not about knuckling down to study art history (which some people might find just as boring as tackling famine). Nor is it even, necessarily, about the so-called fine arts. We may want to paint or make sculpture, certainly, but many would prefer to learn a few guitar chords and start a band. Or we may be drawn to traditional handicrafts, in the widest sense: not just embroidery or jewellery-making but also customizing second-hand clothes, doing DIY or inventing amazing things in a secret workshop. Taking an even wider look at creative engagement, we may dream of opening a small cafe or running a hotel.

These wishes may seem initially entirely selfish. But we needn't beat ourselves up about this, because when we engage creatively with the world, we are having an impact. Our work can lighten hearts, console, and give people a reason to think of life as something to savour rather than just endure. Works of art (in this widest sense) are ways of building a meaningful community, tools of communication – and thus not unconnected to the more overtly 'serious' mission of peacekeepers and global diplomats.

History shows that as soon as people's most basic needs are taken care of, the aesthetic impulse kicks in. We want to write stories, sing of our pain (or make people laugh), and create works of harmonious and delicate craftsmanship. These needs are at the heart of what we are, and should never be sacrificed to a misplaced notion of seriousness – or put away for ever just because a teacher, years ago, said something unkind about our early efforts.

All too often, we think of art as a luxury, or something that should be left to 'artists', but the distinction between artists and the rest of us is false. (Was Van Gogh an artist? During his lifetime, nobody wanted to buy his paintings.) Everybody belongs somewhere on a spectrum of creativity, from Mozart performing his most complex works to a toddler taking a first piano lesson. We may think that solving world poverty is the more important pursuit, but changing the world is also about considering our own interests and skills – we will be most effective if we do what comes naturally to us.

Taking part in the aesthetic side of life doesn't mean trying to be famous or make a career of it. Most of us won't make our fortune from art, but we all have the chance, indeed usually the need, to create something beautiful. And if we find that enjoyable, we may find ourselves irresistibly compelled to share it.

Rachael Matthews is an artist and a 'Brother' in London's ancient Art Workers' Guild (there are no 'Sisters'). In her own art, Matthews happens to work with textiles, particularly knitting and crochet. She feels strongly that the satisfaction she derives from her work comes not merely from the finished product but the process involved in making it. And that too is something she wants to share with others. In order to do so, she and her friends sometimes conduct 'knit-ins' on the London Underground. They teach strangers to knit or crochet and let them take away wool and needles if they enjoy it.

A wider-ranging attempt to share the joys of creativity is *Learning To Love You More*, which was devised by the artists Miranda July and Harrell Fletcher. In their own work, Fletcher and July have to come up with original ideas every day, but they realized over years of practice that some of their most joyful and even profound experiences arose through following somebody else's instructions. By letting go of the need to be original, and by following another's idea, they were able to create works of delightful originality.

In order to share something like that sense of liberation – to help others do away with the oppressive instinct for originality – Fletcher and July hit on the charming idea of getting the general

Assignment 63: Make an encouraging banner. (This is one by Sarah Corbett of the Craftivist Collective.)

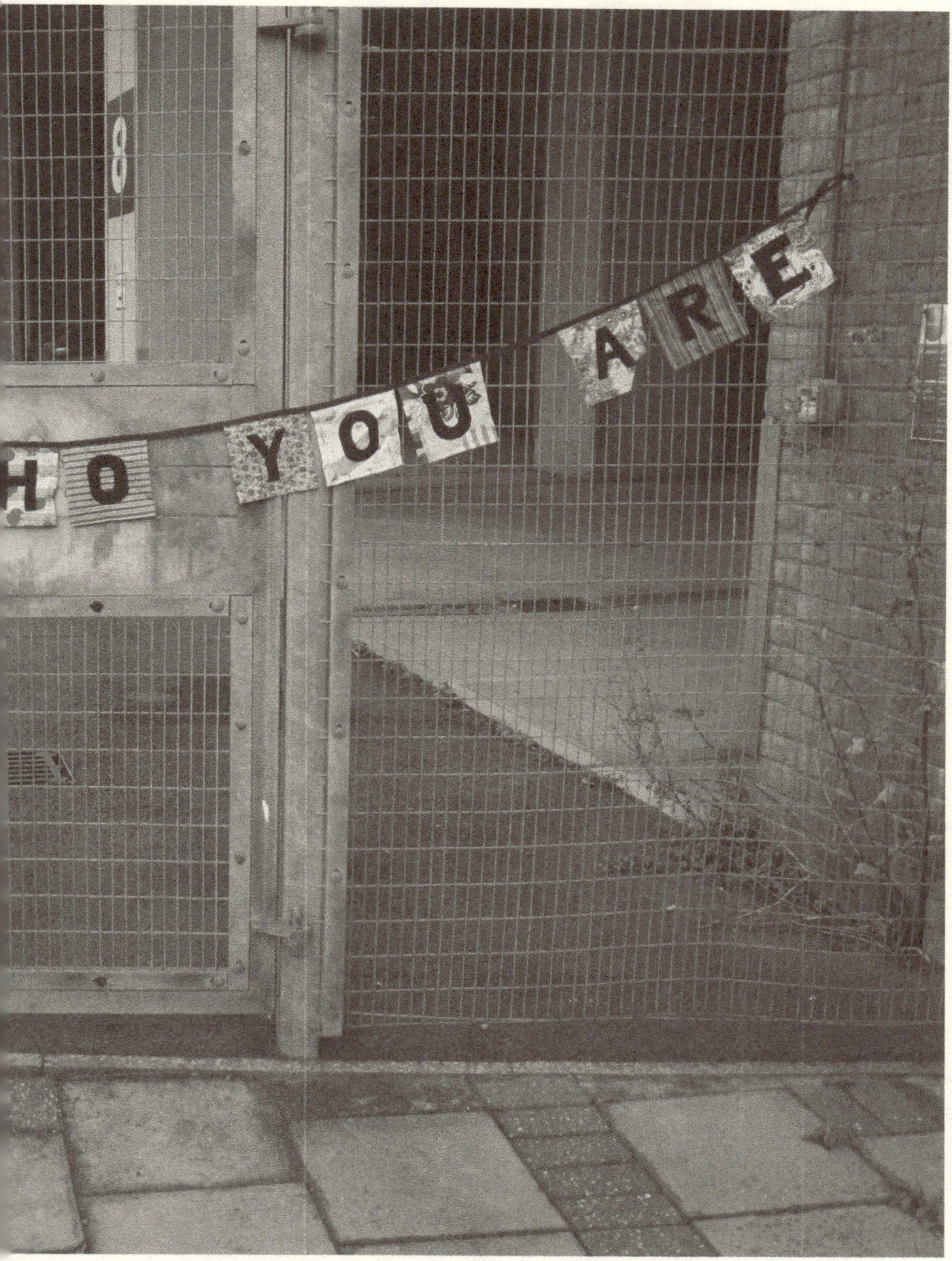
HO YOU ARE

public to do a number of quasi-artistic and psychological assignments, and then to post their results on a website (www.learningtoloveyoumore.com).

There were seventy assignments in all. They included: 'Draw the news', 'Make an encouraging banner', 'Start a lecture series', 'Give advice to yourself in the past', 'Spend time with a dying person', 'Perform the phone call somebody else wished they could have', 'Photograph strangers holding hands' . . .

Some of the other assignments were more introspective, but all shared the quality of inviting people to engage directly with their community and the wider world. In the course of carrying out the assignments, the thousands of people who uploaded reports needed to overcome fear (think of what it takes to ask two people who don't know each other to hold hands!) and to use their creativity. Having done that, they became just as 'expert' as Fletcher and July. One American family successfully completed every assignment and was invited to put on a show at a local gallery. The family's lecture series took the theme 'Art Is Where You Find it, and Everyone Can Do Art'.

I mention this project because it seems typical of what the best works of art can do: reconnect us to sources of energy and engagement that can be stifled by routine and habit.

A good world is not a world where everybody fixates on global problems according to some externally imposed framework of 'importance'. A good world is one in which people find meaning in the particular things they do – and that means a world that has a place for beauty, creativity and play.

2. How Does Money Fit In?

Of all the things that hold us back, our thoughts about money are perhaps the most confusing. And one reason for this is that it can feel as if we face a choice between doing good and making a decent living – we think that we can't choose both.

For most people, this dilemma appears only some time after we embark on our career. We may have started out with excitement in a job that offered glamour or financial rewards, but gradually found it unsatisfying, and have come to envy people whose work seems more meaningful. Alternatively, we may have taken the path of meaningful good works, and have come to resent our low wages and lack of other benefits.

Either way, if this worries us we must work to fix the situation, perhaps change our career. But is it really necessary to make a choice between making a useful contribution and earning a decent living? I don't believe it is. And I'm not going to suggest that the way round the problem is to change the world in our spare time, in evenings and at weekends. (Though we can do that too.) I'm going to insist that we can do good even when we are at work – and we must. Because as we saw in this book's first chapter, we make a difference all the time, and that necessarily includes the time we are at work.

If we are lucky, we may find a way to make a living – perhaps an extremely comfortable living – precisely by doing good. One who has managed that is Dale Vince, a former hippy who made it his mission to generate 'clean' electricity and reduce carbon emissions (because he felt he could not wait for the British government, or anybody else, to do this). He built his own wind turbine, then another, and many more, and set up a company, Ecotricity, to sell his 'green' energy to households and businesses. In the process, he made a fortune.

Making a fortune was not Vince's specific aim, but he has always insisted that his business should succeed *as a business*, for the reason – obvious but worth stating clearly – that otherwise it will fail. (People who consider themselves 'progressive', and instinctively distrust 'business', may want to reflect on this.) And many others have done something similar, finding a mechanism to make meaningful change that generates income, and creates jobs.

But not everybody is naturally inclined to be an entrepreneur. And only a relatively small number can find employment with the likes of Vince. What about the rest? What if the only local employer is rather less admirable?

One way to change how we think about this is to consider honestly how we make our living. Are we serving people's real needs, like Vince, or artificial and unhelpful desires?

Anyone who has raised children will know that it's sometimes necessary to step between them and the things they wish for – such as late bedtime and sugary treats. Sadly, that tendency to behave or consume in ways that are unhelpful is not something we grow out of, and great fortunes have been made by selling things that people do not really need, and may cause harm.

We could all draw up our own list of what those nasty things are. I'm not here to impose my own list on you, but many people would agree that weapons, unhealthy foods and pornography are among them. Nevertheless, the people involved in making and selling these things would usually argue (if you could get them onto the subject, which I suspect they would try to avoid) that they are serving a legitimate need. They might argue that their weapons are needed to keep the peace, their food is a great convenience to people who lack time to make healthy meals from scratch, and their pornography consoles people who are lonely. Are they deluding themselves? Perhaps. But that's not what concerns me here. What I want to propose is that there is no absolutely categorical way to distinguish between 'good' and 'bad' ways to make a living.

This may puzzle some people. Surely I can see that somebody working in an investment bank has sold their soul to the devil? And that somebody who works for an NGO in developing countries is a saint? And haven't I just held up Dale Vince as a paragon?

In reality, it is not so simple. Having met Vince and talked to him for a long time, I do believe that he has built his company, Ecotricity, out of the best intentions, rather than merely a selfish determination to get rich (he pays himself a small salary, less than some colleagues, and has a modest home). But many other people, even if they acknowledge Vince's good intentions, say that wind energy may not be the solution to the energy crisis. They raise arguments against his approach that cannot be dismissed out of hand. Such is the complexity of the relationships between intentions and outcomes that I've discovered it often becomes rather meaningless to attach the labels 'good' and 'bad' to individuals, and perhaps even more so to do that with companies, and entire industry sectors.

Let's consider, as I have already mentioned them, banks and NGOs. I met a man recently who runs the British branch of a Dutch bank that has uncommonly high ethical standards (regarding the kinds of investments they will make), and sometimes lends to good causes that can't provide the customary forms of security. (The loan is made on what essentially amounts to trust, and personal relationships.) On both counts, Charles Middleton and his investment bank, Triodos, deserve applause. I have also met people who told me of NGO activities in developing countries that are downright unhelpful. To give just one quick example: well-known and respected NGOs in developing countries frequently offer a dollar to anybody who attends their events. This enables them to report back to global headquarters that they are winning large audiences – success! But in the process it skews the local economy, because it can be more lucrative to attend a talk than to work, and it puts people off attending other, non-paying events, which may be very important.

But to say that no job or industry is *necessarily* good or bad is not to say that anything goes. It's to insist on personal responsibility. Whether we work in an investment bank or an NGO, the things we do as individuals are either helpful or unhelpful. Speaking for myself, I suspect that I would not find a way to be happy working with weapons, unhealthy food or pornography, and would try hard to find other work elsewhere, but I accept that there may be people working in those areas trying to make real improvements – perhaps by changing the direction of the company, or industry, from within.

Whatever our own position, it's always tempting to be judgemental about other people. To give a perhaps far-fetched example, a highly professional assassin might sneer at a hopelessly un-businesslike charity worker, and vice versa. It's also tempting to justify ourselves ('I only assassinate bad guys' or 'I haven't time to be businesslike').

But we must resist these temptations and look carefully and honestly at what we ourselves actually do, to judge whether we have what Buddhists call a 'right livelihood'.

The way we support ourselves can either allow us to live by our real values or it can distort them. If we decide that our living is unwholesome, we must find another. But the Buddhist idea of right livelihood extends beyond our own job, because we can't be living by our real values while we depend on others to carry out jobs that distort those same values. A teacher may congratulate herself for nurturing children, for example, but would breach her own values if she bought products from companies that use child labour.

In other words, right livelihood is not just a personal matter, but a form of collective responsibility. We are partly responsible for the way others support themselves, because in our daily lives we buy products and services from them or support them through our taxes.

If we hear about companies that breach our values, and if we care about that, it is not enough just to blame others. We should ask what we are doing ourselves to remedy the situation. We should resolve to help create a society where there is more right livelihood and less wrong livelihood, says the Buddhist philosopher Thich Nhat Hanh.

But he adds that nobody, in the real world, can have entirely right livelihood. Once we recognize that, we acquire the humility to stop judging others and ourselves – and get on with our good work.

Another way money can trouble us is related to the idea of giving it away. This is a proven mechanism for making change, but it's often done without the careful attention it deserves.

Specifically, there are three things to consider: how much we can afford to give, whether our donations are truly effective, and whether we should tell others about our donations or remain silent.

Toby Ord has investigated these points thoroughly, not only in his work as a tenured academic philosopher, but in his private life. He has made calculations, and drawn up arguments, that can help us all to understand the distribution of money better.

When Ord was an undergraduate, he often used to make idealistic statements about politics. 'And people would say "Well, if that's what you think, why don't you give all your money to Africa?"' This usually shut him up, he told me, but over time he thought about it. 'If we care about suffering and we want to help people then how much can we achieve?'

He was also directly inspired by something Peter Singer had written, which might make anybody sit up: 'Are you opposed to the present division of resources between the wealthy nations and the poor ones? If you are, and you live in one of the wealthy nations, what are you doing about it? How much of your own surplus income are you giving to one of the many organisations that are helping the poorest of the poor?'

As an academic, Ord does not enjoy massive wealth, but on the other hand he is not badly off. This is how many people would describe their situation. But exactly how well off are we? Ord has set up a movement, Giving What We Can, and a website (www.givingwhatwecan.org) that allows visitors to do the same sums he did himself. Simply type in your annual income (after tax) and the number of people in your household, and the site will generate a report showing how much you can realistically afford to give.

In Ord's own case, the calculations showed that he was among the richest 4 per cent of people in the world, *even taking account of how much further money goes in developing countries*; and that if he gave away 10 per cent of his income, he would still be among the richest 5 per cent.

'Most people are very surprised to find out how rich they really are because we typically compare our wealth only with that of our peers,' Ord said in an interview with me. 'We may or may not be richer than our friends or colleagues, but we are nevertheless richer than the great majority of the world's population. Did we *earn* this position? No. It is certainly true that we can increase our incomes with hard work, but the biggest factor is simply that we were born in the right place – something we can take no credit for at all.'

On his website, Ord has incorporated a graph showing just how unevenly income is distributed. The graph isn't entirely accurate, because to take the super-rich into account it would reach a kilometre above your computer screen.

The more he learned, the more Ord was determined to give money. He felt inspired to set up Giving What We Can, and others joined him – pledging to give away at least 10 per cent of their income – forever.

We may not feel ready to go so far. But if we are resolved to give money, we come to the second problem: how can we be sure that our donations will be effective?

For Ord, the answer came after he happened to read a friend's medical textbook, which compared the efficacy of various medical interventions, and their cost. He was astounded to find that some interventions are 10,000 times more effective than others, but carry the same price. 'Imagine how you would feel if you went into the high street and found one shop selling the same thing as the shop next door for 10,000 times as much!' Of course that wouldn't happen, because the market wouldn't allow it. 'But with charities it does. Two people could each give £1,000 to two charities and one would save a single person's life for a year and the other might save many people a total of 10,000 years of life. And they wouldn't know!'

Ord realized that, by supporting the most cost-effective interventions, he could personally secure 400,000 years of good-quality life for people less privileged than himself. Four hundred thousand? 'That's a lot of life!'

According to the medical textbook, those most cost-effective interventions can buy somebody a whole year of good health for about the price of a decent loaf of bread – by tackling neglected tropical diseases that cause blindness, kidney damage and disfigurement.

It's not very glamorous, but glamour wasn't Ord's motivation. By choosing something this cost-effective, he found he could save a life *every day*. 'You might think that to achieve these amazing things you have to give up your career and move to another country to work for an NGO. But you don't have to do that. You can carry on with whatever career you like.'

When Ord told me this, I was impressed, and glad that I didn't need to give up my work. But also confused. These neglected diseases may have been the most sensible use of my money, but I didn't feel drawn to them. They weren't for me. Anyway, if everybody tackled these tropical diseases they would no longer be neglected, which would be great, but every other cause would suffer. Is it bad to give money, sometimes, to people who shake collecting tins outside train stations for causes we haven't investigated thoroughly?

Ord does not propose that everybody should give money to the same causes as him. But he does suggest that we think carefully about the money we give away – just as we would think carefully before giving somebody a birthday present. It isn't the amount of money we spend that determines a good result, it's the amount of time we're willing to think about what the recipient actually needs – what they're like and what might benefit them individually. Good philanthropy is no different from good birthday-present buying. To help those who wish to donate to causes other than the fight against tropical disease, Ord is working on providing models of cost-efficiency relating to a variety of other interventions in health, education, sanitation and political change.

Another source of advice on giving money effectively is the Institute for Philanthropy. This was set up to advise people with large sums to disburse, but offers insights that would help anybody. Indeed, a key point made on its courses and in its literature is that philanthropy does not always come down to giving money – we can also share our time and expertise. But giving money is important, and the institute was set up precisely to promote that practice by raising awareness of others who do it – because, as we've seen, one of the things that may hold us back when it comes to making any kind of change is the feeling that others are not doing it – and we don't want to feel like suckers.

This raises a crucial question: if we give money, should we speak openly about it, or keep it secret?

Most religious traditions entreat us to avoid making a show of giving alms. 'Do not sound a trumpet before thee, as the hypocrites do,' Jesus said, 'that they may have glory of men.' Making our gift secret preserves the identity of the recipient, notes the Koran.

We should bear these points in mind before giving money in return for, say, a glittering plaque on the wall commemorating our generosity. But giving money publicly does not need to be showy, and nor does it need to humiliate the recipients. 'Public giving can be annoying,' Ord concedes. 'But there is a middle way – doing it without being boastful.'

And the key to not being boastful is to remember that all of us stand in need of charity. It might not be you right now, and you may never contract a tropical disease, but none of us get through life without occasionally relying on the help of others, help that we can't just buy. It's useful to bear this in mind, if you are prone to embarrassment about giving. You may be giving now, but one day you will be at the receiving end – and so have no reason to feel either proud or self-conscious.

If we care about a cause enough to give our own money to it, we would presumably like others to do the same. We can help that to happen by speaking out about the cause itself, and mentioning, modestly, that we have given it our own support. The idea is not to corner people into an awkward position where they feel obliged to follow suit, but only to give them a kind of 'permission' – to stop *them* feeling that they are doing something strange or boastful.

3. Make It Appealing

When we talk about the solving of 'problems' we may put people's backs up or bore them, because most of us naturally associate problems with what is grim and unpleasant. Indeed, if we present only the negative aspects of what the future holds, people will switch off altogether. To change that, we must learn to seduce our audiences into seeing the upsides of a challenge – and one of the best ways to do this is to build networks of friendship around problems.

The environmental movement has been particularly guilty of making us despondent, with seemingly endless tales of doom. And as we've seen, to put people in a place of despondency – to draw attention to danger without also giving a sense of agency – does nothing but render them lethargic, rebellious or depressed. It can actually make people ill, as Frankl observed. Worse, when environmental groups do suggest solutions, they tend to be presented as duties – we are given lists of things we must not do, joys we must surrender. This can be counter-productive.

In recognizing what drives *us*, we must accept that other people too are more likely to pursue personal interests rather than duty. So the great challenge is to make duty coincide with personal interest. To ask: how can we make doing the right thing *appealing*, rather than merely necessary?

If we want to get people to help us in our projects, we should create a movement for change that provides an opportunity for community and togetherness. And to do this we need to identify social benefits as well as purely technical and financial ones.

When environmentalists lecture us about the need to save the planet, they sometimes emphasize the importance of saving strangers in distant lands, or the generations that will come after us. Alas, the very distance of these 'other people' works against any attempt to motivate us to help them: we just can't get excited about saving the livelihoods of people we've never met and cannot even picture. Humans are deeply sociable creatures, and will seize the chance to help others – but our capacity to do this depends on an imaginative engagement that is hard to sustain over great distances of time or place.

When environmental initiatives have been life-enhancing, even fun, they have usually allowed people to confront an issue by forging communal bonds around it. The underlying reason for coming together might have been to save the world, but for many of those involved the driver will have been nothing more or less than a desire to be with people. We should never underestimate the value of this social instinct when we try to change things. If we offer people a chance to say hello to their neighbours, our projects will be infinitely more successful.

To understand this, consider the Green Belt Movement founded by Wangari Maathai in Kenya in 1977. It's a non-profit organization that promotes environmental conservation among lower-income rural Kenyan women. The movement's female members have planted more than 45 million trees across their country, thus preventing large stretches of it from turning into shrub and desert. But for the individual women who have been involved in the project, it hasn't just been about reforestation and the alkaline levels in the soil. It is the social side of the movement that has had the most immediate benefit for them and been the greatest motivator of their efforts. They speak of the deep connections they forged during tree-planting sessions with women they might otherwise never have met – and how this communal work, outside of the presence of male relatives in a highly patriarchal Kenyan society, gave them a new confidence and stature.

Perhaps the greatest environmental and economic challenge of our age is the fact that we have substantially depleted our oil reserves, and may even have passed the peak of global production – or, in the language of geologists, that we have entered the era of 'peak oil'.

When we read about this in the abstract, the problem sounds both dreary and chilling – a reason to retreat into ourselves and do nothing in particular besides panic. But some people have found ways to turn this catastrophic prospect into an opportunity to rethink our economic arrangements and, in the process – to the delight of many who've become involved – to adjust how we relate to our neighbours and make new friends.

The Transition Town movement was launched in England in 2005. It's a grassroots organization of volunteers that spread by word of mouth to towns and villages around the country. The people involved – there is no official membership – devote themselves to preparing, with thought and imagination, for the day when the world will need to get by with considerably less oil – a world in which transport and much that depends on it will be prohibitively expensive. Rather than presenting this as a disaster, the Transition Town movement stresses the possibilities that will arise as people start to think more ecologically and locally – growing food in their own locality, building homes that are less wasteful of energy, and supporting their local economy as much as possible.

It's hard to see how to be upbeat about a world in which energy will be so scarce, but the Transition Town network is founded on the notion of finding an upside in the combined threat of peak oil and climate change. 'Realistically, only a very small percentage of people will think that life beyond abundant oil could be preferable to what we have now,' one of the founders of the Transition movement, Rob Hopkins, told me. 'But I don't think it has to be a dark age. It could be a most extraordinary renaissance.'

It has to be admitted that, when they first read up about the facts around oil, Hopkins and his allies went through something like the classic grief cycle described by the psychiatrist Elisabeth Kübler-Ross – from despair to anger, then bargaining, depression and finally acceptance – before they were able to be so optimistic. Realizing that most other people have not gone through that – and don't want to – Transition Towns try to find ways to nudge society towards more sustainable practices *that are also fun.*

To begin, Hopkins and his allies used a technique that we could all use to find motivation, whatever our mission of change: they sent themselves, in effect, a cheerful postcard from the future. They used 'imaginary hindsight' to picture what the world could be like in a hundred years if humankind gets it mostly right – and they concluded that local communities will all be much more self-sufficient than today, and more close-knit.

Then they worked out, backwards, how to get there, year by year. The steps for change included: teach people to grow food and make and mend clothes (and other items), hold workshops to give energy-conservation advice, and form clubs to install renewable-power facilities. In each case, as these strategies were put into practice, the leaders of the movement found out something remarkable: that people actually enjoyed coming together with a common purpose, picking up useful and engaging skills and (in the process) building a greater sense of community.

When I first found out about 'peak oil', in 2005, I was desperately worried. I told my wife that the future as we had always imagined it was an illusion. (This didn't go down very well.) I wanted to act, but felt lost until I heard about the startlingly upbeat approach of Hopkins and the other Transition pioneers. I happened to tell friends about Transition, and was thrilled when one of them asked me to help him set up a group in his area, near where I live. (See how bearing witness, on its own, can pull us into being a part of what we observe and tell others about.) Soon others joined us, and it was enormously reassuring to see that people shared our concern.

The high point was a meeting in a crowded hall in north London. Hoping to spread awareness, and find allies, we had invited everybody we could think of who might have an interest in joining forces: local members of environmental lobby groups, people who promote fair trade, church groups, members of the local barter network, political parties, as well as anybody else who lived locally. We explained what we were doing, and then – as Chris Johnstone recommends – explicitly asked for help.

In the months that followed, our group achieved a great deal, organizing film screenings, talks and even a street fair. But I was impatient to do more than preach to the converted. With peak oil and climate change looking increasingly menacing, I wanted to see *everybody* growing their own food. What to do?

My next step was substantially inspired by a book called *Soil and Soul*, by Alastair McIntosh, who has been involved in extremely successful community groups in Scotland. A practising Christian, McIntosh has written about the imperative to re-imagine and act upon the old Christian dictum to love your neighbour. When it comes to trying to change the world, he has argued, it's no good campaigners shouting through a megaphone at anonymous millions. They must start with those closest to them. If they are not good neighbours, then why should anybody listen?

I was powerfully struck by this point. Transition Towns emphasize local engagement, and McIntosh took that to the logical conclusion: I would try to work with my neighbours. And not just the handful of people in my street who might be inclined towards environmentalism already, but my actual next-door neighbours.

I had moved into my house a few years earlier, and knew Martin and Val enough to say hello and have little chats. (The house on the other side was empty.) We'd been into each other's houses, but not often or for long. We looked after each other's spare keys. I hadn't the faintest idea what they thought about peak oil.

So I walked round one afternoon and knocked on the door, which was opened by Val. I told her I had got hold of a film about how the world was going to run out of oil soon, and I wondered if they might like to pop round and watch it one day – any day. How were they fixed next week?

This may not have been the most attractive invitation Martin and Val ever received, but to their eternal credit they said they'd like to come round the following Tuesday afternoon. They would bring a friend too, Val said, if that was alright, because she was interested in that kind of thing.

So the day came, and I bought some biscuits and made tea and we watched the film, *A Crude Awakening*, which is pretty devastating, because it destroys all possibility of the future we might previously have hoped for. I was a bit worried about this, because, as Raymond Williams put it, the key thing is not to make despair convincing.

Afterwards we had a little chat. I can't remember exactly what we said. But a few weeks later workmen came round and installed solar panels on Martin and Val's roof.

I was stunned. This loving-your-neighbour business was more powerful than I could have imagined. I had learned for myself that it's possible to extend your support network into unexpected places.

To be clear, I don't mean to suggest that we think of our neighbours as merely *useful*. At every moment, we choose to see others either as people like ourselves, or as objects in our own life's drama. They either count like we do, or they don't. I'm glad to report that Martin and Val counted very much. In fact, with hindsight, I think I am less pleased by their installation of renewable energy than by the fact that they agreed to come and watch a rather unpromising film; and that Martin subsequently invited me to lunch. Simone Weil once wrote that the sense of being rooted is a greatly overlooked human need – and, as I found, getting to know your neighbours is a great way to feel more rooted.

I wondered if I might get any more locals involved in my positive change. That September, I collected apples from my apple tree and put them in a huge box, which I carried under one arm while holding my young daughter's hand in my other hand. We walked up and down the street, telling our neighbours we had more apples than we could use, and would they like some? I had calculated that a man holding a toddler's hand, and offering fruit at no cost, is not unduly frightening. Most neighbours seemed glad to take a handful of apples.

A few months later, I sowed dozens of tomato seeds in small pots. When the young plants appeared, I got hold of another box, grabbed my daughter's hand, and went up and down the street again. I told my neighbours I had grown 'too many' tomato seedlings. Oh dear! Would they like one? Nobody refused, and that year, several people in my street enjoyed growing their own food for the first time. Perhaps they were going to do that anyway – but I like to think I gave them a little push – and without even mentioning peak oil.

Your ideas for changing the world may feel desperately important. They may *be* desperately important. But if you can't find a way to engage the interests of the people around you – including your next-door neighbours – they may never take off.

And perhaps they don't deserve to.

Grown too many vegetables? Leave them on your neighbours' doorsteps, and next year they might grow their own.

4. Love Helps

As we grow more comfortable engaging with other people, and building a stronger community, we eventually come up against individuals who are difficult, not merely apathetic and resistant to our themes, but burdened with problems of their own, including personal problems that can make them very hard to engage with and can lead to them being marginalized in the community.

Instinctively, we may wish we could avoid these kinds of people, because dealing with them can be extremely hard work, but dealing with them teaches us an important lesson; that we may be better equipped, as individuals, to deal with social problems than governments or other official bodies. That's because state agencies, when they're confronted by social problems, usually respond by throwing money – it is difficult for them to act in any other way.

But not all people's needs are material. Sometimes what is really needed is help of a more personal kind. Sometimes what is needed is love.

No one needs this more than children, whatever their background. It's in the care of children that we see the limitations of purely cash-based assistance. Somebody who knows a great deal about this is Camila Batmanghelidjh, a woman who worked for years as a nanny in rich but sometimes troubled or neglectful families, but also has extensive qualifications in psychotherapy and has in recent years helped London's most impoverished children through her own pioneering charity, Kids Company.

Many of the children's individual stories are heartbreaking, but the really shocking thing is the sheer *number* of children involved: Kids Company has thousands on its files. They include the sort of young people we might cross the street to avoid – and with good reason, because despite their age many have been involved in violent crime. But Batmanghelidjh is plainly happy among them. Meeting her is to be confronted with the possibility of a totally different way of thinking.

Many of the children come from severely impoverished homes. In fact, 85 per cent would not have an evening meal if it weren't for Kids Company. But having seen dysfunction in rich homes, too, Batmanghelidjh knows that the childrens' problems are not *only* financial. 'I saw terrible neglect in those homes,' she told me. Money alone can't give children what they need most.

Underlying everything Kids Company does is a belief in love. In particular, the organization is indebted to what is known as Attachment Theory, which was first elaborated by the child-psychologist John Bowlby. This essentially holds that children develop as the direct result of how their first carers engage with them. Physically and emotionally neglected children expect others to be unresponsive, unavailable, and unwilling to meet their needs. Abused children expect others to be rejecting, hostile, and unavailable. Both types behave in ways that increase the likelihood that others will treat them in the ways they expect. And once a child has established a model of its relationships, Bowlby suggested, changing it can be difficult.

Fortunately, not all is lost if early love was missing. A study by the University of Minnesota showed that 61 per cent of mothers who had been sexually abused as children went on to maltreat their own children. However, the same study found that the availability of emotionally supportive individuals and involvement in long-term, intensive psychotherapy could substantially reduce the chances of the repetition of abuse. And that is precisely what children get from Kids Company.

Many of these children have lost the ability to empathize. It's no good merely instructing them in conventional morality. If troubled children are to care for others, they first need to hear someone apologize to them for everything they've been through. Kids Company staff do that: they apologize. Then they attempt to remodel children's ability to empathize by helping them to form intensive-attachment relationships with trained adults.

It would be a mistake to suppose this process goes smoothly. At first, the children often become more aggressive, not less. 'They don't want that attachment to develop,' Batmanghelidjh told me. 'They say we are making them soft, and they won't be able to survive on the streets.' But eventually most of the children are turned around.

I once spent several months observing Kids Company at work. Some of the children I met had been extremely troubled. One was a girl who used to be uncontrollably wild, and would stop on the street to pick fights with strangers. Through the loving care of Kids Company workers, Cleo had learned to stop doing that. Indeed, staff had recently started taking her to restaurants, to learn things that would not otherwise be in her behavioural repertoire – from engaging with waiters to holding the cutlery correctly. Another time, the invitation to dine out came from the children: Batmanghelidjh was taken out by a group of young immigrants, formerly child soldiers, who had just been granted places at university and wanted to repay her years of kindness with a pizza.

We don't need to set up a charity to make a difference of this kind. We could volunteer to help somebody like Batmanghelidjh who has already done that – or just decide to do something ourselves.

That's what Fenella Rouse did. 'It started with me and my hairdresser,' Rouse told me. 'We were talking about things that need to be done, and what could we do ourselves. And we were struck by the number of young people who aren't in paid employment.'

Resolving to act, Rouse walked into a jobcentre near her home in north London and announced that she'd like to help some young people to find work. (She had recently reached retirement age, and had a bit of spare time.) She said she particularly wanted to help youngsters with no qualifications, and no family tradition of work. A government-funded jobcentre could not afford to overlook the lack of qualifications, but Rouse, a mother of young adults herself, knew that formal qualifications aren't everything.

The jobcentre staff suggested a few names, and Rouse approached the young people. She told them what she wanted to do, explaining that she would try to find them placements with her friends, or in offices that seemed interested in helping.

It was immediately apparent to the young people that this was a woman offering nothing but kindness. They accepted it.

The work proved to be more time-consuming than Rouse expected. She travelled far across the city to meet the young people's families. She also found it necessary to collect them from home and accompany them all the way to the workplace, on the first day, having learnt by experience that, no matter how confident they sounded beforehand, not one of them was able to find their way around London by public transport. She also gave pep talks, and explained basic office conduct. (Some young people needed to be told during their placements not to spend so much time arranging their social lives when they were at work.) One or two of the youngsters panicked, leaving their placement early and never going back. Rouse would phone them several times before they eventually took her call. She gently told them they would look back on this as the moment they decided to stop letting themselves down. And that's what happened: one girl having been thus gently rebuked, went out to find a new job herself and thrived in it.

Like Batmanghelidjh, Rouse was motivated by love to help young people who badly needed it. Unlike Batmanghelidjh, she did not set up an organization, with staff and premises and other overheads. She was just an individual, with a mobile phone. But she almost single-handedly transformed the prospects of several 'unemployable' youngsters by finding work placements that led to real jobs.

One of the young people she helped said to me, afterwards, 'She's a lovely person. Anyone could try to do what she has done, but to be able to get along with people like she does . . . She's one of a kind.'

But Rouse doesn't see herself as unique. 'Anyone could do what I've done,' she says modestly, 'if they like young people and have a bit of spare time.'

Being short of money can seem to let us off the hook: we'd dearly like to help, but economic circumstances won't allow us. But Rouse and Batmanghelidjh show that true generosity consists of more than writing a cheque, or putting coins in a tin. And the resource they distribute is one we all have in abundance. It may not be in our power to build new schools, but it is definitely always an option to give our care, attention and love.

5. Aim for a Peace Prize

When we want to change the world, we frequently realize early on that there are groups of people who are standing in our way. And typically we respond by categorizing them as The Enemy – pure evil in contrast to our own perceived purity – and we set about trying to overcome them in whatever way we can: by defeating them in an election, outsmarting them at a dinner party, mocking them in a newspaper article, punching them in the stomach or killing them in battle. We associate getting our way, and forcing through the benevolent change we are looking for, with being able to vanquish The Enemy.

Much of the change the world has seen in its history has come through violent conquest of one kind or another. But there are plenty of examples, which I want to highlight, of remarkable changes that have come about when two camps learn to see each other as legitimate human agents who hold positions which, while divergent from their own, are not intrinsically evil or worthy of being trampled upon.

The other day, in a left-of-centre newspaper that usually opposes war and violence, I read an article written by a woman who supports Britain's Labour party. The identity of the writer doesn't matter, and nor does the specific point of her article. It's just an article I happened to read. I was shocked by the quantity of warlike language in it. The headline urged Labour to 'take the fight' to the Conservative government, 'day in, day out', to use their 'considerable fire power' for 'daily cannonades', to 'deliver smart bombs' and devote themselves to 'devastatingly forensic attacks', in order to 'knock the hell out of government'.

Nobody was physically harmed by the article and I'm sure the writer would have been appalled if Labour politicians did start dropping bombs. But to write in this way is to dehumanize the government, and the individuals within it. We hear similar things in conversation every day.

If we agree with them, rallying cries like this make us feel like part of a select group and capable of great action. But it also sets us up as 'against' the rest of the world – including people we may need to convince if we want to make a difference. So one way to make a difference is to start to take these small but significant examples of dehumanization seriously; if we want to live in a less violent world, we could write letters to people like that newspaper writer and, in the gentlest ways, ask if she might reduce the use of bellicose metaphor a little in the interests of making positive change. And we might try not to use the same kind of language ourselves.

The need to halt our dehumanizing impulses is never more urgent than when it comes to the threat of armed conflict. Those who've worked most closely with warring parties tend to report a small but fascinating truth: if you get them into the same room, get them to have a meal together, shake hands, look into each other's eyes or take a walk together, you have a much higher chance of resolving conflict than by merely holding debates in parliament or calling for UN troops. It's those gestures that remind each party of the other's fundamental humanity that are key to any attempt to make peace take hold.

A famous example of this kind of re-humanization took place in what was then Rhodesia, at the time of its transition to Zimbabwe in 1980. Fighting had been going on for years between blacks and whites. Under white minority rule the government, led by Ian Smith, had unilaterally declared Rhodesia independent of Britain in 1965. Sanctions by Britain and the UN followed, while internally the country was riven by guerilla war. Killings, torture, rape and pillage became common and one in six of the black population were displaced. Some twenty initiatives had been made to establish peace – to no effect – when the parties agreed, at a conference in London, to hold an election. Whatever the result of the election, few expected peace to follow. The head of the armed forces was understood to have prepared a coup in case it went against the white minority, while African nationalists confided years later that they had been waiting 'to kill every white in sight' if the order were given.

Fortunately, the disaster that could have occurred was averted in the simplest way possible: Smith and Robert Mugabe got together in the same room and had a drink together. A group of citizens, both white and black, realized what was in danger of ensuing after the election and persuaded Smith to meet Mugabe at his headquarters. As Smith walked in, he passed fifty heavily armed guards. One shouted out 'Let's get rid of him now!' and raised his gun at Smith – only to be sent sprawling by one of his own commanders. Inside, something extraordinary happened that we might think about whenever we are confronting a seemingly intractable problem within our own social circle: Mugabe invited his former enemy to sit beside him on a couch and for several hours they talked about themselves and their love and hopes for their country. In other words, they found a context in which

Bitter enemies: but a private meeting between Ian Smith and Robert Mugabe enabled them to make terms.

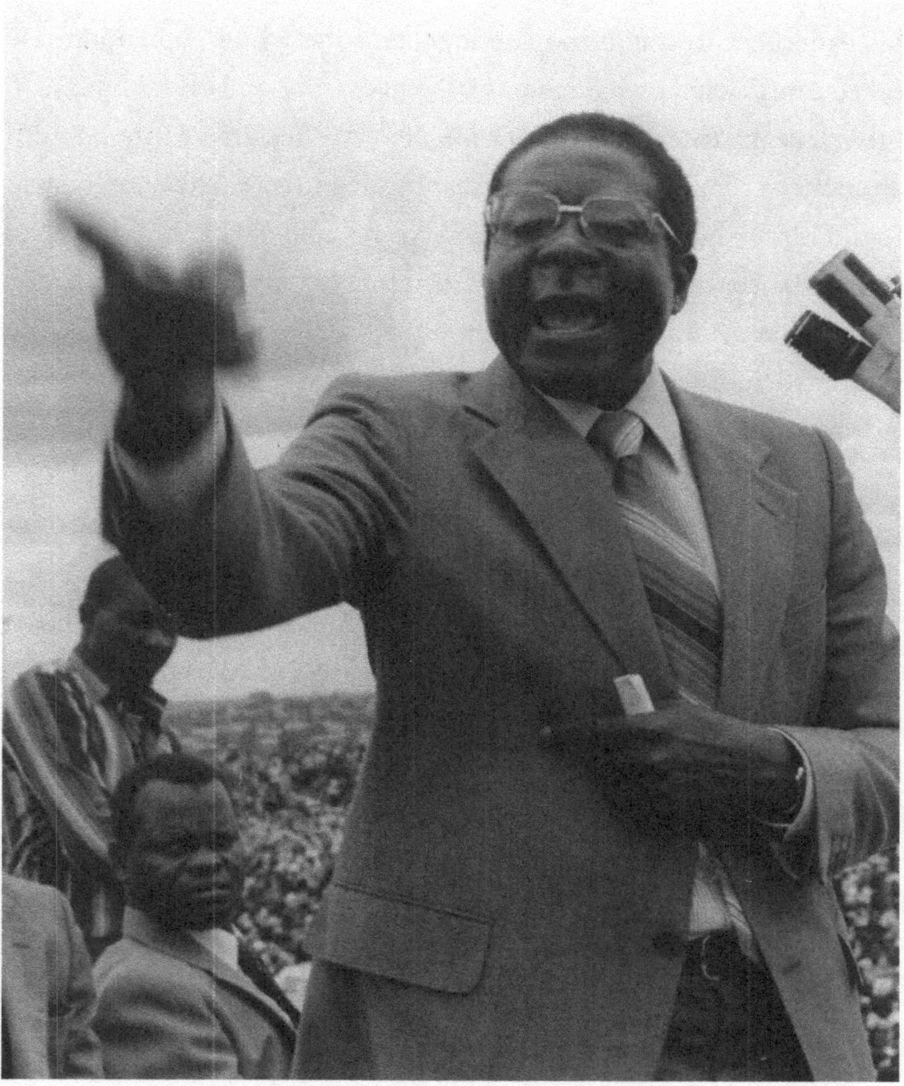

to realize they were both human. They both knew Mugabe was likely to win. He outlined the policies he intended to pursue, and stressed his eagerness to retain the confidence of the white population. He asked Smith what measures might be necessary, and offered him two cabinet seats. Immediately after Mugabe was declared winner, Smith announced that he accepted the results, had met Mugabe and he had found him to be a 'reasonable man'. Smith added that he intended to stay in the country and recommended that other white people do the same. That evening, Mugabe addressed the nation. 'I urge you,' he said, 'whether you are black or white to join me in a new phase and to forget our grave past. Forgive others and forget.'

It sounds simple, but neither Mugabe nor Smith had felt able to call for this kind of meeting without losing face. They needed outsiders, unaffiliated with either side, to do it for them. Reading this years later, you may feel confused. Is this a story about Robert Mugabe as peacemaker? The recent history of Zimbabwe makes such a possibility hard to believe. Surely Mugabe is a monster? But what happened in Rhodesia is instructive because it shows that change is possible even in the most unlikely circumstances. We don't get to choose the people who pose a problem – they're just there. We might feel more comfortable reading about peace breaking out elsewhere, with more attractive protagonists. But resolving conflict is not about making even closer friends with people who already behave nicely. We may one day have to deal with individuals who behave like monsters. It's more startling, and more impressive, to learn that somebody like Mugabe could be persuaded to make peace. It starts to put our own quarrels and disagreements into perspective.

If we are going to find lasting solutions to external conflict, we first need to find a way out of the internal conflicts that poison our thoughts, feelings and attitudes towards others. No conflict can ever be solved so long as all parties are convinced they are right. A solution is only possible when at least one begins to consider how he or she might be wrong. And the deepest way in which we tend to be right or wrong is not in the intellectual positions we adopt but the attitude we have towards the other person. If we don't respect them as a person with real interests and vulnerabilities of their own, we will get nowhere.

We also have to realize that we may not get everything we want, but we can get something more than we'd feared. Peter Emerson has devoted his life to promoting peace by championing this kind of realism. His ideas have been tested in conflict zones such as Bosnia and Emerson's native Northern Ireland, a territory long divided by armed violence between sectarian groups. Emerson promotes a decision-making process that, rather than entrenching division, works towards consensus and shared interests. The system was originally conceived in pre-revolutionary France, by a scientist called Jean-Charles de Borda. Because it relies on complex maths, it was hard to put into practice until the advent of computers. But the Borda count, or 'preferendum', will be familiar to anybody who has ever watched the Eurovision Song Contest: voters simply express their preference on a range of options, ranking them from highest to lowest. The winning option may not have been any individual voter's first choice, but will have won higher overall approval than any other option. The losing option, though it may have been some voters' first choice, will have the lowest overall approval. The multi-option preferendum can be used either to elect individuals or to choose between policies. It can be used in formal politics, but also among friends, in clubs or at the office. Whatever the context, people usually have the same basic interests, Emerson says, but in a different order of priority. The preferendum allows them to recognize this. They may not agree on each other's first choice, but will quickly agree on the second or third.

What is particularly interesting about Emerson's experience is that adopting a different technique for finding common ground can change the way individuals regard people they formerly saw as opponents. They start to see them as more like colleagues. This is because, in the preferendum, nobody votes *against* anything. Instead, you vote for every option, but in your own order of preference. No matter how strongly voters disagree, they must give at least one point to those of an opposite persuasion. 'The effect of having to accept literally everyone as a neighbour may make an incalculable contribution towards mutual understanding and accommodation,' says Emerson. 'Every individual starts the reconciliation process . . . with himself.' If someone wants a particular policy to be adopted, he or she must persuade not only the mild supporter to become more committed, and give 9 or 10 points instead of just 6 or 7 – but also the opponent must be warmed a little, to give 6 or 7 instead of 1 or 2. Rather than merely preach to the converted, there is more to be gained by gently wooing those who would previously have been seen as political adversaries, and ignored. Thus the very use of a consensual system will in itself promote consensus, both in the course of a civilized debate and in the resolutions that may follow.

Eventually, as people discover their common interests, they find themselves able to overlook differences that previously seemed so important. In Northern Ireland, a consequence of this is that previously bitter enemies like the loyalist Ian Paisley and the nationalist Martin McGuinness are able to work together successfully.

What is going on here is essentially an unfolding of compassion. Individuals are starting to see things from the other's point of view. The writer (and former nun) Karen Armstrong believes that compassion is the key to changing the world. In 2008, Armstrong was awarded the TED Prize for her work in this area over many years. At the award ceremony, she asked TED to help her create, launch and propagate a Charter for Compassion, to be written by leading thinkers from a variety of major faiths around the world. The charter was launched the following year.

Compassion does not mean 'to feel sorry for somebody' (a mistake Armstrong frequently encounters). It means to endure something with another person, to put ourselves in somebody else's shoes, to feel his or her pain as though it were our own, and enter generously into his or her point of view. Every faith insists on compassion as the true test of spirituality, and has a version of the so-called Golden Rule, which requires us to treat others as we would like to be treated by them, and not to treat them in ways we would find unwelcome. And we must do this for everybody, including our enemies.

'Sceptics say the Golden Rule just "doesn't work" but they don't seem to have tried it,' Armstrong says. 'It's not a doctrine that you decide either to agree with or not. It's a method, and the only way to test it is to put it into practice.' When people have done this they have reported experiencing deeper, fuller levels of existence – and insisted that anybody could do the same if they tried.

To develop greater levels of compassion, it may be necessary to work on it, like sports professionals in training. There are many exercises we might try. One is to imagine a relative or friend in the place of a person who is suffering. It is hard to disregard a homeless man if you imagine that he might be your father, or your brother or son.

Wishing for your enemy's well-being and happiness is harder. Indeed, Armstrong says, developing a sense of responsibility for your enemy's pain is the supreme test of compassion. At first it may seem impossible. (How can we feel compassion for Robert Mugabe?) If we do manage it, briefly, it is all too easy to fall back into our old ways. The attempt to become compassionate is a lifelong project. Nearly every day we will fail, but we cannot give up.

But the great danger with altruism generated in the seclusion of one's own thoughts is that it might become a subtle means of evading actual interpersonal responsibility, and justify a life of peaceful, uninvolved isolation from others: 'We proclaim to ourselves our love and compassion for such abstract entities as "humanity"', says the Buddhist writer Jack Kornfield, 'in order to avoid having to love any one person.' Or to put that another way, we may be tempted to say we feel love for everybody – but without actually engaging with the real people whom we find difficult or unpleasant.

Which brings me to a story of what happened some years ago between me and a friend, and our own painful falling out. I would like to describe how our dispute arose, and what its consequences were.

I mention this in the context of armed conflicts because it is petty everyday resentments that, if they're left unchecked, grow into cold hatred, then violence. If nothing is done to dismantle these resentments, they may even lead to bombing campaigns. Or, expressed differently: large-scale violence always grows out of private resentments.

I had known Paul since childhood. From as early as either of us could remember, we were very close – like brothers. But he grew up to be a big drinker, and when he was drunk tended to be very unpleasant. We would have tetchy conversations, in which he said things that were unreasonable. Instead of ignoring them or laughing them off, I argued back. At the time, this seemed the right approach: here was a man wasting his life drinking and he needed to be put right. In short, we wound each other up – inviting the very behaviours we hated in each other. (This is why conflict-resolution specialists speak of enemies as being in collusion, rather than merely in conflict.)

I can't remember now exactly what caused me eventually to lose my temper, one evening soon after Christmas, but it started with his accusation that I was not sufficiently grateful for a gift. He was very drunk, he was shouting, and then – I'm ashamed to say that I punched him in the stomach before I knew what I was doing.

We hardly spoke for three years afterwards. You might think I was better off without him, but we had always been close, and our estrangement was a lingering shadow over my daily life. It was painful for people who knew us, too. It would be neat if I could say that one of those other people brought us together – like Mugabe and Smith. Only the situation isn't quite the same. Mugabe and Smith needed third-party assistance because, as leaders of a wider movement, neither man could risk losing face by reaching out to the other and being rebuffed. Private disputes between individuals are different. When you don't represent anybody else, it's easier to take that kind of risk yourself.

But if you are waiting for me to reveal that I reached out to him, and nobly set about putting our relationship in order, I'm afraid I can't do that, because it was Paul who reached out to me.

In doing so, he made it possible for me to feel compassion for him. In fact, I think it would have been very hard, in the circumstances, *not* to show compassion.

It was a Saturday afternoon. He was at a football match. He told me he'd been out drinking all night, in a park. Then he said he'd had enough. He mentioned his recent divorce, and spending his birthday alone. And at the top of his voice – shouting to be heard over the din of the football crowd – he said he was going to kill himself.

Before he called, I had carried resentment and hostility towards him. I resented his drinking particularly. Now he was calling and he was obviously very drunk. But it was clear that his call for help was sincere, and this had a powerful effect: in an instant, I became his old friend again. I have since met people who work in restorative justice who tell me this kind of thing happens often: criminals brought to meet their victims may break down in tears – and victims are surprised to find themselves moved to help the criminals put their lives on the right track. I'm not suggesting that Paul and I were criminal and victim – it was I who hit him, not the other way round – but his call for help transformed my feelings towards him at a stroke.

I urged him not to do anything rash and after hanging up, I found a phone number for Alcoholics Anonymous. The woman who answered the phone told me Paul must call AA himself.

I drove to see him. I was shocked by the squalor of his home – a single room overlooking a busy main road in a poor district – and the powerful odour of alcohol he gave off, but I tried to hide this feeling. Over the next hour or two, I assured him that I, for one, cared for him and couldn't bear the idea of his suicide – and that I was sure many other friends felt the same way. That was only half-true: his behaviour, over the years, had reduced those 'many other' friends to just a few.

I urged him to call AA, and summarized what I knew about it. As I left, I pressed into Paul's hand AA's phone number, scribbled on a Post-it note.

I doubted that he would call. And for a week, he didn't: people don't always do what we want them to do. But then he did. He went to one meeting, then another. Suddenly he was going every day, and talking at length about AA and its celebrated Twelve-Step program. With support from strangers who have been through a similar experience, he stayed sober for a week, then a month, and now nine years. He met someone else, moved into a house, and they had a child – a little girl.

We are close friends again, and he has since returned the favour by giving me support when I needed it.

I mention this personal story to point out something extremely important: that resolving conflict is not only about making peace between nation states. It's about looking at our own situation, among friends and relatives, and asking if there may be somebody with whom we should try to straighten things out. Because, as I pointed out at the very beginning of this book, the things we tend to think of as historically significant – achievements of the sort credited to Julius Caesar, Genghis Khan and Christopher Columbus – aren't really any more important than the small things we can all do, every day.

IV. Conclusion

In the first part of the book, we saw that we do not need to accept the way things are. In the second part, we looked at a variety of ways to engage with the world and with other people – and, by extension, to cultivate an ever greater sense of community. But these were only examples, and while you were reading this book I hope you will have had your own ideas about how to make a positive change. You may perhaps have had these ideas for a long time. In which case, you must do something about them.

Before you start, a final word of caution. We need to accept that even our best efforts will have unintended consequences, and may even be harmful.

To give an example: the 'Green Revolution' in agriculture enabled farmers to increase massively the amount of food they grew, and thus saved many people from starvation. Norman Borlaug, one of the scientists most closely involved, was given a Nobel prize for his work. But the very success of this scientific approach to food-growing made it possible for the global population to reach unsustainable proportions. Likewise, the inventor of the motor car indirectly made it possible for humankind to emit the most incredible quantity of carbon dioxide into the atmosphere. Trade unions that improved wages and working conditions may thereby have pushed employers to export jobs overseas. The creators of financial instruments that vastly improved liquidity inadvertently contributed towards an international financial system that poses a threat to the world economy.

The list could go on. But the point is not to be clever at the expense of people who almost certainly believed themselves to be doing something of real value (and not only for themselves). If we had been in their shoes and had their capabilities, we would probably have done the same, and accepted the plaudits of people who told us we were changing the world in a good way.

The fact is that *anything* we do might be characterized as unhelpful, if only by people far away from ourselves, in time or space, who must deal with consequences that are hidden from us. Being aware of this, we are less likely to get carried away with messianic zeal, and that's no bad thing. In changing the world, we can proceed with a degree of humility.

But this awareness does not stop us from acting. It merely reinforces the importance of the here and now. If we can foresee problems likely to be caused by our actions, we should of course draw back and think again, but if we sincerely can't imagine what those problems may be, we should humbly accept that they might arise, hope that somebody else will think of a way to deal with them when the time comes, and get on with doing whatever needs to be done *now*.

And if we are to do anything, we need first to accept that we can't fix *everything*. When we accept that, we allow ourselves to stop feeling daunted by the scale of what we hope to achieve. This kind of anxiety is understandable, but unnecessary. 'Nobody made a greater mistake than he who did nothing because he could do only a little', said Edmund Burke, the Irish statesman.

Change the world by doing what you can. Rob 'The Rubbish' Kevan picks up the litter near his Welsh home town every day.

If we make the mistake Burke describes, we're likely to postpone action, deluding ourselves that we will do our great works at a later date, when circumstances are more favourable – when we get a new job, perhaps, or move to a bigger house, or retire.

When we wish for the landscape to change in this way we're using 'static' thinking: imagining our goals as, essentially, finished paintings, beautifully framed, that we hope one day to hang on our wall. But the trouble is that nobody is doing any painting.

It helps to use 'process' thinking instead. As Nietzsche said, 'Not every end is a goal. The end of a melody is not a goal.' Which is to say: we don't go to a concert and wish that the music would hurry up and finish, so that we can enjoy it. We enjoy it *as it goes along*. So instead of imagining your mission as a painting, think of it as a piece of music. By all means keep an eye on the long term. (Indeed, you must, if you're to know where you are going. Nietzsche continued: '. . . If the melody had not reached its end it would not have reached its goal either.') But having identified your long-term target, focus on the present. Ask yourself: what can I do in the next 24 hours? Because if you don't do anything in 24 hours, what makes you think you ever will?

If Wangari Maathai had not focused on the small steps, her group would never have planted all those millions of trees: 'Until you dig a hole, you plant a tree, you water it and make it survive, you haven't done a thing,' she said. 'You are just talking.'

Mother Teresa of Calcutta took much the same view: 'I never look at the masses as my responsibility,' she said. 'I look at the individual. I can only love one person at a time, just one, one, one. I began, I picked up one person. Maybe if I didn't pick up that one person, I wouldn't have picked up 42,000. The whole work is only a drop in the ocean. But if I didn't put the drop in, the ocean would be one drop less.'

Nobody ever achieved anything except in small steps, one after another. That stone mason who built the magnificent cathedral for others to enjoy, long after he'd gone, did so exactly like his colleagues: by squaring off stones and moving them – again and again and again.

Small actions are important. Sufis teach that every act can be done for the Beloved. Others might choose to fold laundry as if it were the robes of Jesus or Buddha. Gandhi called these small acts 'blessed monotony'. His own great achievements developed slowly, and we know that he frequently sought reassurance from a passage in the Baghavad Gita, in which Lord Krishna urges us to practice karma yoga – to do work independently of the anticipated outcome.

If we follow this advice, removing our focus from the end, a happy result is that we are less likely to use the end to justify questionable means. We make each step enjoyable and valuable in its own right. And by focusing properly on the small steps, we come to recognize them as what they are: mini-victories, each one giving us confidence to move on to the next challenge – just as protesters in Montgomery, Alabama, moved, gradually, from calling for minor changes to the rules about who sits where on local buses to demanding an end to segregation entirely; a previously unthinkable ambition.

It's worth building a time into your schedule to focus on the mini-victories properly, and recognize their true worth. Make an appointment to ask yourself, at the end of each week, what you have achieved – and what you are looking forward to next week. This modest practice will benefit anybody.

As you notice how much you have achieved, you may wish to raise your longer-term ambitions. But be careful not to get too wrapped up in thinking of those small steps only as a part of something bigger. Really enjoy them *in their own right*.

The principles in this book will only work if they come from the heart. What is proposed is not a bag of tricks, but a new way of living. If you are genuinely interested in forming new habits, keep this book nearby after you have finished it and look through it again every so often. Ask yourself what you have done recently that you might have done better, but also make a note of the things you did well. Actually write down your triumphs, with specific details. Because it is those details, as much as any stories you find written in here, that will give you the courage to go even further.

Changing the world is a job that never ends. In that sense, it's not so much a job as a state of mind: attentive to the way things are, willing to share responsibility for it, and determined not to make despair convincing, but hope possible.

People engaged in this work try to look for the upside, find resources where others might overlook them, and recognize allies in sometimes unexpected places. They focus on the long term but always think how to take small actions right now. They are compassionate and even humble, but experience life as an adventure, rather than a series of oppressive incidents entirely beyond their control. And rather than complain that the work never ends, they see reason to be glad: because there will always be something else to do.

You can be one of them.

Homework

A very large number of books, articles, films and conversations contributed towards the ideas in this book. The following were very useful, not only in the chapters where they are first cited – and are all highly recommended.

II. How to Start to Make a Change

1. Overcoming Defeatism

Leo Tolstoy wrote essays about the importance of absolutely everybody's actions and omissions but he first became aware of it when writing fiction, particularly the epic *War and Peace*. A similarly hefty volume, with narrative drive and global sweep, is *A Force More Powerful*, Peter Ackerman and Jack DuVall's compendium of non-violent campaigns in the last century or so. Gene Sharp's magnum opus, *The Politics of Non-Violent Action*, is more academic but it's hard not to be impressed by the breadth of his research, and the force of his case that power is enjoyed only by the consent of those over whom it is exercised. Of course, he got the idea from Gandhi, whose own writings were extensive: you could start with *The Story of My Experiments With Truth*. For an English-language account of the group that did so much to rattle the Nazis, do read Annette Dumbach and Jud Newborn's *Sophie Scholl and The White Rose*.

2. What Drives Us?

The idea of a life well lived is a cornerstone of philosophy, psychology and every religious tradition. In *How Are We To Live?* Peter Singer gives a broad overview of the philosophical ideas, with many challenging insights of his own. You may also want to look into the original writings of Immanuel Kant, David Hume, Albert Camus, Jean-Paul Sartre, and Iris Murdoch. Viktor Frankl, Martin Seligman and Chris Johnstone provide extremely practical ideas from psychology and other clinical disciplines (and raw personal experience). Of the religious traditions, I rely here mostly on Buddhist writings (though I recommend others too). Stephen Batchelor is a British Buddhist of long-standing: he combines that expertise with existentialist ideas in *Alone With Others*. Thich Nhat Hanh is a Vietnamese monk who has lived in the west for years; *The Heart of the Buddha's Teaching* is clear, and comprehensive, but for a more accessible read try *The Miracle of Mindfulness*. Richard Nelson Bolles' *What Color is Your Parachute?* is written for job-seekers, but contains excellent self-assessment tests.

3. Some Thoughts on Strategy

In *Eradicating Ecocide*, Polly Higgins explains in detail why she thinks a law, like the law against genocide, is needed to protect the planet. Rebecca Solnit's *Hope in the Dark* is less direct, and contains many memorable formulations about change-making. The examples of non-violent techniques are taken from Gene Sharp: it would be wonderful if somebody started a wiki site allowing people all over the world to upload other instances of each technique. The book to read about the Scouts is of course Robert Baden-Powell's *Scouting For Boys* (though things have moved on a bit). The story about the businessmen pretending to be hippies is from Keith Johnstone's remarkable book on creativity, *Impro*.

4. Bearing Witness

The place to read about prophets is of course the Bible, though it is less up-to-date than Trenna Cormack's book of interviews with contemporary voices of hope, *Be the Change*. Jung Chang's memoir about a family in China, *Wild Swans*, is painful to read but gripping, and illustrates just how badly things can go wrong if people don't recognize their own power to effect change. Precisely the opposite effect is achieved by Dale Carnegie's *How To Win Friends And Influence People* – a book that is easy to mock until you actually read it. The advice it contains is practical, upbeat and relentless.

5. What You Will Need

Richard Reynolds has written a lovely book about his exploits, *On Guerilla Gardening*. To find out more about how Peace Direct supports former child soldiers in their new roles, see www.peacedirect.org

6. Taking a First Step

The exercise used by Joanna Macy is mentioned in her book with Molly Young Brown, *Coming Back to Life*. To find out more about her work and other exercises, see www.joannamacy.net. The man at the music festival can be found dancing eternally on YouTube. The civil-rights struggle is well documented in Gene Sharp's work and in Ackerman and DuVall's *A Force More Powerful*; but the quote from the Women's Political Council is from *The Montgomery Bus Boycott and the Women Who Started it: The Memoir of Jo Ann Gibson Robinson*, and Diane Nash's quote is from Catherine Ingram's *In The Footsteps of Gandhi*.

III. What Needs Changing, and How

1. Add Beauty – and Fun

Rachael Matthews' blogs at www.prickyourfinger.com. Do give yourself plenty of time to look around www.learningtoloveyoumore.com if you are really to appreciate the hundreds of submissions from around the world. (They're not accepting any more, but that needn't stop you from having a go.)

2. How Does Money Fit In?

Dale Vince, founder of Ecotricity, blogs at www.zerocarbonista.com. Toby Ord's website is www.givingwhatwecan.org.

3. Make It Appealing

The insightful and moving autobiography of Wangari Maathai is *Unbowed: One Woman's Story*. Rob Hopkins first set out his ideas in *The Transition Handbook*; *The Transition Companion* brings the story up to date. He blogs at www.transitionculture.org. After *Soil and Soul*, Alastair McIntosh published the equally inspiring *Hell and High Water*.

4. Love Helps

Camila Batmanghelidjh has written a powerful, but academically robust account of her work with several young people, *Shattered Lives*.

5. Aim for a Peace Prize

The story of Ian Smith's secret meeting with Robert Mugabe is told by Ron Kraybill in Douglas Johnstone and Cynthia Sampson's fascinating *Religion: The Missing Dimension Of Statecraft*. If you want to find out more about the organization that inspired it, Moral Re-Armament, it has changed its name to Initiatives of Change (www.iofc.org). Peter Emerson's ideas about consensus voting systems are promoted through the de Borda Institute (www.deborda.org). Karen Armstrong's book, *Twelve Steps to a Compassionate Life* borrows the Twelve Step framework from Alcoholics Anonymous (www.aa.org), which was itself substantially inspired by Moral Re-Armament. Jack Kornfield's quote is from his book *After the Ecstasy, the Laundry*.

Appendix

This list is an excerpt from Gene Sharp's *The Politics of Nonviolent Action, Part II: The Methods of Nonviolent Action,* Boston: Porter Sargent, 1973, available for purchase at www.extendinghorizons.com. The book contains detailed descriptions and historical examples of each of the methods.

198 Ways to Act

The following menu of non-violent actions was drawn up by Gene Sharp over a period of several decades. It is known to have been influential in several non-violent revolutions – but also less dramatic social, artistic and political change.

Raising Awareness/Protest

FORMAL STATEMENTS
1. Public Speeches
2. Letters of opposition or support
3. Declarations by organizations and institutions

4. Signed public statements
5. Declarations of indictment and intention
6. Group or mass petitions

COMMUNICATIONS WITH A WIDER AUDIENCE
7. Slogans, caricatures, and symbols
8. Banners, posters, and displayed communications
9. Leaflets, pamphlets, and books
10. Newspapers and journals
11. Records, radio, and television
12. Sky-writing and earth-writing

GROUP REPRESENTATIONS
13. Deputations
14. Mock awards
15. Group lobbying
16. Picketing
17. Mock elections

SYMBOLIC PUBLIC ACTS
18. Displays of flags and symbolic colours
19. Wearing of symbols
20. Prayer and worship
21. Delivering symbolic objects
22. Protest disrobings
23. Destruction of own property
24. Symbolic lights
25. Displays of portraits

26. Paint as protest
27. New signs and names
28. Symbolic sounds
29. Symbolic reclamations
30. Rude gestures

PRESSURES ON INDIVIDUALS
31. 'Haunting' officials
32. Taunting officials
33. Fraternization
34. Vigils

DRAMA AND MUSIC
35. Humorous skits and pranks
36. Performances of plays and music
37. Singing

PROCESSIONS
38. Marches
39. Parades
40. Religious processions
41. Pilgrimages
42. Motorcades

HONOURING THE DEAD
43. Political mourning
44. Mock funerals
45. Demonstrative funerals
46. Homage at burial places

PUBLIC ASSEMBLIES
47. Assemblies of protest or support
48. Protest meetings
49. Camouflaged meetings of protest
50. Teach-ins

WITHDRAWAL AND RENUNCIATION
51. Walk-outs
52. Silence
53. Renouncing honours
54. Turning one's back

Non-Cooperation

OSTRACISM OF PERSONS
55. Social boycott
56. Selective social boycott
57. Lysistratic non-action (withholding sex)
58. Excommunication
59. Interdict

NON-COOPERATION WITH SOCIAL EVENTS, CUSTOMS, AND INSTITUTIONS
60. Suspension of social and sports activities
61. Boycott of social affairs
62. Student strike
63. Social disobedience
64. Withdrawal from social institutions

WITHDRAWAL FROM THE SOCIAL SYSTEM
65. Stay-at-home
66. Total personal non-cooperation
67. 'Flight' of workers
68. Sanctuary
69. Collective disappearance
70. Protest emigration (*hijrat*)

ACTIONS BY CONSUMERS
71. Consumers' boycott
72. Non-consumption of boycotted goods
73. Policy of austerity
74. Rent withholding
75. Refusal to rent
76. National consumers' boycott
77. International consumers' boycott

ACTION BY WORKERS AND PRODUCERS
78. Workmen's boycott
79. Producers' boycott

ACTION BY MIDDLEMEN
80. Suppliers' and handlers' boycott

ACTION BY OWNERS AND MANAGEMENT
81. Traders' boycott
82. Refusal to let or sell property
83. Lockout

84. Refusal of industrial assistance
85. Merchants' 'general strike'

ACTION BY HOLDERS OF FINANCIAL RESOURCES
86. Withdrawal of bank deposits
87. Refusal to pay fees, dues, and assessments
88. Refusal to pay debts or interest
89. Severance of funds and credit
90. Revenue refusal
91. Refusal of a government's money

ACTION BY GOVERNMENTS
92. Domestic embargo
93. Blacklisting of traders
94. International sellers' embargo
95. International buyers' embargo
96. International trade embargo

SYMBOLIC STRIKES
97. Protest strike
98. Quickie walkout (lightning strike)

AGRICULTURAL STRIKES
99. Peasant strike
100. Farm Workers' strike

STRIKES BY SPECIAL GROUPS
101. Refusal of impressed labour
102. Prisoners' strike

103. Craft strike
104. Professional strike

ORDINARY INDUSTRIAL STRIKES
105. Establishment strike
106. Industry strike
107. Sympathetic strike

RESTRICTED STRIKES
108. Detailed strike
109. Bumper strike
110. Slowdown strike
111. Working-to-rule strike
112. Reporting 'sick' (sick-in)
113. Strike by resignation
114. Limited strike
115. Selective strike

MULTI-INDUSTRY STRIKES
116. Generalized strike
117. General strike

COMBINATION OF STRIKES AND ECONOMIC CLOSURES
118. Hartal, or total civic shutdown
119. Economic shutdown

REJECTION OF AUTHORITY
120. Withholding or withdrawal of allegiance

121. Refusal of public support
122. Literature and speeches advocating resistance

CITIZENS' NON-COOPERATION WITH GOVERNMENT
123. Boycott of legislative bodies
124. Boycott of elections
125. Boycott of government employment and positions
126. Boycott of government depts., agencies, and other bodies
127. Withdrawal from government educational institutions
128. Boycott of government-supported organizations
129. Refusal of assistance to enforcement agents
130. Removal of own signs and place-marks
131. Refusal to accept appointed officials
132. Refusal to dissolve existing institutions

CITIZENS' ALTERNATIVES TO OBEDIENCE
133. Reluctant and slow compliance
134. Non-obedience in absence of direct supervision
135. Popular non-obedience
136. Disguised disobedience
137. Refusal of an assemblage or meeting to disperse
138. Sit-down
139. Non-cooperation with conscription and deportation
140. Hiding, escape, and false identities
141. Civil disobedience of 'illegitimate' laws

ACTION BY GOVERNMENT PERSONNEL
142. Selective refusal of assistance by government aides

143. Blocking of lines of command and information
144. Stalling and obstruction
145. General administrative non-cooperation
146. Judicial non-cooperation
147. Deliberate inefficiency and selective non-cooperation by enforcement agents
148. Mutiny

DOMESTIC GOVERNMENTAL ACTION
149. Quasi-legal evasions and delays
150. Non-cooperation by constituent governmental units

INTERNATIONAL GOVERNMENTAL ACTION
151. Changes in diplomatic and other representations
152. Delay and cancellation of diplomatic events
153. Withholding of diplomatic recognition
154. Severance of diplomatic relations
155. Withdrawal from international organizations
156. Refusal of membership in international bodies
157. Expulsion from international organizations

Providing An Alternative, And Other Interventions

PSYCHOLOGICAL INTERVENTION
158. Self-exposure to the elements
159. The fast
    a) Fast of moral pressure

b) Hunger strike
   c) Satyagrahic (Gandhian) fast
160. Reverse trial
161. Non-violent harassment

PHYSICAL INTERVENTION
162. Sit-in
163. Stand-in
164. Ride-in
165. Wade-in
166. Mill-in
167. Pray-in
168. Non-violent raids
169. Non-violent air raids
170. Non-violent invasion
171. Non-violent interjection
172. Non-violent obstruction
173. Non-violent occupation

SOCIAL INTERVENTION
174. Establishing new social patterns
175. Overloading of facilities
176. Stall-in
177. Speak-in
178. Guerilla theatre
179. Alternative social institutions
180. Alternative communication system

ECONOMIC INTERVENTION
181. Reverse strike
182. Stay-in strike
183. Non-violent land seizure
184. Defiance of blockades
185. Politically motivated counterfeiting
186. Preclusive purchasing
187. Seizure of assets
188. Dumping
189. Selective patronage
190. Alternative markets
191. Alternative transportation systems
192. Alternative economic institutions

POLITICAL INTERVENTION
193. Overloading of administrative systems
194. Disclosing identities of secret agents
195. Seeking imprisonment
196. Civil disobedience of 'neutral' laws
197. Work-on without collaboration
198. Dual sovereignty and parallel government

For further details, visit Sharp's Albert Einstein Foundation: www.aeinstein.org.

Picture and Text Acknowledgements

The author and publisher would like to thank the following for permission to reproduce the images used in this book:

Page 306–7 Berlin wall © Caro / Alamy; Page 318–19 Manuscript illumination (detail), *The Legend of the Three Living and the Three Dead*, Ms.Arundel 83, fol.127 © akg-images / British Library; Page 323 Dog walker © Arnd Wiegmann / Reuters / Corbis; Page 326–27 Tank man © Jeff Widener / AP / Press Association Images; Page 338–39 Optimistic graffiti © Mario Tama / Getty Images; Page 365 Rosa Parks © Bettmann / Corbis; Page 374–75 Encouraging banner © Craftivist Collective and Robin Prime (photograph); Page 406 Ian Smith © Gamma-Keystone / Getty Images; Page 407 Robert Mugabe © Sipa Press / Rex Features; Page 421 Rob the rubbish man © Howard Barlow

All other images provided courtesy of the author.

Every effort has been made to contact the copyright holders of the material reproduced in this book. If any have been inadvertently overlooked the publisher will be pleased to make restitution at the earliest opportunity.

Pages 309 and 310 extracts are taken from *Mahatma Gandhi and Leo Tolstoy Letters*, Mahatma Gandhi (Long Beach Publications/ Navajivan Trust, 1987); Page 316 extract is taken from *How Are We*

To Live?, Peter Singer (Text Publishing, © Peter Singer, 1993); Page 321 extract is taken from *Man's Search for Meaning*, Victor Frankl (Beacon Press, 1946); Page 348 extract is taken from *Wild Swans*, Jung Chang (HarperCollins/Touchstone, © Jung Chang, 1991); Page 360 extract is taken from *Coming Back to Life*, Molly Young Brown and Joanna Macy (New Society Publishers, 1999); Page 363 extract is taken from *The Montgomery Bus Boycott And The Women Who Started It: The Memoir of Jo Ann Gibson Robinson*, ed. David J Garrow (University of Tennessee Press, 1987); Page 367 extract is reprinted from *In the Footsteps of Gandhi: Conversations with Spiritual Social Activists* (1990) by Catherine Ingram with permission of Parallax Press, Berkeley, California, USA, www.parallax.org

Notes

Notes

Notes

Notes

Notes

Notes

Notes

Notes

Notes

Notes

Notes